ROUTLEDGE LIBRARY EDITIONS:
SPORTS STUDIES

Volume 5

SPORT, LEISURE AND SOCIAL RELATIONS

SPORT, LEISURE AND SOCIAL RELATIONS

Edited by
JOHN HORNE, DAVID JARY AND
ALAN TOMLINSON

Routledge
Taylor & Francis Group

LONDON AND NEW YORK

First published in 1987

This edition first published in 2014
by Routledge
2 Park Square, Milton Park, Abingdon, Oxon, OX14 4RN

and by Routledge
711 Third Avenue, New York, NY 10017

Routledge is an imprint of the Taylor & Francis Group, an informa business

British Library Cataloguing in Publication Data
A catalogue record for this book is available from the British Library

ISBN: 978-1-138-02613-1 (Set)
eISBN: 978-1-315-77279-0 (Set)
ISBN: 978-1-138-77755-2 (Volume 5)
eISBN: 978-1-315-77253-0 (Volume 5)

Publisher's Note
The publisher has gone to great lengths to ensure the quality of this reprint but
points out that some imperfections in the original copies may be apparent.

Disclaimer
The publisher has made every effort to trace copyright holders and would
welcome correspondence from those they have been unable to trace.

Printed and bound by CPI Group (UK) Ltd, Croydon, CR0 4YY

SOCIOLOGICAL REVIEW MONOGRAPH 33

SPORT, LEISURE AND SOCIAL RELATIONS

Edited by John Horne, David Jary and Alan Tomlinson

Routledge & Kegan Paul
London and New York

First published in 1987 by
Routledge & Kegan Paul Ltd
11 New Fetter Lane, London EC4P 4EE

Published in the USA by
Routledge & Kegan Paul Inc.
in association with Methuen Inc.
29 West 35th Street, New York, NY 10001

Set in Times
by Hope Services, Abingdon
and printed in Great Britain

Library of Congress Cataloging-in-Publication Data
Sport, Leisure, and social relations.
(Sociological review monograph; 33)
1. Leisure – Social aspects – Great Britain.
2. Sports – Social aspects – Great Britain.
I. Horne, John. II. Jary, David. III. Tomlinson, Alan.
IV. Series.
HM15.S545 no. 33 301 s   [306'.48'0941]   86–22104
[GV14.45]

British Library Cataloguing in Publication Data
also available
ISBN 0–7102–1167–8

Contents

Introduction: The sociological analysis of sport and leisure

John Horne, David Jary and Alan Tomlinson

The sociology of sport and leisure still promotes sceptical and even amused responses in some quarters. To some eyes, leisure is a 'trivial' or marginal phenomenon, and simply unworthy of serious sociological study. Many commentators would seem to regard leisure as a mainly individual matter, with little requirement or scope for sociological explanation.

The history of sociology shows, however, that apparently marginal social phenomena, the minutiae of social life, have many times been demonstrated to possess central and surprising socio-logical significance. In recent years developments both in the sociology of leisure and in society have amply demonstrated this point in relation to sport and leisure. Not only has the work of numerous individual sociologists focusing on leisure succeeded in establishing the fruitfulness of a sociological analysis of leisure phenomena, but changes in society – including the twin extremes of affluence and unemployment – have also made sport and leisure more central. While not in any simple sense leisure societies, modern advanced societies have become consumer societies in which individual and collective rights and opportunities have become increasingly central, including a widespread demand for expanded leisure opportunities. Under these circumstances, (and especially when an expansion of consumption and leisure opportunities made available to many is denied to others), a heightened awareness of the social and the sociological significance of leisure has become inevitable. As Max Weber (1949:106) pointed out 'advances in the sphere of the social sciences are substantively tied up with the shift in practical cultural problems'. Sociologists have responded to the new prominence of leisure with sociological analysis of many types. But a sociology of sport and leisure has not been arrived at easily.

Early sociological accounts of sport and leisure

The early stages in the growth of a sociological specialism tend to concentrate on establishing simply that the phenomenon in question can be understood as a social product. The sociology of sport and leisure in Britain and elsewhere has been no exception. As late as 1973 the authors of a pioneering but disparate collection of reprinted and original readings on the sociology of leisure (Smith, Parker and Smith (eds), 1973) remained largely content to demonstrate that leisure was located in a social content and could be subjected to sociological analysis.

If the sociology of leisure as a whole at first struggled merely to establish and to gain recognition for the possibility of a sociological perspective on leisure, the sociology of sport remained even more marginal. In its early years the sociology of sport was often crudely abstracted empiricist in method. In Britain it was virtually a ghetto subject, almost wholly taught in colleges of physical education and dependent on the idiosyncratic tastes of a relatively few influential but isolated sociologists such as Norbert Elias and Eric Dunning (see Dunning (ed.), 1971).

Only in the last decade or so has the sociology of sport and leisure grown more confident and extended its range and also its critical edge. The later writings of Stanley Parker (especially see Parker, 1976) and Ken Roberts (1978) have played some part in this. But more striking than the valuable but relatively eclectic and only loosely theorised work of these authors has been the rise of new groupings of researchers and theorists in the 1980s.

It is a feature of all of the articles contained in this volume that they now challenge or even ignore earlier conceptualisations of the sociology of leisure as formulated by amongst others, Stanley Parker and Ken Roberts. It is remarkable now how little these two primary sociologists of leisure in Britain engaged in any attempt to construct a systematic theoretical orientation for the sociology of leisure. Parker in particular has continued to regard the sociology of leisure as 'in its infancy' and therefore confined largely to 'sociographic' accounts. His recent overview and listing of ten sets of sociological questions about leisure (Parker, 1986) is still not framed in any interpretively consistent or integrated manner. His lack of a systematic conceptualisation of leisure research also undermines his efforts to communicate an understanding of the work of sociologists of leisure who do have greater ambition.

Leisure studies

Although Parker's view can no longer be considered representative of the range of work and the current state of debate in the sociology of sport and leisure, his style of thinking remains close to the heart of a good deal of the approach and 'conventional wisdom' which still survives in the wider field of leisure studies – far wider than sociology alone. One of the aims of a collection of articles such as this is to seek to make inroads into this conventional wisdom. The most formative period in leisure studies was based upon a particular set of alliances, in which three types of interest (at least) were represented. First, a reformist strand in liberal sociology suggested that to identify social problems, cracks in the social structure, could diagnostically suggest social changes. Second, and at the same time, the provision of organised sport and recreation was elevated into a new area of providing-cum-caring professional expertise, for example, the Sports Council and the new frameworks of Local Authority provision. Third, an environmentalist concern – and also new agencies in this area – stressed issues of access to and conservation of the countryside. It is not surprising, in these circumstances, that in the early 1970s the emerging interest in leisure studies was largely dominated by public sector providers of leisure and also geographers as well as by sociologists of liberal persuasion, often associated in their teaching and research with the providers of leisure. The Leisure Studies Association, founded in the early 1970s, reflected the synthesis of these interests.

One effect of all this was to produce a conventional wisdom about leisure research. But it was a new specialism which lacked the impulse adequately to review its inherited patchwork of conceptual and interpretive perspectives or to move beyond them. In general, much thinking remained permeated by idealist conceptions of leisure deriving from European thought (see Dumazedier, 1974), resulting in a continuing stress on the 'autonomous' character of leisure and sports forms, an approach inimical to the strong development of sociological perspectives. In the work of sociologists and social historians there were honourable

3

exceptions to this pattern, including the work of Elias and Dunning on sport. Otherwise, however sociologists mainly shared in the production of the valuable, but nonetheless limited, official and unofficial 'mappings' and 'sociographies' of sport and leisure (e.g., Sillitoe, 1969). Elsewhere – the most coherent element in Parker's work but still a limited perspective – leisure was seen as an adjunct to work: merely an added specialist topic for the industrial sociologist. Within the rich community studies traditions of 1950s and 1960s the sociology of leisure was also treated as an adjunct, in this instance as an epiphenomenon of community. In total then, approaches to the sociology of leisure remained partial and fragmented. It is also notable that there was relatively little integration of work on leisure and work on sport. The ideological role of sport and leisure in wider relations of power and domination was barely considered.

New directions in the sociology of sport and leisure

In sociology itself and also in the social history of leisure there were early exceptions to these predominant patterns, notably the work of E. P. Thompson (1967), the focus on sport and leisure provided by the Centre for Contemporary Cultural Studies at Birmingham (e.g., Hall and Jefferson (eds), 1976) and questions raised and work inspired by the new influence of feminist research and theory (e.g., McIntosh, 1981). Arising from such influences, the challenge thrown down by numerous sociologists and also social historians in the last decade (e.g., by Gruneau, 1983; Clarke and Critcher, 1985; Hargreaves, 1975) is that conventional approaches to the study of sport and leisure sociology must be reconstructed or transcended.

The collection of essays in this volume continues this process. The work presented is intended as continuing the process of bringing the study of sport and leisure more into the centre of current sociological debates concerning theory and methodology. In more general terms, the collection is a call for a more sociologically informed study of leisure, rather than for a new version of a discrete 'leisure sociology' or any new 'orthodoxy'. These essays we would see as characterised by a greater openness to sociological ideas and to a wider range of methods than earlier approaches.

Structure and content of the present volume

The articles assembled in this collection, although not fully representative of the entire spectrum of current research and perspectives in the sociology of sport and leisure in Britain, nevertheless have been chosen with the intention of reflecting the range of work which now exists. (For further useful overviews of the range of work in the sociology of sport and leisure viewed from varying perspectives see Parry and Coalter, 1981; Parry, 1983; Rojek, 1985; and Hargreaves, 1982.)

Since the beginning of the 1980s the Leisure and Recreation Study Group of the British Sociological Association/Leisure Studies Association has offered a forum for presentation of new work and the consideration of work in progress. A number of the articles in the present volume have been presented in some form or another at Conferences or Workshops of this Group.

The pieces in this volume have been arranged into four general categories:

i) *extended summaries of empirical data which also provide illustration and critical discussion of the value of conventional survey methods and 'secondary analysis' in leisure research –* articles by Jonathan Gershuny and Sally Jones, and Joan Smith. Analysis of survey data, including the careful use of much maligned official statistics, allows these authors to convey much of the general shape and more detailed patterns of modern leisure in summary statistical form, whilst also demonstrating both the strengths and the limitations of conventional survey analysis in leisure research. These two articles (as well as that of Deem later) also display some interesting differences in the interpretation of change or lack of change in the potency of gender differences as well as in the sharing of domestic responsibilities between men and women as factors exerting a major influence on leisure behaviour. Whilst Gershuny and Jones appear prepared to point to potentially significant changes in these areas, Smith's analysis does not seem to support this suggestion.

ii) *theoretical analysis and consideration of theoretical and metho-dological issues –* articles by Mike Featherstone, John Horne and David Jary, and John Hargreaves. Featherstone's article covers part of the same ground as that of Gershuny and Jones, but whereas their aim is to summarise and to analyse empirical data, his aim is unashamedly theoretical and conceptual, providing a set of analytical distinctions and illustrations pertaining to contemporary leisure behaviour which are derived mainly from the work of Bourdieu. There is an obvious value to theoretical and conceptual work of this *genre* in suggesting new and perhaps provocative hypotheses about leisure behaviour, even if the broad sweep and only illustrative use of supporting data raises many issues – for example, the different view of class or the relative neglect of the influence of gender in Featherstone's article compared with the treatment of these by Gershuny and Jones or Smith and other authors. While Featherstone's article, like much recent theory in sociology, is properly concerned with establishing an analytical perspective which also achieves an adequacy of purchase on historical change, a concern with the historical dimension in sociological analysis is even more in evidence in the other two theoretical articles. The purpose of Horne and Jary's essay is to outline and to evaluate the seminal influence on the sociology of sport and leisure exerted by Norbert Elias and Eric Dunning, arising in particular from Elias's work on the role of sport in the historical 'civilising process'. Whilst acknowledging the importance of this work in helping to establish a genuinely sociological frame of reference in the analysis of sport and leisure, the relatively restrictive form of the *Figurational* approach to sociology propounded by Elias and Dunning is strongly criticised by Horne and Jary and the advantages of alternative general approaches identified, including the work of Gruneau (1983) and that of researchers and theorists at the Centre for Contemporary Cultural Studies. Hargreaves in his analytical, theoretical and historical discussion of the body in sport and power relations can equally be seen as representing an alternative, more critical theoretical approach in the sociology of sport and leisure than that conventionally provided. Hargreaves in particular – but also the article by Whitsun – provides a good indication of the character of the new wave of more critical, more *engagé* work which has come to the fore in the sociological analysis of sport and leisure.

iii) *case studies of particular areas of leisure and sporting activity* – articles by John Sugden and Sheila Scraton provide illustration of the great value of the combination of analytical sharpness and empirical groundedness which becomes possible above all in a sociological case study approach. John Sugden's discussion of the culture of boxing stands in a long tradition in sociology of carefully focussed ethnographic case studies leading up to a tight conceptual formulation of relations within a particular social context. Case studies of this care and precision of sociological focus have been rare in the sociology of sport and leisure. Sheila Scraton provides a somewhat different example of the case study method: a more practically and politically oriented *exposé* of the underlying social relations in a specific context, in this case the implications of formal physical education in schools in relation to girls' subcultures.

iv) *consideration of the practical and political implications of research and theory* – here the articles by Rosemary Deem and David Whitson which conclude the volume provide the prime examples. Whilst David Whitson elaborates a justification for a concern with praxis as well as analysis in relation to the sociological study of sport and leisure in general terms, Rosemary Deem presents the same case with specific reference to issues of gender.

However, a concern with the practical and the political implications of a study of sport and leisure is far from confined to these articles. The same concern, if in differing degree, is also evident in almost all of the pieces included. Although there is thus a general agreement with Weber's view that an academic discipline like sociology grows in close relation to such practical concerns, it should also be noted that most of the authors in this volume would probably not accept many of the strictures with which Weber surrounded his conceptualisation of 'involvement and detachment' in sociology. It is only a partial response to practical cultural problems to identify them and then sit on the sidelines. This volume represents a fuller response, in a more comprehensive as well as analytically rigorous approach than has been evident in previous studies in the development of the sociology of sport and leisure.

References

Clarke, J. and Critcher, C. (1985), *The Devil Makes Work*, London, Macmillan.
Dumazedier, J. (1974), *Sociology of Leisure*, Amsterdam, Elsevier.
Dunning, E. (ed.) (1971), *The Sociology of Sport*, London, Cass.
Gruneau, R. (1983), *Class, Sports and Social Development*, University of Massachusetts Press.

John Horne, David Jary and Alan Tomlinson

Hall, S. and Jefferson, T. (eds) (1976), *Resistance Through Rituals*, London, Hutchinson.

Hargreaves, Jennifer (ed.) (1982), *Sport, Culture and Ideology*, London, Routledge & Kegan Paul (particularly see the Introduction by Jennifer Hargreaves and the chapter by John Hargreaves 'Sport, Culture and Ideology').

Hargreaves, John (1975), 'The political economy of mass sport', in Parker, S. et al. (eds), *Sport and Leisure In Contemporary Society*, London, Leisure Studies Association.

McIntosh, S. (1981), 'Leisure studies and women', in Tomlinson, A. (ed.) (1981), *Leisure and Social Control*, Brighton Polytechnic.

Parker, S. (1976), *The Sociology of Leisure*, London, Allen and Unwin.

Parker, S. (1983), *Leisure and Work*, London, Allen and Unwin.

Parker, S. (1986), 'Leisure', in Burgess, R. (ed.), *Key Variables in Social Investigation*, London, Routledge & Kegan Paul.

Parry, N. (1983), 'Sociological contributions to the sociology of leisure', *Leisure Studies* 2.1:57–81.

Parry, N. and Coalter, F. (1981), 'Sociology and leisure: a question of root and branch', *Sociology*, 16.2:220–31. (Also see Coalter, F. and Parry, N. (1982), *Leisure Sociology or the Sociology of Leisure?*, Polytechnic of North London.)

Roberts, K. (1978), *Contemporary Society and the Growth of Leisure*, London, Longmans.

Rojek, C. (1985), *Capitalism and Leisure Theory*, London, Tavistock.

Sillitoe, K. (1969), *Leisure in Britain*, London, HMSO.

Smith, M., Parker, S. and Smith, C. (eds) (1973), *Leisure and Society in Britain*, London, Allen Lane.

Thompson, E. (1967), 'Time, work-discipline and industrial capitalism', *Past and Present*, 38:56–97.

Weber, M. (1949), *The Methodology of the Social Sciences*, New York, Free Press.

The changing work/leisure balance in Britain, 1961–1984

Jonathan Gershuny and Sally Jones

1 Time use and time budgets

We know a great deal about what goes on in the realm of work (using the term in its narrowest sense of 'paid employment'). We know how many jobs there are, of what sorts, in which industries. We know in great detail which goods and services are produced in 'the economy', and who buys them. And we know how these characteristics have changed over the recent past. Using this knowledge, we can construct generalisations about the way work is changing – knowing the distribution of employment between branches of production, for example, we have firm grounds for asserting that we are at present becoming post-industrialised, or de-industrialised, or a service society or information-based or dual or whatever. We have evidence that, for instance, an increasing proportion of those who want jobs cannot find them, or that more women have jobs now than previously, or that there are more non-manual workers than there were. But outside this very narrow span of human activity, we are surprisingly incapable of making general statements. We have no firm basis for generalising about such issues as the extent and distribution of unpaid work, the total amount of work (in the broader sense which includes unpaid production) done in the society, or about the composition of leisure activities. The intention of this paper is to provide some of the raw material out of which such generalisations might be constructed – in the form of evidence about the society's changing pattern of use of time. And in particular it will probe a question which seems simple, and yet is surprisingly difficult to answer: How has the balance between leisure and work time (in the broad sense) changed over recent decades?

People asked to describe their own activities naturally include a temporal dimension. They sometimes describe an activity sequence: 'First I got up, then I washed and made breakfast . . . .'; or the duration of events: 'I spent an hour at the art gallery'; or a statement of frequency of participation: 'I go swimming once a week.' Actions are, it seems to us, *made of* time, since it is the passage of time that makes us aware of them. And we can do no actions out of time, so all of what we do should be found in our accounts of how we spend time.

Everyday language is a highly appropriate medium for carrying such accounts. We are all trained to use it for these purposes from childhood ('What did you do at school today?'), and it would be reasonable to speculate that the reliable transmission of retrospective summaries of past events may have been one of the reasons that the human species first developed language. Certainly such summary accounts may be more or less detailed with respect to the content of the activities ('housework' vs 'cleaning, polishing, dusting, hoovering'), and more or less comprehensive with respect to circumstances ('what else were you doing?', 'where?', 'with whom?'), but the common experience of those engaged in the collection of this material is of the ease of providing cues as to the desired levels of detail and comprehensiveness. In short, people's own accounts of their daily activity patterns should yield a uniquely comprehensive and revealing view of the patterns of physical activity which (together with their associated mental events) constitute a society.

Time-budget research comprises a wide range of different approaches, undertaken for a number of different purposes: common to all of them is the collection and analysis of peoples' accounts of their own activities. The field has a very long history, internationally and in the UK: it is usual to trace its ancestry back to the Russia of the 1920s, entering western sociology as a result of the work done by Lundberg (1934) and the Russian emigré Pitirim Sorokin, whose *Time Budgets of Everyday Life* was published in 1937. But in fact time diary techniques had been used as a device for mapping the pattern of daily life in Britain during the first decade of this century (Bevans 1913; Pember-Reeves 1979) and a larger (though by modern standards, still very small) time budget exercise was carried out as part of the 1930 Social Survey of Merseyside (Jones 1934). And the technique has been very widely used; at least fifty national studies have been carried out in at least twenty countries (Robinson 1984; Gershuny 1985).

This is a rather large body of empirical work, and considering the fundamental and comprehensive nature of the data it yields, it ought to have had a substantial effect on social science: in fact its impact has been less than impressive. With a few honourable exceptions, the publications that emerge as a result of time-budget research are blandly descriptive and theoretically uninformed and uninformative. There are two connected reasons for this: the practical complications of time budget analysis and the almost complete absence of appropriate theory.

The data are enormously difficult to collect and analyse. The great diversity of life circumstances and of individual lifestyles mean that very large sample sizes are needed for even the most straightforward of analyses. If the raw data are collected in the form of manuscript diaries, the natural language descriptions must be translated into a closed activity coding frame. The data must then be reorganised, perhaps transforming the initial sequential form of the diary ('7 am, got up, washed; 7.15 had breakfast . . .') into an aggregated form (30 minutes per day spent washing and dressing, 70 minutes eating, and so on). And then, as we shall see in the following pages, the behaviour that is described by the data is very complicated; very careful model specification is necessary before any clear patterns begin to emerge; the analysis of time budgets is in fact anything but straightforward. The literature in the field often gives the impression that researchers have been exhausted by the rigours of data collection and preparation, and have only the meagerest residuals of intellectual energy to devote to analysis.

Running parallel with the practical complications of time-budget analysis is the lack of appropriate theories. The theoretical hiatus is in fact a double one. We have as yet *no adequate theorising about the determination of time use patterns*; the elegant and ever-more-sophisticated models produced by economists, which seek to explain cross-sectional differences and historical changes in time-use patterns by wage differentials (e.g., Becker 1965; Gronau 1977), while internally consistent, bear little relation to the patterns of behaviour exhibited by the data. And perhaps more important, there are *few theoretical applications of time use information*. The data has in the past been used by sociologists examining the sexual division of labour (Meissner et al. 1974), and by economists estimating the value of household production (Hawrylyshyn 1974; Schettkat 1985). But these are rather limited applications, which do not exploit the potential of the material for providing a comprehensive set of indicators of the full range of activities that constitute life-style.

2 Time budgets in the UK

Descriptions of 'how people spend their time' *are* bland and banal – until we bring normative or policy concerns to bear on them. Do women have less leisure time than men? Is leisure becoming more home-centred, less sociable? What are the consequences of improving the accessibility of leisure facilities? Our answers to these sorts of questions would unquestionably be improved if we could draw on appropriate grand sociological theories. But in the absence of grand theory, we can still arrive at reasonably clear answers, organising the time use data on an *ad hoc*, pre- or proto-theoretic basis.

A single time-budget survey, conducted at a particular historical juncture, can, however, only give somewhat equivocal answers to these sorts of questions. It will describe the current pattern of daily activity – but give no clues about *change*. We can use such material to tell us, for example, what is the current disposition of work and leisure between men and women, but not the historical trend. There are of course sociological tricks that we can play: we can, for instance, identify a 'leading class' and assume that activity patterns diffuse from it into the mass of society (this is the technique used by Young and Willmott in *The Symmetrical Family*, 1975). But the results this technique yields are no better than the theory that underlies it – and the theory can only be confirmed by the empirical evidence of differences in activity patterns over time.

Many of the most interesting questions involve historical change in some form or other; we want to know about the development of the gender division of work and leisure, about the changing nature of work activities and so on. And yet the time-budget research instrument is essentially unsuited to long-term retrospection – few people can recall detailed sequences of activities from ten or twenty years ago. How then are we to use time budget evidence to answer questions of social change, other than by waiting for history to happen?

One clear solution is: the combination of survey analysis with the secondary analysis or re-analysis of existing historical time-budget material.

The UK has a very long history of time-budget research. In addition to the material already mentioned, there was an (until recently unanalysed) diary collection by Mass Observation in 1937, and sample surveys by the same organisation in 1951 and 1957. There was a small survey of working-class women, carried out by Claus Moser in 1948 (*Population* 1949), a national sample from Mark Abrams in the mid-1960s (Abrams 1969), the 1970 'Symmetrical Family' survey of couples in the London Metropolitan Region, the 1981 Scottish Leisure Survey, and a number of other surveys of special groups such as students (Tomlinson et al. 1973), shiftworkers (Aubrey et al. 1986), or the unemployed (Miles, 1984). And in addition, there is a long series of so-called 'viewer/listener availability surveys' carried out by the Audience Research Department of the BBC (in 1938, 1951, 1961, 1974/5 and 1983). These surveys were intended to tell the BBC when their potential audiences were available for transmissions: however, until the most recent, the techniques of data collection were precisely the diary completion methods of time budget analysis. And finally, there is the national time-budget sample, funded by the ESRC during the winter of 1983/4 (Gershuny, Miles et al. 1986).

This article is the first publication of results from a historical time-use data series reconstructed from these resources, as part of a project, funded by the Joseph Rowntree Memorial Trust, undertaken at the Universities of Bath and Sussex. At the core of this series is the raw data from seven surveys (the 1938 Mass Observation collection, the 1961 BBC survey, the 1971 Symmetrical Family survey, the 1974/5 BBC survey, the 1981 Scottish sample, and the 1983/4 ESRC and BBC surveys), though this evidence can be supplemented from published material from other UK sources (of particular importance are the two 1950s Mass Observation studies).

We are at present at an intermediate stage of the project, with the most recent data (the ESRC 1983/4 Survey) just becoming available for integration with the earlier material. The evidence that follows is drawn from the three most important surveys from the Bath/Sussex archive: the 1961 and 1974/5 BBC Surveys, and the 1983/4 ESRC material. This paper will not deal with the validation of these national sample surveys (evaluation of the 1983/4 sample will be found in Hedges 1986 – which contains

13

strong support for the seven-day diary techniques used – and in Gershuny, Miles et al. 1986; the 1961 and 1974/5 material is evaluated in Gershuny and Thomas 1981).[1]

A major problem, in inter-temporal comparisons of time-use patterns, is the inconsistency of activity classifications. What, for example, does 'housework' include – clothes washing? painting a wall? gardening? The seven survey data archive employs a common forty-category activity classification (see Table 1); this was designed to be consistent with the slightly more detailed classification systems used in the Symmetrical Family and 1974/5 BBC surveys (and also the 1965 Multinational Time Budget Survey). The original manuscript diaries for the 1937 Mass Observation and the 1961 BBC Surveys are still in existence; these were obtained and coded into the forty-category classification. And the organisations responsible for the 1981 Scottish Survey and the two 1983/4 surveys, all adopted coding systems based on our forty categories. (We are also currently processing pairs of surveys from Holland, Denmark, Norway, and Canada – with material from France and the USA expected soon – into the same classification system.)

Intertemporal time-use comparisons have been carried out in the USA, using published tables from early surveys (Robinson and Converse 1972), and for the USA, Holland, Norway and Japan, employing series of time-budget surveys collected by the same organisation (Robinson 1977; NHK 1976; Knulst 1983). The UK series is the only example which uses reconstructed data from surveys originally collected for other purposes. And the extended time-span of the UK data, combined with the fact that (unlike all of the other national data except the Dutch) it consists largely of week-long diaries rather than day diaries, makes it perhaps the most powerful time-budget research resource available anywhere (the advantages of seven-day over one-day diaries are argued in Gershuny, Miles et al. 1986, pp. 14–25).

3 Work, leisure, and change over time

The empirical part of this paper is devoted to a description of changes in leisure patterns in the UK over the last three decades. There are two different sorts of change which can take place over historical periods: 'type 1' changes, in the composition of the population, and 'type 2', behavioural changes; we must consider

Table 1: *The eight and forty-category activity lists*

A	*Formal Work*	
	1) At Work	2) Work at home
	3) Second Job	4) School/Classes
	5) Travel to/from Work	
B	*Domestic Work*	
	6) Cooking/Washing up	7) Housework
	8) Odd Jobs	9) Gardening
	10) Shopping	11) Child Care
	12) Domestic Travel	
C	*Personal Care*	
	13) Dressing/Toilet	14) Personal Services
	15) Meals/Snacks	16) Sleep/Naps
D	*Outdoor Leisure*	
	17) Leisure Travel	18) Excursions
	19) Playing Sport	20) Watching Sport
	21) Walks	
E	*Civic Activities*	
	22) At Church	23) Civic Organisations
F	*Out-of-Home Leisure*	
	24) Cinema	25) Dance/Party, etc.
	26) Social Clubs	27) Pubs
	28) Restaurants	29) Visiting Friends
G	*Passive Leisure*	
	30) Listening to Radio	31) Watching TV
	32) Listening to Music	
H	*Other Home Leisure*	
	33) Study	34) Reading Books
	35) Reading Papers/Magazines	36) Relaxing
	37) Conversation	38) Entertaining Friends
	39) Knitting/Sewing	40) Pastimes/Hobbies
I	*No Information*	

these separately. But before considering change over time, let us first consider the problem of description of time-use at a single point in history.

One traditional view of empirical research is that descriptions run logically prior to explanations; time-budget data requires exactly the opposite treatment. Simply listing the results of time-budget surveys as, say, overall averages of amounts of time spent in particular activities, produces quite meaningless pictures – since these averages are across different sorts of people with quite different life circumstances. Survey or population average estimates of amounts of time spent in childcare or outdoor sport, compound the activities of young mothers with those of widowers living on their own, young athletes with one-legged pensioners. To make sense of time-use data it is necessary to disaggregate the sample by those social categories which 'explain' the variance in the activity averages – we need to look separately at the mothers and the widowers. Of course these 'explanations' are often rather tautologous: we do childcare 'because' we have children, we do paid work 'because' we fall into the category of the full-time employed. And in other cases they are not explanations in any sense at all: we do not keep house 'because' we are women, but because of a norm attached to that gender category – the explanation is the norm, not the sex. But nevertheless, we have to arrive at 'explanations' (in the variance-explaining sense) as a prerequisite for giving sensible descriptions.

At a given historical juncture we have a set of cross-cutting explanatory classifications, some of them determined wholly externally ('exogenously') to the individual (sex, age), some of them ('endogenously') determined in part at least by the individual (employment status, stage in the family/life-cycle). And associated with each of the categories defined by these cross-cutting classifications is a particular pattern of behaviour.

So, a first sort of change between historical junctures may come about as a result of a change in the proportion of the population which falls into each particular category, while the pattern of behaviour associated with that category remains unchanged – a *change in the composition of the population*. The number of one-legged widowers decreases and that of fit young mothers increases, so there is more sport and more childcare – even though each population category maintains exactly the same pattern of behaviour as before. Simple demographic change (change in the population's distribution across exogenously determined categories) can produce this sort of effect, and in principle at least, change in endogenously determined categories (e.g., employment status) may produce the same sort of effect. This first category is in a sense not really social change at all (though see the brief mention of the problem of boundaries of explanation below).

Second, we might expect to see *change in the patterns of behaviour specific to particular categories*. The widowers are found to play more sport, at a later point in history, the young mother spends more time with her child. This is much closer to what we think of as social change. It may reflect a pure change in tastes (as when we find an increase in the number of people in the various categories going to pubs). Or it may reflect a combination of changing tastes and change in the range of options available to people (increasing domestic travel and shopping time reflecting the decline of neighbourhood shopping). However it is not just tastes and the opportunities for exercising them that can lead to changes in the behaviour patterns of particular categories.

There may be a change in the 'sorts of people' who are recruited to the category. Thus over time we find an increasing number of mothers with young children *within* the category of part-time employed women, which has the effect of increasing the amount of childcare done by these women over the historical period. This suggests the need to introduce new sorts of classifying variables (to continue the example, the system of social categorisation should then be elaborated to include some family status variable such as the age of the youngest child).

These two categories of change are not, unfortunately, quite as distinct as they may initially seem. To differentiate between them we need a prior clear distinction between 'explanatory categories' and 'effects to be explained' – between 'sorts of people' and 'patterns of behaviour'. And yet quite often the very variables we use to identify 'sorts of people' are themselves particular 'patterns of behaviour'. Employment status falls into both categories, and so does family status (having a child is after all 'behaviour'). Depending on the sorts of initial judgements ('theories') which inform the initial choice of classificatory dimensions (and which in turn result from the choice of the boundary of what is to be explained), the same decrease in domestic work over a historical period could be viewed in two quite different ways: as a result of a change in the composition of the population (fewer housewives, more part-time employed women with children) with no change in the behaviour of either category; or as a change in women's behaviour (women deciding to have jobs *and* children). Neither explanation is self-evidently better than the other; which we choose depends on whether we take the choice of family and employment status as externally determined 'givens' – or as a life-style requiring explanation.

4 Overall change in time use, 1961–1984

Table 2 sets out an extremely aggregated view of change in activity patterns over the last twenty-five years for adults (aged 25–60) in the three surveys. The first subtable (headed 'Minutes per average day') gives the mean time allocation for members of these samples. If we add together, for each sample, the five different categories of activity, we arrive as we should at a total of 1440 minutes in the average day. There are some apparent changes in time use over the historical period. Paid work (categories 1 to 5 in Table 1) has reduced from an average of 272 minutes per day (just over four-and-a-half hours) across working age adults, to 239 minutes, about four hours. What does this mean? More women have jobs, with an increasing proportion working part time, more people are unemployed, people with jobs work a different length of working day: the reduction in the samples' averages of paid work time is constituted by a mixture of such changes. For domestic work and childcare (categories 6 to 12), a 25-minute reduction between 1961 and 1974 is followed by an almost equivalent increase up to 1984 – has each 'sort of person' experienced a reduction and then an increase in unpaid work? The 'personal care' category (13 to 16) including sleep, personal toilet and non-social eating shows a small variation. Leisure outside the home (categories 17 to 29) shows an increase of nearly 40 minutes through the 1960s and early 1970s, followed by a small decline to 1984, while leisure at home (categories 30 to 40), shows a steady increase to an overall average of just over four hours per day in 1984. In each case the change in the average may reflect a similar change for each 'sort of person' over the period, or alternatively, a complex pattern of quite distinct intertemporal changes.

Plainly, in order to make sense of these changes, we must take a view as to which characteristics serve to constitute a 'sort of person', and then look at change on a rather more disaggregated basis. There is an empirical procedure for establishing such a view, through the process of variance explanation; those characteristics which best serve to explain variance in the activity categories, must provide the appropriate basis for 'elaborating' the analysis. (This procedure has of course a substantial hidden theoretical content: those who designed the 1961 BBC enquiry had theories, based on thirty years of collective experience of 'audience research', about what determines viewers' and listeners' availability, which in turn determined the choice of descriptive characteristics collected for the diary respondents. Theories – in this case, other peoples' theories, concerning a somewhat irrelevant issue – actually determine which sorts of characteristics are available for variance explanation.) The results of the procedure are, however, strikingly clear. In these three surveys, in the other eight surveys in the British archive, and indeed in every other modern time budget, irrespective of what other classifying variables are available, three sorts of characteristic emerge as being of crucial importance in the determination of the overall pattern of time use: sex, employment status, and stage in the life-cycle (particularly, the presence or absence of small children).

Notable for its absence from this list is 'occupational social class'. This has not always been the case: it has been argued that until the 1950s class differences in time use were quite pronounced – middle-class women, it appears, did less than half as much housework as did working-class women, but the virtual end of private domestic service and the diffusion of domestic equipment, meant that the differences had disappeared by the early 1960s (Gershuny and Miles, 1986). Most modern evidence shows very little differentiation by class, at least in terms of a binary manual/non manual split, either for the very broad activity categories given in Table 2, or at the more detailed activity classification given in Table 1. Obviously, at a very detailed level of classification, there are highly class-specific activities; though we might find no substantial class differences in playing or watching sport, we would certainly expect to find them once we adopt finer activity classifications that include such categories as Real Tennis or the Henley Regatta. The rich can afford activities which the poor cannot. But by 1984 the division of time between the main activity classifications, as represented by Table 1, is altogether quite surprisingly similar for manual and non manual groups.

Table 2 is constructed from a Multiple Classification Analysis (MCA), taking sex, family status and employment status, together with the binary social class indicator, as the independent variables. The overall proportions of variance explained (R^2) for each

Table 2: *Broad activity changes GB 1961–1984*

Minutes per average day

	1961	1974/5	1983/4
Paid Work	272	251	239
Domestic Work	225	200	222
Personal Care	648	653	638
Leisure Outside Home	69	107	99
Leisure at Home	225	228	243

Multiple R²

	1961	1974/5	1983/4
Paid Work	.91	.9	.9
Domestic Work	.78	.7	.63
Personal Care	.2	.17	.21
Leisure Outside Home	.05	.06	.08
Leisure at Home	.19	.19	.32

Sex Effects

	Male			Female		
	1961	1974/5	1983/4	1961	1974/5	1983/4
Paid Work	29	21	12	-29	-19	-13
Domestic Work	-71	-68	-60	70	63	55
Personal Care	7	10	8	-7	-9	-7
Leisure Outside Home	6	17	11	-6	-16	-10
Leisure at Home	30	20	27	-30	-19	-25

Family Status

	Younger, no children			Children < 5			Children 5–14			Older, no children		
	1961	1974/5	1983/4	1961	1974/5	1983/4	1961	1974/5	1983/4	1961	1974/5	1983/4
Paid Work	8	8	-2	3	2	6	-5	-5	5	-1	-1	-6
Domestic Work	-20	-33	-48	33	32	56	17	17	13	-27	-14	-17
Personal Care	2	2	14	6	0	-14	-2	-3	-7	-2	-5	6
Leisure Outside Home	28	37	34	-10	-8	-14	-8	-8	-8	1	-7	-4
Leisure at Home	-18	-14	2	-32	-26	-34	-2	-1	-2	30	28	22

	Employment Status								
	Working Full-time			Working Part-time			Others		
	1961	1974/5	1983/4	1961	1974/5	1983/4	1961	1974/5	1983/4
Paid Work	160	149	161	−91	−69	−67	−244	−231	−224
Domestic Work	−81	−60	−66	31	17	22	128	100	96
Personal Care	−30	−30	−36	56	34	31	37	35	41
Leisure Outside Home	−6	−19	−9	4	12	6	10	29	11
Leisure at Home	−42	−38	−49	−1	5	9	70	67	77

	Social-Class					
	Non-manual			Manual		
	1961	1974/5	1983/4	1961	1974/5	1983/4
Paid Work	−12	5	(−2)	6	3	(2)
Domestic Work	10	7	(−1)	−5	−4	(1)
Personal Care	9	6	(+1)	−4	−4	(−1)
Leisure Outside Home	13	(+1)	(+6)	−7	(0)	(−6)
Leisure at Home	−19	−10	(−4)	10	6	(+4)

(Effects not significant at .05 level in parentheses)

category of activity remain very similar across the three surveys. Unsurprisingly, the level of explanation of paid work is high, at around .9 – only to be expected given the inclusion of employment status among the independent variables! But in fact, if we exclude employment status from the model, we still find more than half of all the variance explained by the interaction of sex and family status. The proportion of variance explained by the model in the case of domestic work time seems to have declined over the period, from .78 in 1961, to .63 in 1984. This reflects the increasing number of women with children in the paid workforce (i.e. the reduction of unpaid work consequent on the increase of the mothers' paid work weakens the association between life-cycle stage and unpaid work time). And very little of the overall variance in out-of-home leisure is explained by the independent variables, these being very highly dependent on individual motivational factors and geographical location.

The bulk of Table 2 is taken up with the 'effect parameters' from the MCA analysis (the coefficients of the effect of each category on the mean estimate of time allocation, adjusted to take account of the effect of each of the other independent variables). Thus in 1961, men of any given employment and family status did on average 29 minutes *more* paid work than the average person of that status, whereas women did 29 minutes *less* than the average; men did 71 minutes less unpaid work, and had 42 minutes leisure and personal care time above the average. Note that, allowing for rounding errors, for each survey the effect parameters, for each social category, sum to zero: clearly any extra time spent by men in one activity on the average day, must be matched by less time in other categories. The MCA scores give us a rather neat summary of the life-styles of different social groups: the overall average distribution of 24 hours between the set of activities, together with deviations of each category from the average.

The general structure of the effect parameters is quite remarkably stable. The signs of the effects only change in a very few cases. There is some convergence between men's and women's paid and unpaid work times, but in general the magnitudes of the effects of belonging to each category remains constant from 1961 to 1984. This might, in the light of the discussions in the previous section, encourage the view that most of the change over the period may be described in 'type 1' terms. However, the effect of the interactions between categories (particularly interactions between sex and employment status) are not shown in this table. When we look at the sub-categories individually we will be able to see some more distinct changes in behaviour.

It is the magnitude and stability of these effects that provides the basic justification for using the three categories of sex, family status and employment status as the main basis for disaggregation of the time-use data (and incidentally reinforces our confidence in the usefulness of these three samples for tracing social change). The binary social class variable has only rather small effects (which become insignificant at the .05 level for all five broad activity categories by 1984), and so is not very frequently discussed in the following pages, although it is possible that future analysis will reveal more important differences in behaviour patterns among groups distinguished by more elaborate educational or occupational categorisations.

5 Domestic production

We see from Table 2 that domestic work activities show an apparently irregular trend over time, declining overall throughout the 1960s, apparently increasing again from the mid-1970s to the 1980s. Table 3 looks at some slightly less aggregated activity categories, and breaks the sample down by sex and employment categories (looking only at full-time employed men because of small numbers in the part time and non-employed categories).

The irregular overall trend in domestic activities seen in Table 2 is revealed in Table 3 as being composed of a number of really quite different, but individually quite clear and consistent, changes over time. For women in each of the categories of employment, the time in routine domestic tasks has declined consistently over the period, whereas for men, the average amount of routine domestic work time nearly doubled between 1974/5 and 1983/4 – albeit from a very low base. Domestic travel and shopping time have grown substantially over the period, reflecting the decline of local shopping facilities. And time spent in odd jobs around the home has increased for all the categories.

The change in these activities can be seen most clearly when we consider the participation rate statistics in Table 3. Almost all women were involved in the routine cooking and cleaning activities, and (with the exception of full-time employed women) in shopping activities in 1961; by contrast, a minority of men were engaged in these activities in 1961, and they show a very

Table 3: *Domestic Tasks 1961–1984*

a) Minutes per average day

	Cooking Washing Up Housework	Domestic Travel Shopping	Child Care	Odd Jobs	Gardening
Men, Full-Time Employed					
1961	13	9	4	24	28
1974/5	13	17	5	29	11
1983/4	24	28	11	31	(4)*
Women, Full-Time Employed					
1961	133	23	4	13	5
1974/5	130	30	6	10	4
1983/4	117	37	10	13	(1)*
Women, Part-Time Employed					
1961	252	41	19	13	10
1974/5	207	48	14	12	4
1983/4	199	64	34	20	(2)*
Women, Non-Employed					
1961	308	54	39	17	14
1974/5	250	60	36	18	8
1983/4	226	71	58	29	(2)*

b) Participation Rate %

	Cooking Washing Up	Housework	Odd Jobs	Gardening	Shopping	Child Care	Domestic Travel
Men, Full-Time Employed							
1961	38	28	58	60	36	18	7
1974/5	55	28	70	40	61	27	42
1983/4	86	57	85	16	77	32	65
Women, Full-Time Employed							
1961	100	92	45	26	80	15	8
1974/5	100	97	44	20	91	27	46
1983/4	100	98	72	9	96	35	74
Women, Part-Time Employed							
1961	100	98	46	45	93	38	11
1974/5	100	100	57	24	96	46	59
1983/4	100	100	83	14	97	72	88
Women, Non-Employed							
1961	99	100	50	45	95	51	8
1974/5	99	100	65	34	97	57	61
1983/4	100	99	83	11	98	61	84

substantial increase in participation over the period of our surveys. Domestic travel – in almost all cases, travel connected with shopping – involved around 10 per cent of the sample in the diary week in 1961; this participation rate had risen to about 65 per cent for full-time employed men, and nearly 90 per cent for part-time employed women by 1984 – the drive to the shopping centre or the supermarket replacing the brief walk to local shops. The participation in non-routine jobs about the home has increased most markedly for women, to the point that, part-time and not-employed women at least, are very nearly as likely to engage in these supposedly male-specialised tasks as employed men are.

The apparently very steep decline in gardening suggested by Table 3 is in fact a statistical artifact. Budgetary constraints in the ESRC meant that the interviewing for the most recent survey had to be concentrated in November 1983 and February 1984, the low points in the gardening year. From the 1974/5 survey, which had both winter (February) and summer (July) interview waves, we know that gardening is the activity which is most affected by seasonal factors. (But luckily, this evidence also suggests that the seasonal effects are not very widespread; it is mainly gardening and outdoor sport that is depressed by winter – and these are pretty directly substituted for, in terms of time allocation, by watching television.)

The most unexpected result, however, is the increase in time devoted to children. Time spent looking after children, or playing with them, more than doubles for full-time employed men and women over the period, and almost doubles for the other two categories. Participation rates in this activity also rise dramatically. Why? This phenomenon has, as far as we are aware, gone unnoticed in the British sociological literature until now (though there is a somewhat similar result for the USA to be found in Robinson 1977), and we are unaware of any explanation for it.

Of course, as presented so far, there could be compositional explanations for these trends. It could, for example, be some change in the composition of households that leads to the increase in childcare; it could be the increase in women's employment that entirely explains the reduction in women's domestic work time. In fact we can demonstrate that such compositional explanations do not account for these trends.

One potential explanation for the decrease in domestic work might be a shift in the population such that less people live in the sorts of households that have a lot of domestic work as a result of

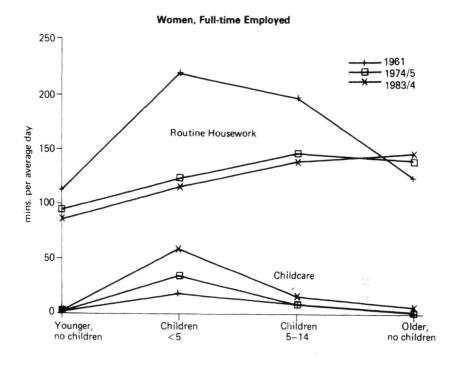

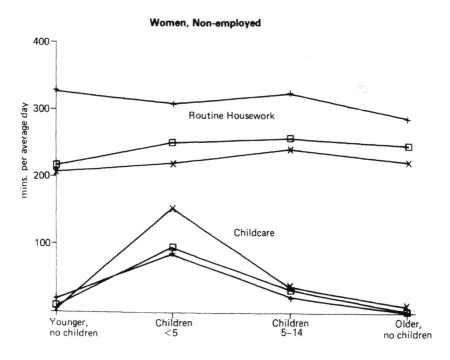

Figure 1: *Domestic work at four points in the family cycle*

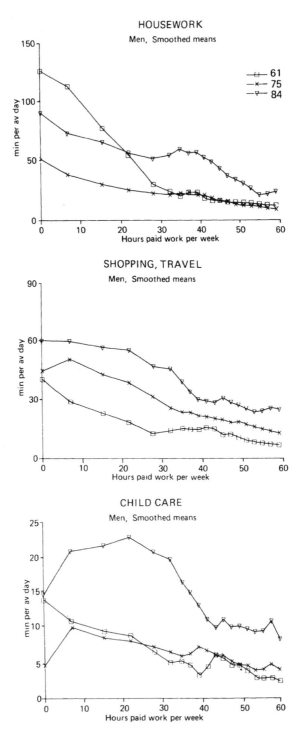

Figure 2: *Domestic work elasticities 1961–1983/4*

reduction in family size, or in the number of households with small children. Figure 1 shows the average time spent in domestic tasks by full-time and non-employed women at different points in the family cycle. Take the 'routine tasks' (cooking, cleaning, house-work) first: for all life-cycle categories (except for some reason the older childless women) time in these activities has been declining regularly since 1961. For full-time employed women, altogether the most substantial decline is among those with small children, presumably reflecting the effect of the diffusion of new consumer capital equipment (automatic washing machines, food preparation and storage equipment) on the very substantial workloads in such households. For the non-employed women, the reduction in routine domestic work time is quite evenly distributed across each of the categories. Whatever the shift of population *between* the family cycle categories, we are clearly observing here changes of behaviour *within* the family cycle categories.

There is an analogous 'compositional' query relating to the childcare activities. The increase in childcare *could* be a product of an increase in the number of households with children, or of households with very young children (who are particularly demanding of adult time). Again, Figure 1 shows us that the increase in childcare time over the period is still apparent when we break the samples down by the family cycle – though in this case the change is very largely concentrated in households with children below the age of 5. It is not that there are more households with toddlers, or more toddlers per household with children; people, it appears, are spending more time looking after their children.

It might perhaps be thought that the reduction of routine domestic work is all to be explained by the increased participation of women in paid work. What happens to domestic work over time if we control for the amount of paid work? Figure 2 attempts to answer this question, by looking, for each of the three surveys, at the relationship between paid work time and domestic work – it shows, in effect, the elasticity of time spent in the various domestic activities, how much of a decrease in domestic work comes with each increment of paid work. (The three samples are each divided into a large number of subgroups according to the respondents' hours of paid work; the numbers of respondents in each working-hours category tend to be small, so the curve is smoothed by averaging the domestic activities time in each working-hours group with those in adjacent groups.)

Consider the negative slope of the elasticity curve for women's routine housework in 1961. Clearly, even if this curve had remained unchanged over the historical period we are considering, the growth in women's participation in paid work would have had a consequence in the decline of domestic work time. But in fact, Figure 2 gives us a second and quite independent sort of explanation. For women, between 1961 and 1974/5, the whole curve is shifted downwards. For equivalent amounts of paid work, women in the mid-1970s did 50 to 100 minutes per day less routine housework than women in the early 1960s. The change between the 1974/5 and the 1983/4 surveys is negligible by contrast (though the very close similarity between these two quite independent samples does itself speak for the quality of the data in both cases). While there is no direct evidence in the surveys to support this, it seems quite reasonable to infer a technological explanation for these changes. The 1960s and early 1970s saw the diffusion of the basic domestic capital equipment into households, which led to a decline in the amount of time necessary to provide given levels of domestic service to the household; by the mid-1970s, however, most households had installed the equipment which contributes most significantly to domestic productivity, so subsequent changes in domestic work time are less marked.

Now consider the equivalent elasticity curve for men. Two things emerge with extreme clarity. The first is already widely known, and can be demonstrated with much simpler data constructions: the inequitable 'dual burden' of paid work and unpaid housework on employed women. The men's curve shows a negative elasticity, as the women's did, but in all the surveys, the slope is much less steep, and in each category of working time, women do between two and three times as much routine domestic work as men. The second finding may have been suspected, but has certainly not previously been documented: there is a clear rise in the amount of routine domestic work done by men in each paid work category, between the mid-1970s and the mid-1980s. Again, we have no direct evidence to support our proposition, but we can certainly speculate that this shift is related to a change in the ideological basis of the domestic division of labour. (The apparent decline between 1961 and 1974/5 in hours of domestic work for men in very short-time employment, is in fact a compositional effect – there are very small numbers in these groups in 1961, and these may be single parents, or other men with heavy family care responsibilities.)

So the routine domestic work elasticities, controlled for paid-work time, show, for men and women, two distinct and quite contrary trends: women's domestic work reducing during the 1960s, presumably as a result of the diffusion of domestic technology, and remaining unchanged through the later 1970s and early 1980s; men's domestic work staying constant through the 1960s, and then increasing between 1974/5 and 1983/4, perhaps as a result of ideological pressures. Had the survey evidence suggested that the two sorts of change were simultaneous, then either (though hardly both) of them could perhaps have been explained away as resulting from a difference in survey techniques or activity coding practices. The fact that in each case a different pair of elasticities show almost no change (1974/5–1983/4 for women, 1961–1974/5 for men), and that the change in the elasticity curves take place over different periods for the women and the men, virtually excludes the possibility that these results stem from systematic differences in the samples.

We saw previously that childcare time appeared to have increased over the late 1970s and early 1980s. Figure 2 shows that, though in the earlier pair of surveys the pattern of change is less regular than in the routine domestic work case, the increase in childcare over the later period is quite clear and unequivocal, with people at each level of employment doing more in 1983/4 than in 1974/5. In the shopping and domestic travel category, the trend is consistent over the whole period for both sexes: at each employment level, travel and shopping time increases through the three surveys.

In Table 2 (taking the samples as representative of the population) we saw the society's average of domestic activity time decreasing overall for 1961 to 1974/5, then increasing again from 1974/5 to 1983/4. We have now decomposed this irregular pattern of change, into a number of separate components, each having a rather more consistent, and certainly quite explicable, pattern of evolution. Some of the change in time use does fall into the 'type 1', change in population composition, category. Families have certainly got smaller over time, more women had paid jobs in 1983/4 than in 1961. But nevertheless we have seen a number of substantial 'type 2' changes in the behaviour of particular 'sorts of people'. Some of these changes may be explained by the diffusion of new technologies (reduction in women's housework 1961–1974/5), some by changes in social norms (increase in men's domestic work 1974/5–1983/4), some by changes in the spatial organisation of society (the increase in shopping), others by what we might have to put down to simple changes in tastes and preferences (the increase in childcare time). In sum, it seems reasonable to conclude that the irregularity in the change in domestic work time over this period results from the balancing of the technologically generated *reduction* in women's routine domestic work, against the *increases* in childcare, shopping time, and men's domestic work.

6 Change in the work/leisure balance

We are now in a position to put together a preliminary view of how the balance between work and leisure time has been developing in Britain over the last two-and-a-half decades. As we have seen from the discussion of the domestic activities, the patterns of change are very complex, so the following discussion will concentrate on the four subpopulations: full-time employed men, and full-time, part-time, and non-employed women. This leaves out one important group, the unemployed, who figure largely in only the last of the three surveys; a brief discussion of the time-use pattern of the unemployed in 1983/4 is found in Gershuny, Miles et al. (1986) and a substantial study of time use by unemployed men in Miles (1984).

So, how has the work/leisure balance been changing in Britain? Time-use statistics from sources other than time-budget studies are rare; the one exception that might have been expected are statistics on paid working time. In fact comprehensive data on this topic, covering the whole population, are only available from the 1970s (the standard UK source, the 'New Earnings Survey' was first carried out in 1968, and then yearly from 1970). But there is a much longer data series covering only adult manual employees, collected by the Department of Employment and its predecessors, stretching back in some form for just about a century. From these data we know that, taking full-time manual adult men's hourly paid working week in 1961 (47.9 hours) as 100, paid work time fell to 92.9 in 1974, and 90.4 in 1984. The equivalent calculation for women's paid work time shows a fall to 93.2 in 1974, and a subsequent small rise to 95.7 in 1984.

Of course, from a time-budgeting point of view, there is more to paid work than just the work time paid for by the employer. The 'paid work' category in the first column of Table 4 includes travel to work, and direct preparation for work, so, for example, the full-time

Table 4: *The work/leisure balance (adults, 25–60)*

	Paid Work	Domestic Work	All Work	Personal Care	Child Care	Out of Home Leisure	At Home Leisure	All Leisure	Child Care + All Leisure
a) Minutes per average day									
Men, Full-Time Employment									
1961	466	74	540	618	4	69	209	278	282
1974/5	427	72	499	627	5	102	207	309	314
1983/4	422	98	519	602	11	98	209	307	318
Women, Full-Time Employment									
1961	388	183	570	631	4	61	173	234	238
1974/5	365	174	540	630	6	82	183	265	271
1983/4	372	167	539	612	10	90	188	278	288
Women, Part-Time Employment									
1961	164	316	481	661	19	72	207	279	298
1974/5	169	271	440	665	14	99	221	320	334
1983/4	165	284	449	645	34	89	222	311	345
Women, Not Employed									
1961	4	392	395	679	39	70	257	327	366
1974/5	6	336	342	677	36	116	268	384	420
1983/4	7	327	335	667	57	95	286	381	438

b) Changes 1961 to 1983/4 (Changes significant at the .05 level underlined)

Men, Full-Time Employment

61–74/5	–39	–2	–41	9	1	33	–2	31	32
74/5–83	–5	26	20	–25	6	–4	2	–2	4
61–83/4	–44	24	–21	–16	7	29	0	29	36

Women, Full-Time Employment

61–74/5	–23	–9	–30	–1	2	21	10	31	33
74/5–83	7	–7	–1	–18	4	8	5	13	17
61–83/4	–16	–16	–31	–19	6	29	15	44	50

Women, Part-Time Employment

61–74/5	5	–45	–41	4	–5	27	14	41	36
74/5–83	–4	13	9	–20	20	–10	1	–9	11
61–83/4	1	–32	–32	–16	15	17	15	32	47

Women, Not Employed

61–74/5	2	–56	–53	–2	–3	46	11	57	54
74/5–83	1	–9	–7	–10	21	–21	18	–3	18
61–83/4	3	–65	–60	–12	18	25	29	54	72

employed men's daily average work time, at 466 minutes (54.4 hours per week) is substantially higher than the Department of Employment estimate. It also includes white collar employees and the self-employed in addition to manual workers. But all in all the *trends* in paid work time exhibited by the three time-budget surveys are really quite satisfactorily similar to those in the Department of Employment statistics. The full-time employed men move from 100 in 1961, to 91.6 in 1974, to 90.6 in 1984; the equivalent group of women decline from 100 in 1961, to 94.1 in 1974, and then rise to 95.9 in 1984. Clearly the time budgets and the Department of Employment statistics are describing the same reality.

Let us now add together the change in paid work, for these groups, with the change in unpaid work time, so as to see the overall trend in leisure time. We have chosen to include as unpaid work, for this purpose, all of the domestic tasks other than childcare, making this exclusion on the grounds that the apparently unconstrained increase in childcare indicates that the activity has a substantial recreational impact (though in fact, re-aggregating childcare into the work category does not have a very substantial effect on the conclusions of the analysis).

For full-time employed men, we see the jagged pattern, an initial substantial reduction, 40 minutes less work in 1974/5 than in 1961, reflecting mostly the decline in paid work over the period; in the following decade, however, the work total rises by about 20 minutes, largely because of their increase in routine domestic work and shopping. Part-time employed women show a simliar pattern, a 40-minute decline in work followed by a 15-minute increase, this latter again largely explained by domestic travel and shopping. Full-time and non-employed women both show declines in total work time of 30 and 60 minutes respectively between 1961 and 1984, with, in both of these cases, most of the change taking place between 1961 and 1974/5. If childcare is included in the work total, then the reduction in total work time over the whole period is somewhat less; part time employed women and full time employed men have about a quarter of an hour per day reduction in this broader work category over the period, full time employed women 25 minutes per day less work, and non-employed women, a reduction of 40 minutes per day.

But of course 'leisure' is not necessarily the residual of the day once 'work' has been removed. A large part of the day is devoted to what we might consider 'personal care and maintenance' including sleep, personal toilet, and non-social eating. As we see, personal care time shows a regular decline, of 10 to 20 minutes per average day, over the period. Only a small part of this decline is in sleep – for the adult (25–60) sample as a whole this declined from 516 minutes per average day in 1961, to 511 minutes in 1974/5, and remained unchanged in 1983/4. The reduction comes very largely from 'non-social eating', which occupied more than an hour and a half per day for the adult sample in 1961, and less than an hour and a quarter in 1974/5. Apparently, convenience foods reduce consumption time as well as preparation time.

The most generous definition of 'leisure' that we can adopt is simply to take the residual time once work and personal care is removed. On this basis, for the four groups in Table 4, leisure time has increased very substantially through the period. Full-time employed men have 36 minutes extra free time, part-time employed women 47 minutes extra, full-time employed women 50 minutes, and non-employed women 70 minutes extra. If we take the less generous estimate, excluding childcare time, the increases in leisure time still amount to 30 minutes or more per day for every group, and nearly an hour per day for non-employed women.

Tables 5 and 6 outline the changes in average time and participation rates, for out-of-home and at-home leisure activities respectively. Let us work through the activity categories in turn. Leisure travel (i.e. travel to or from leisure activities) has greatly increased for all the groups, reflecting, as in the case of domestic travel, the increased mobility bestowed by private motorcars, which in turn enables a much wider geographical dispersion of leisure facilities. One unexpected side effect of this is the very dramatic decline in the other travel category, 'excursions'. When households did not own their own means of transport, travel *itself* was a leisure activity. We see from Table 5 that in 1961, around 25 per cent of each group went on 'excursions' – trips on a river boat, or on the train to the seaside, or 'up to Town to see the shops', or rides on the bus into the country for a picnic – in which 'going for the ride' was the main purpose of the journey. Domesticating the means of production of transport services, seems to have robbed travel (or at least, local travel) of something of its previous romance; only one-twentieth of our sample reported an excursion in the 1983/4 diary week.

Watching live sport (i.e. not on TV) in 1961 was a clearly sex segregated activity. No more than 2 per cent of the women respondents engaged in it whereas 10 per cent of men did so during the diary week. Over the period to 1983/4, the male involvement

Table 5: *Leisure outside the home*

	1 Travel	2 Excursions	3 Playing Sport	4 Watching Sport	5 Walks	6 Church	7 Civic Duties
a) Minutes per average day							
Men, Full-Time Employed							
1961	5	10	4	3	4	3	6
1974/5	12	5	7	3	5	2	4
1983/4	24	1	10	2	9	2	3
Women, Full-Time Employed							
1961	5	9	2	1	4	4	2
1974/5	12	5	1	1	2	2	3
1983/4	21	0	2	1	4	6	7
Women, Part-Time Employed							
1961	5	9	1	0	3	3	8
1974/5	14	11	2	1	6	2	5
1983/4	24	1	5	1	5	3	5
Women, Non-Employed							
1961	2	8	1	0	5	4	5
1974/5	17	11	1	1	9	2	5
1983/4	23	0	3	1	9	4	6

	8 Cinema, Theatre	9 Discos, Dances, Parties (Bingo)	10 Social Clubs	11 Pubs	12 Restaurants	13 Visiting Friends	10+11+12 Out of Home Sociable
Men, Full-Time Employed							
1961	4	2	4	4	2	19	10
1974/5	2	17	8	14	2	21	24
1983/4	1	5	5	13	4	18	22
Women, Full-Time Employed							
1961	6	3	1	0	1	24	2
1974/5	2	17	6	3	2	27	11
1983/4	2	7	2	10	5	21	17
Women, Part-Time Employed							
1961	6	5	1	1	1	30	3
1974/5	2	17	3	3	1	33	7
1983/4	1	7	2	4	4	26	10
Women, Non-Employed							
1961	4	3	1	0	1	34	2
1974/5	2	18	4	3	2	42	9
1983/4	2	7	3	4	4	29	11

b) Participation rates

	1 Travel	2 Excursions	3 Playing Sport	4 Watching Sport	5 Walks	6 Church	7 Civic Duties
Men, Full-Time Employed							
1961	23	26	9	10	20	15	15
1974/5	60	18	19	11	24	10	12
1983/4	91	5	31	11	31	14	13
Women, Full-Time Employed							
1961	24	25	6	2	15	20	9
1974/5	63	16	6	3	15	9	11
1983/4	91	5	17	6	20	17	21
Women, Part-Time Employed							
1961	24	30	6	2	15	19	13
1974/5	62	21	6	3	15	13	18
1983/4	93	5	17	5	20	24	21
Women, Non-Employed							
1961	15	22	4	1	21	20	13
1974/5	64	24	5	3	39	13	16
1983/4	88	4	16	3	35	17	17

	8	9	10	11	12	13
	Cinema, Theatre	Discos, Dances, Parties (Bingo)	Social Clubs	Pubs	Restaurants	Visiting Friends
Men, Full-Time Employed						
1961	11	6	10	16	8	43
1974/5	6	42	17	39	9	57
1983/4	5	19	16	41	33	60
Women, Full-Time Employed						
1961	16	8	4	3	7	55
1974/5	7	44	13	17	13	69
1983/4	8	34	6	32	40	75
Women, Part-Time Employed						
1961	17	13	2	4	9	55
1974/5	6	52	9	14	12	69
1983/4	7	31	9	20	26	75
Women, Non-Employed						
1961	11	7	5	2	10	64
1974/5	7	45	10	14	11	81
1983/4	6	30	11	21	32	79

Table 6: *Leisure at home*

a) Minutes per average day

	Radio	Watching TV	Listening to Music	Study	Reading Book/Papers	Relaxing	Conversations	Entertaining	Knitting, Sewing	Hobbies etc.
Men, Full-Time Employed										
1961	23	121	1	0	28	20	2	5	0	8
1974/5	5	126	3	1	19	31	7	6	0	7
1983/4	3	129	1	3	24	16	14	6	0	12
Women, Full-Time Employed										
1961	16	93	1	0	13	27	1	5	14	3
1974/5	3	103	1	0	13	31	7	10	8	7
1983/4	2	102	1	2	20	14	21	7	7	11
Women, Part-Time Employed										
1961	21	98	0	0	15	36	3	7	23	4
1974/5	4	112	2	1	14	39	12	15	14	9
1983/4	2	121	1	2	21	21	22	14	12	8
Women, Non-Employed										
1961	25	125	1	0	19	38	3	13	28	5
1974/5	6	132	1	0	19	51	16	18	16	9
1983/4	3	147	2	1	27	32	26	16	18	14

b) Participation Rates (in diary week) %

Men, Full-Time Employed

1961	60	89	5	2	–	53	16	20	0	31
1974/5	32	96	17	2	–	66	49	27	1	41
1983/4	23	98	13	8	–	50	69	41	0	50

Women, Full-Time Employed

1961	56	87	4	0	–	67	10	26	42	22
1974/5	27	95	10	2	–	66	52	40	30	44
1983/4	21	97	8	9	–	58	85	52	25	65

Women, Part-Time Employed

1961	56	88	4	0	–	73	22	33	61	30
1974/5	32	97	13	2	–	83	69	57	41	45
1983/4	19	99	8	7	–	78	83	72	42	52

Women, Non-Employed

1961	63	88	5	1	–	81	20	44	58	29
1974/5	36	96	12	0	–	85	77	58	49	53
1983/4	26	98	11	4	–	77	87	69	47	60

in watching sport hardly increased (and the amount of men's time devoted to it marginally declined), while the female rate of involvement trebled. There was a similar sex bias in playing sport in 1961 – but in this case, male and female participation rates both increased in the following years, so by 1983/4 there were still twice as many men as there were women engaged in the activity. The surveys demonstrate that the most common form of exercise in the population is going for walks – though sport is catching up. By 1983/4 about the same proportion of the employed men in the sample went for walks as played sport, whereas in 1961 there were twice as many walkers as sportsmen. Walking, however, still maintains itself as the clearly dominant source of exercise for women.

Church and civic activities still involve substantial minorities of the population; participation rates in these activities seem, among women at least, to have been increasing over recent years. Cinema and theatre, as we would expect, now account for a rather small proportion of leisure time – hardly more than one twentieth of our sample engaged in this sort of activity during the 1983/4 diary weeks. The next categories form something of a puzzle. The 'dances, discos, parties' group (and to a less marked degree the 'social clubs') showed a really enormous increase over the 1960s and early 1970s – and then declined with almost equivalent rapidity to 1983/4. The 'seasonality' evidence we get from the 1974/5 survey does not lend support to the possibility that this results from the placing of the 1983/4 survey in mid-winter. Does it reflect the end of the Bingo boom? The trend does correspond to the reduction in men's pub-going over the late 1970s and early 1980s: perhaps a reflection of the general economic depression? This puzzle will presumably be solved as we get deeper in the analysis of the full British dataset.

Time spent at the pub showed a substantial increase from 1961 to 1974/5, and then, among men a small decline to 1984; women's pub going increased very substantially during the 1974/5 to 1983/4 period, greatly diminishing the traditional sexual segregation of this activity. Though the rate of participation in 'visiting friends' (in their own homes) increased regularly through the period, the time spent in the activity seems to have declined somewhat between 1974/5 and 1983/4. And while the overall time spent in pubs and restaurants is still rather small when compared to, say, watching TV, the increase in rates of participation (for full-time employed women, for example, from 3 per cent and 7 per cent respectively during the 1961 diary weeks, to 32 per cent and 40 per cent in 1983/4) speak of a real transformation in the pattern of sociability in Britain.

Time spent watching television increased somewhat over the earlier part of the period (mostly as a result of the increase in the participation rate – itself presumably due to households' first acquisition of a set). When, however, we add together TV, listening to radio and listening to music, we find that the overall allocation of time to these 'passive' leisure activities tends to decline. Time spent studying and reading stayed overall about the same for men, but increased for each of the women's categories. A small decline over the period in time spent 'relaxing' was more than compensated for by the time spent in conversations with other household members. And the reduction in the almost entirely sex-segregated knitting and sewing activity group is matched by an increase in the non-segregated 'hobbies' category.

7 Some cautious conclusions

What has been written here is necessarily rather tentative. The process of constructing the recent history of time use in the UK is not very far advanced (the analysis described here employs a comparative dataset that has only been available since February 1986). Further work on this material will certainly modify the results presented. In addition to the three surveys we have been considering, there is more British material waiting to be integrated, and a mass of evidence from Europe and North America to compare it with. But we may nevertheless see the broad outlines of historical change from the survey evidence presented here.

Official statistics indicate that over the past two-and-a-half decades paid work time has declined for men in full-time employment, and that there was a decline in average work time for employed women, connected with the increase in women's participation in part time jobs, followed, from the mid-1970s, by a small increase in women's paid work. The time-budget data from our three surveys shows very much the same picture. But the official data covers only 'the economy'; we are now in a position to move towards similar generalisations for activities outside paid work.

Figure 3 summarises the change from 1961 to 1983/4 for the four

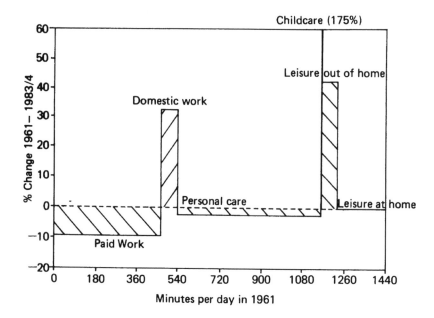

Men in full-time employment

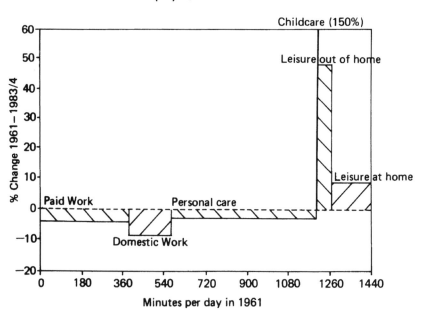

Women in full-time employment

Figure 3: *Change in time use 1961–1983/4*

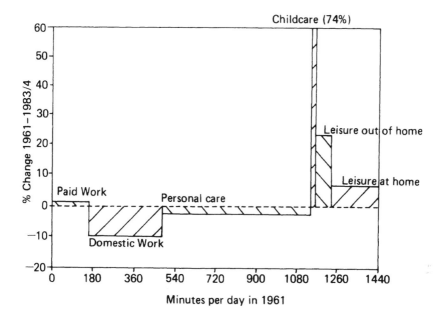

Women in part-time employment

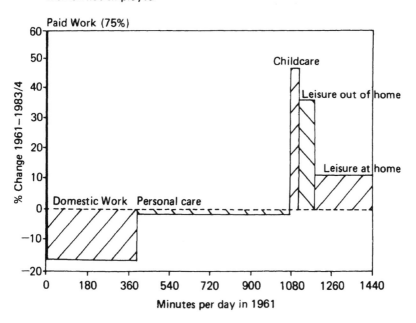

Women not employed

Figure 3 (*cont.*)

groups of adults on which we have been concentrating (it is derived from the data in Table 4). It consists of 'proportional base histograms'; the horizontal axes represent the distribution of time on the average day in 1961, the vertical, the percentage change in time devoted to each activity from 1961 to 1983/4. The area of each bar is proportional to the amount of time that moves to or from the activity over the period.

We see that the near 10 per cent reduction in men's paid work is very substantially offset by the increase in their time spent in unpaid domestic work. Full-time employed women, by contrast, show a rather smaller decline (4 per cent) in their average paid work time, and part-time employed women actually have a small (1 per cent) increase; to set against these, we have approximately 10 per cent declines in domestic work for both these groups. Overall, total work time (paid plus unpaid) declines about 4 per cent for the men, and by 5 per cent and 7 per cent respectively for the two groups of employed women. This sex differential between the rates of reduction of work time will certainly go some way to reduce the, often remarked, extra burden of work on employed women. The non-employed women, despite a very substantial 75 per cent increase on the small amount of paid work they did in 1961, show overall a 15 per cent reduction of their total workload. Childcare time has increased markedly for all four groups, and they all also show a small proportional decline in the personal care category.

So, work, in the broad sense, and personal care, occupy less time – and leisure activities occupy more. On the narrower definition of leisure time (excluding childcare) the men have 10 per cent more leisure time in 1983/4, on the broader, 13 per cent; the full-time employed women have 19 per cent more on the narrower and 21 per cent more on the broader; the part time employed 12 per cent and 16 per cent; the non-employed women, 17 per cent and 20 per cent. Out-of-home leisure shows a much faster rate of growth than leisure in the home, even though it was by far the smaller category in 1961.

Since the late 1960s we have seen a very substantial increase in involuntary leisure in Britain, in the form of unemployment. But the evidence for a growth in leisure that we have been considering has nothing to do with this. It appears that employed and voluntarily non-employed people do a little less work, and enjoy a rather substantial amount more leisure, in the 1980s than they did in 1961, with the increase consisting largely of a growth in out-of-home leisure activities and in reading, hobbies and conversation at home, rather than passive television viewing or radio-listening.

This is of course not a definitive statement of the past evolution of the work and leisure balance in Britain. There remains much detective work, fitting together the survey data to produce improved accounts of historical change. But the most exciting questions concern what these changes *mean*. How does change in activities outside paid work influence the purchase of goods and services – and hence alter the number and nature of jobs in the economy? Could the growth of new sorts of leisure – or indeed unpaid work – activities, serve to stimulate new paid employment? It is in answering these sorts of questions that the time-budget data will find their most important applications.

Note

1 Sample sizes for the three surveys were:
1961   902 men, 1000 women
1975 1117 men, 1270 women
1983   474 men,   691 women

References

Abrams, M., 1969, 'Die Zeit verwendung in der Britischen Gesellschaft', in Meyershon, R. and Scheuch, E. (eds), *Soziologie der Freizeit*, Köln.

Aubrey, P., Herbert, D., Carr, P.G., Chambers, D.A., Clark, S.C. and Cook, F.G., January 1986, *Work and Leisure in 1980s – The Significance of Changing Patterns*, ed. Nicola Lloyd, London, Sports Council.

BBC Audience Research Department, 1965, *The People's Activities*, London, BBC.

BBC Audience Research Department, 1977, *The People's Activities and Use of Time*, London, BBC.

Becker, G.S., September 1965, 'A theory of the allocation of time', *The Economic Journal*, No. 299, Vol. LXX.

Bevans, G., 1913, *How Working Men Spend Their Spare Time*, New York, Columbia University Press.

Bullock, N., Dickens, P., Shapcott, M. and Steadman, P., 1974, 'Time budgets and models of urban activity patterns', *Social Trends*, CSO.

Gershuny, J. November 1985, 'Developing a multinational time-budget archive', Mimeo from University of Bath.

Gershuny, J., Miles, I., Jones, S., Mullings, C., Thomas, G. and Wyatt, S., 1986, 'Time budgets: preliminary analyses of a national survey', *Quarterly Journal of Social Affairs*, 2 (1), pp. 13–39.

Gershuny, J. and Thomas, G., 1981, 'Changing patterns and time use in UK 1961–1974/5', *SPRU Occasional Paper*, No. 13, University of Sussex.

Gronau, R., 1977, 'Leisure, home production and work: the theory of the allocation of time revisited', *Journal of Political Economy*, Vol. 85.

Hawrylyshyn, O., December 1974, *A Review of Recent Proposals for Modifying and Extending the Measure of GNP*, Ottawa, Statistics Canada.

Hedges, B., March 1986, *National Time-Budget Study*, Methodological Report prepared for the Economic and Social Research Council.

Jones, F.C., 1934, *The Social Survey of Liverpool*, London, University Press Liverpool.

Jones, P.M., Dix, M.C., Clark, M.I. and Heggie, I.G., 1983, *Understanding Travel Behaviour*, Aldershot, Gower.

Knulst, W., 1983, *Waar Blijft de Tijd*, Sociale en Culturele Studies – 4, Staatsuitgeverij 's-Gravenhage.

Lundberg, G., Komarovsky, M. and McInerny, M., 1934, *Leisure: A Suburban Study*, New York, Columbia University Press.

Mass Observation, May/June 1951, 'The housewife's day', *MO Bulletin*, No. 42.

Mass Observation, June 1957, 'The housewife's day', *MO Bulletin*, No. 54.

Meissner, M., Humphreys, E.W., Meis, S.M. and Scheu, W.J., 1974, 'No exit for wives: sexual division of labour and the cumulation of household demands', *Canadian Review of Sociology and Anthropology*, 12 (4), Part (pp. 424–39).

Miles, I., April 1984, *Unemployment, Time Use and the Content of Experiences*, Mimeo, University of Sussex, SPRU, Occasional Paper 21.

Moser, C., 1949, 'Le budget-temps de la femme à Londres dans les classes laborieuses', *Population*, 4, pp. 371–3.

NHK, 1976, *A Report on The How Do People Spend Their Time Survey in 1976*, NHK Public Opinion Research Institute.

Pember-Reeves, M., 1979, (originally 1913) *Round About a Pound a Week*, London, Virago.

Robinson, J., August 1984, *Free Time in Western Countries*, University of Maryland, Survey Research Centre.

Robinson, J. P., August 1977, *Changes in Americans' Use of Time: 1965–1975. A Progress Report*, Cleveland State University.

Robinson, J.P. and Converse, P.C., 1972, 'Social change reflected in the use of time', *The Human Meaning of Social Change*, eds, Campbell and Converse Sage.

Schettkat, R., September 1985, 'The size of household production: methodological problems and estimates for the Federal Republic of Germany in the period 1964–1980', *Income and Wealth*, Series 31, No. 3.

Sorokin, P. and Berger, C., 1939, *Time-Budgets of Human Behavior*, Cambridge, Mass, Harvard University Press.

Tomlinson, J., Bullock, N., Dickens, P., Steadman, P. and Taylor, E., 1973, 'A model of students' daily activity patterns', *Environment and Planning*, 5, pp. 231–66.

Young, M. and Willmott, P., 1975, *The Symmetrical Family*, London, Penguin.

Men and women at play: gender, life-cycle and leisure

Joan Smith

I Leisure and the social obligations of men and women

Defining the concept of leisure has posed problems for sociologists. Traditionally in Britain leisure was often defined in negative terms: leisure was *not* work. Nor was it the labour necessary for home and child-care. Consequently leisure pursuits were often considered as 'left over' after the 'real' worlds of work and home. Outside Britain, however, some sociologists in America and France took a quite different approach, arguing that leisure was a meaningful goal in its own right (Kaplan 1960; Dumazedier 1967). Dumazedier argued that in leisure 'relaxation gives recovery from fatigue, entertainment spells deliverance from boredom', and personal development 'serves to liberate the individual from the daily automatism of thought and action' (Dumazedier 1967:16). In such perspectives leisure needs were seen as less separate from 'real' life than in the British approach and it was not inconceivable that leisure needs might dominate a person's approach to work, or be central to family life. More recently Kelly, following Cheek and Burch (1976), has argued that the quintessential nature of leisure is not only freedom of choice, and engagement in a leisure pursuit for its own sake, but also its role in constructing such 'real' worlds, particularly in constructing family and friendship circles (Kelly 1983:5–19). Leisure is seen as central to all processes of 'social bonding' and it is for this reason that the most 'constrained' type of leisure activity, with family members and friends, is often valued most by participants.

But moving from the question of *what* is leisure to *who* is leisured raises real problems for leisure research. What if the individual is a woman and not a man: what are her means of deliverance from fatigue, boredom and the 'daily automatism of thought and action'? Has leisure research taken seriously her choice of 'means of deliverance' – a choice that might lead to resting and reading, rather than rock-climbing? How far is a woman's 'choice' of leisure constrained by her social status and relationships; her predominant responsibility for home and child-care; her often limited financial resources and lack of financial autonomy; her circles' expectations of 'what women do and don't do'; the influence of sexual and domestic partners over her leisure choice; and of her own self-perception and previous history of self-development?

In this article two approaches to the study of leisure behaviour will be reviewed: first, the influential work of the Rapoports, Kelly, and Young and Willmott on the importance of life-cycle stage for leisure activity; and second, the more recent work by feminist leisure researchers on the relationship between gender and leisure activity. The aim of the article will, then, be to provide an assessment of these approaches in the light of a secondary analysis of the leisure data made available by the 1980 General Household Survey (GHS).[1] In doing this, the article will also provide an evaluation of the GHS data from the point of view of the leisure researcher.

The GHS leisure data sets do have considerable limitations and these are reviewed later. The data sets are, however, the best national data set on leisure, and cover approximately 10,000 households. (For a general discussion on using the GHS for secondary data analysis see Gilbert, Dale and Arber, 1983.) They are more than adequate for an initial exploration of the dual impact of life-cycle and gender on the leisure experience of men and women, allowing answers to two key questions. First, how different are the participation rates in different leisure activities of *men and women* in the *same* family circumstances in any one year? Second, how different are participation rates of *women* in *different* family circumstances? A comparative investigation of these different participation patterns using the 1980 GHS data set will demonstrate how far gender and how far stage of the family life-cycle constrains women's leisure behaviour. Moreover, the sheer size of the GHS data set allows for simple controls on age and occupation of respondents, also making it possible to question Kelly's suggestion (see below) that social status and social class are poor indicators for predicting leisure behaviour.

a) *The family life-cycle and leisure behaviour*

Early British leisure studies often omitted the variable of gender altogether in analysing patterns of participation. Research into gender differences in patterns of leisure stemmed mainly from community studies and the sociology of the family (see Talbot 1979). Other, apparently more gender-aware leisure studies remained problematic. In concentrating on *the family* as a centre for leisure, they underemphasised the importance of the differences in the experience of leisure *within* the family.

In Britain, for example, the Rapoports (with Ziona Strelitz) in their study *Leisure and the Family Life Cycle*, began with Wilensky's summary of American studies, which indicated that leisure behaviour was patterned by class, as well as by individual orientation and family-home-local influences. From their review of British and American leisure studies the Rapoports argued that family situation, especially the particular stage of the family life-cycle, should be placed at the *centre* of three overlapping areas of social life – work, family, and leisure (Rapoport, Rapoport and Strelitz 1975:1–20). Their research, however, failed to focus on the differences between men's and women's experience of leisure, despite the fact that, in contrast to previous research, each person's leisure experience *was* placed in the context of their particular stage in their family life-cycle.

It is John Kelly's work both here and in the United States that has extended and strengthened the Rapoports' case-study approach by directing attention to the utility of survey data. Kelly's United States data demonstrates that the only activities in the top twenty leisure activities that do not usually take place with other family members are reading, arts and crafts, non-familial conversations and hobbies. Of activities with one other person, 70 per cent are with another family member (ibid., p. 23). In a three-community survey in the United States Kelly found that family life-cycle was a major variable in leisure, especially becoming a parent (Kelly 1981:16). Such arguments may appear obvious but, as Kelly suggests, a weakness of leisure research in Britain is that family structure has not been considered as critical a discriminating variable as, for example, social class (Kelly 1981:21).

Kelly, however, fails to identify gender as a key variable. In his *Leisure Identities and Interactions*, he produces tables on family leisure patterns for adults at different stages of their life-cycle, but fails to distinguish between male and female (Kelly 1983:134), providing only two pages on gender differences in leisure (ibid.: 38–40). The heart of the book is about the centrality of the family life-cycle to leisure experience, yet gender differences are virtually ignored. This contrasts sharply with recent feminist orientated leisure research which has taken the experience of women in the family as its starting point (Deem 1982, 1984a, and this volume: Green, Hebron and Woodward 1985; Wimbush 1985).

If Kelly's work is thus one-sided, so also is one of the earliest British surveys of leisure, which put both family and class at the centre of a leisure survey, Young and Willmott's *The Symmetrical Family: A Study of Work and Leisure in the London Region* (1973). Although Young and Willmott argued that social class did not influence leisure behaviour as much as age, marriage and gender, their study failed to develop a full analysis of the relation between family life-cycle and leisure, or the differences between men's and women's leisure, largely because of its central concern with the 'symmetrical family' thesis (see Oakley's critique, Oakley 1974). The Young and Willmott survey was grounded in two central arguments: (i) the rise of a 'symmetrical family' ('a third stage' beyond the 'segregated industrial family', and the earlier 'pre-industrial family') and (ii) the existence of a process of 'stratified diffusion' through which middle-class styles of life were adopted by the working class. 'Stratified diffusion' was also seen as leading women to adopt the styles of life of men: women, like the lower social classes, have demanded the same lives as others and have found the means in technology to attain those lives.

Young and Willmott's analysis of their data can be seen as distorted by the 'symmetrical family' thesis, in particular by the concentration of their main analysis on men. The 411 time-budget diaries (collected from married men and women aged between 30 and 49) did allow confirmation of Szalai's cross-national findings about women's leisure, for example, that women not working outside the home spent *more* time at home at the weekend than either men or women working outside the home, and that women working full-time had the least leisure of all and the most hours of labour, including both work and household tasks (Young and Willmott 1973:99–113 and Appendix 3, Szalai et al. 1972). Nevertheless, the overall conclusion Young and Willmott drew from their analysis was of a greater symmetry in the family, with the gap between the behaviour of men and women narrowing:

The gain for symmetry has been a loss for home-centredness

. . . . But the door is a revolving one, men coming in, women going out. (ibid.: 122)

This narrowing, they argue, is a result of women *reducing* their commitment to housework on entering employment.

In one respect at least, Young and Willmott's research is of great value. It provides a list of those activities that respondents thought were 'work' or 'leisure' and those they thought were 'mixed' (Young and Willmott 1973, p. 210). Paid work was overwhelmingly 'work'; housework and also for men DIY, were mainly 'work'; travel to work, child care, shopping, personal care, eating, sleeping, meals and breaks at paid work, adult education, and civic and collective activities were mixed 'work' and 'leisure'; non-work travel was mainly leisure; entertainment, social contacts, sports, walking and other leisure activities were overwhelmingly leisure. This list is important because there are considerable differences between Young and Willmott's 'subjective' classification of leisure and the GHS, in some respects, more 'imposed' definitions.

b) *Women and leisure – recent research*

Research that emphasises the importance of family life-cycle in determining leisure behaviour poses problems particularly for those theoretical approaches that stress the 'self-actualising' nature of leisure. As Kelly argues:

Joffre Dumazedier proposed that most family activity is at best *semi-leisure* and too laden with obligations to be leisure for its own sake. Family activity is just not free enough to be authentic leisure according to this view. The other pole of the paradox is represented by the accumulated evidence that a high proportion of non-work activity is done with other family members as companions or is essentially familial in its substance. Further, such activity is generally valued most among all the range of leisure choices. How can family-related leisure be both constrained and preferred, least free and most valued. (Kelly 1983: 124)

In an attempt to integrate work on the family life cycle with such theoretical emphasises on the role of freedom in 'authentic' leisure

Kelly has advanced three general propositions for future leisure research. First, leisure is not secondary to work, it is a 'primary social space' in which individual and community identities are developed. Second, the two critical aspects of the meaning of leisure for individuals are freedom to choose activity *and* 'community' participation with significant others, both family and friends. Third, the context of leisure choice is multidimensional; leisure choice is based on more than social position and personal resources, it is also based on opportunities, particularly opportunities governed by ethnicity and gender (Kelly 1981: 8).

Kelly's propositions must be taken seriously but they must also be transformed. Given the centrality of the family to both leisure, and the construction of gender, the gender dimension of leisure cannot be seen as just one more opportunity variable! It is important to integrate the family life-cycle approach with more recent work on the pattern of women's leisure.

In her research review, *Women and Leisure* (1979), Margaret Talbot argued that one of the most important contributions to the study of women's leisure was Sillitoe's (1969) study – which was also used by Young and Willmott as a starting point. She distinguished three elements which Sillitoe's research indicated as significant in women's leisure: a) the home-based domestic nature of much women's leisure, with women more likely to engage in crafts and hobbies, and in social activities and reading; b) the emphasis women themselves placed on domestic or family circumstances curtailing their leisure activities; and c) the quite different club membership of men and women. She also cautioned against the simplistic assumption that removing 'constraints' on women (the provision of crèche facilities, for example) would readily reverse gender differences in participation patterns (Talbot 1979:7).

A further problem identified by Talbot was that standard leisure research techniques might be singularly inappropriate for women: time-budget surveys for example 'tell us little about the way that time is perceived and decisions made by women about its use' (ibid.: 12). For Talbot, 'the perception of free time is a topic which has not been examined in depth' (ibid.: 12) by feminist researchers who have concentrated on what they see as the 'real worlds' of work, family and education. Only since 1979, with the work of Deem, Green, Hebron and Woodward, Wimbush, and Hobson among others, have researchers begun to fill out the picture of women's leisure lives. Of necessity this research has often been small scale, qualitative research. As we shall suggest their findings can be contextualised by a secondary analysis of the GHS data.

Rosemary Deem argues strongly that women have a different attitude to leisure than men:

> Many women do not think of themselves as having leisure time or leisure activities, precisely because they cannot point to any particular time periods or regular activities which are unambiguously pleasurable and not work-related.
> (Deem 1984a:3–4)

Her research into the leisure patterns of employed, non-employed and unemployed women in Milton Keynes was not into leisure *activity* but leisure *space*. She used three hypothetical questions to explore women's attitudes to leisure spaces: How would you use a small amount of time free during the day?; a free day?; a free evening? To fill a small amount of time women in her study would choose to read, sit, watch television or listen to the radio. To use a free day, women would choose to go on an outing to the country, the park or the seaside.

Deem concluded that specific social obligations structure the leisure, or lack of leisure, of women:

> Thus it is not necessarily *paid work* which interferes with leisure (although it may obviously do so), but rather unpaid work and a myriad of other obligations which women, through the sexual division of labour in and outside the household, are subjected to in societies where male dominance is widespread. (Deem 1984a:13)

The ongoing work of Eileen Green, Sandra Hebron and Diana Woodward would appear to reinforce Deem's conclusions, but additionally they argue that women's leisure is actually and actively *controlled*:

> feminist analysis reveals that the area which is portrayed by capitalist ideology as representing the ultimate in freedom from constraint, i.e. leisure, is actually one of the arenas where women's behaviour is regulated the most closely. Women living with male partners are, we would argue, subjected to particular forms of control in this field. (Green, Hebron and Woodward 1985:1)

Joan Smith

From their in-depth interviews the processes by which social constraint is 'genderised' are made visible. They would argue that it is not simply that male domestic partners often refuse to contribute to childcare and domestic labour, it is also that women constitute a part of male leisure and that men actively seek to limit their domestic partner's autonomous leisure, especially with respect to drinking.

Moreover, although women are 'policed' by the men they live with they also 'police' themselves, particularly after the birth of their first child. They may decide, for example, that going to nightclubs is no longer 'suitable' behaviour for a mother. This attitude is likely to be reinforced by the attitude of other women in their social circles (ibid.:8,14). Women are also aware that 'Men not only dominate public places, but also control access to them', and are especially aware of the dangers of being alone on the streets at night. Dixey, for example, has argued that a major reason for the popularity of bingo amongst women is that bingo halls are acceptable places in which women can be seen alone (Dixey 1983: Dixey and Talbot 1982).

Wimbush's (1985) research into the role of leisure in promoting the health and well-being of women concentrates on women at a particular stage in the family life-cycle (mothers with pre-school children). This research addresses many of the questions raised by Kelly but with specific reference to women. Of the seventy women in Wimbush's exploratory study, 'social support' and 'getting on with partner' were ranked as important elements in well-being along with physical fitness, but so was 'time for yourself':

> a commonly-found leisure strategy among mothers in two-parent families was to encourage and welcome their partner going out since his absence enhanced her opportunities for leisure. (ibid.:37).

In such circumstances it is important to ask how far Kelly's findings, often presented as applying to all adults, have a different meaning for men and women. What is leisure for the man may indeed be obligation for the women, (see also Comer 1974). Such research raises once again the question of gender differences in the *meaning* of leisure.

A superficially identical activity may actually be a different activity for men and women when viewed more closely. In Dorothy Hobson's research into the television viewing patterns of

58

young working-class women at home it is clear that television viewing and radio listening were completely interwoven with other activities (they were never mentioned as leisure activities), and also highly selective. Her women viewers rejected news (which was depressing and boring but important), current affairs and documentaries. Serials were particularly important because they were 'something to look forward to next day'; serials were appreciated whether they were realistic, or fantasy, or situation comedy. This may be a quite different use of radio and television compared with men (Hobson 1983).

The GHS data can offer only indirect evidence on these important questions of differences in the way men and women view leisure time, and on differences in the elements of social obligation and social control for men and women represented by leisure behaviour. However, changes in patterns of activity (e.g., from dancing to bingo, from drinking to not drinking) can provide inferential support for suggested differences. Using the GHS data in this way it is possible to explore the influence of gender on participation in different leisure activities, and the impact of different stages in the family life-cycle on gender and leisure participation.

II Using General Household Survey data for leisure research

a) *The leisure section of the GHS schedule*

The annual General Household Survey included questions on leisure in 1973, 1977, 1980, and 1983. Reports on leisure behaviour were provided in the GHS reports of 1973 and 1977 but not in the 1980 Survey Report. There are, however, problems in using the GHS leisure data. First, since 1973 the questions on leisure in the GHS schedule have become more directive. Second, only leisure data for individuals is collected and respondents are not asked with whom they engage in leisure activities. Third, there are statistical problems inherent in the low participation rates reported for some activities.

In the 1973 survey:

no attempt was made to define leisure activities for informants; instead interviewers were told to accept virtually anything that

59

Joan Smith

the informant considered to be a leisure activity. Therefore the assessment of leisure was subjective and varied from one person to another. (GHS 1973:74)

However, in practice the OPCS team excluded as leisure 'reading, non-creative writing, going for a short walk, shopping and sitting around' – at least three of which Deem identified as especially valued leisure activities for women (Deem 1984a). Believing that some activities were under-represented to 1977 the OPCS team changed the questions on leisure. Certain activities – watching television, gardening, listening to the radio, among others – were transferred from an 'aide-memoire' (a flash card handed to the respondent) and were prompted verbally by the interviewer, and other activities – such as playing darts and long-distance walking – were newly specified on the 'aide-memoire'.

Following the first question on leisure, asking whether the respondent had a holiday in the previous four weeks, the second leisure question on the GHS schedule now became:

> Now can you tell me if you have done any of the following things in your leisure time in the 4 weeks ending last Sunday?
> Watched television?
> Listened to the radio?
> Listened to records or tapes?
> Read books?
> Visited friends or relations, or had them come to see you?
> Gone out for a meal or a drink to a restaurant, pub or club (*not* in working hours)?
> Done any:
> gardening
> dressmaking, needlework or knitting
> house repairs or do-it-yourself?

The major impact of these changes for the reported rates of those leisure activities now verbally prompted by the interviewer are indicated by the following table:

	1973%	*1977%*
Visiting or entertaining friends and relations	64	91
Listening to the radio	49	87
Gardening	38	57

60

	1973%	*1977%*
Home Repairs/DIY	11	37
Long Distance Walking	8	22
Playing Darts	3	10

Source: GHS 1977:105

Such changes in participation rates demonstrate the important influence of question wording, and prompting procedures, on reported leisure activities.

The third question on leisure activities was:

> What other things have you done in your leisure time (or on holiday) in the four weeks ending last Sunday?.

All activities mentioned were fully recorded, checking whether the respondent was a participant or an observer and whether the activity was indoor or outdoor, and then the 'aide-memoire' or list of activities was handed to the respondent. This 'aide-memoire' remained the same in 1977, 1980 and 1983:

> Taking part in any form of sport, game or racing
> Watching any form of sport, game or racing (not on TV)
> Going swimming
> Playing darts, billiards, bowls, table tennis
> Walking, rambling, climbing, fishing, camping, etc.
> Outings to the seaside, country, parks, a zoo, etc.
> Other outdoor activities
> Visiting historic buildings, sightseeing
> Going to museums, exhibitions, fairs
> Going to the cinema, theatre, concerts, circus
> Dancing or other entertainment
> Doing a hobby
> Taking part in amateur music or drama
> Doing the pools, betting and gambling, or bingo
> Playing cards, chess or other games of skill
> Going to clubs, societies or meetings
> Doing voluntary work
> Going to leisure classes
> Any other recreational activity?
> (GHS 1983:221)

In 1977, as in 1973, 'no attempt was made to distinguish activities mentioned spontaneously from those mentioned after presentation of the card' (GHS 1977:103). But with the increased specificity of the 1977 prompt and card the interview can be seen as substantially defining 'leisure activities' for the respondent. Finally it is worth noting that not *all* leisure activities offered by respondents were accepted by the interviewer, for example, sitting or resting. These problems remain for more recent data. Questions, prompts and card remained unchanged between 1977, 1980, and 1983, despite the fact that changes were known to have taken place in some patterns of leisure behaviour such as the availability of videos and home computers.

A second problem that arises from the leisure section of the GHS schedule is that leisure activities were recorded for *individuals* only – no leisure information was collected for the household as a whole, or on children under 16 because of the unreliability of leisure information collected by proxy. This omission is compounded by the lack of any question on joint leisure activity with family members or with others. Such a question could accompany or replace the question as to whether a particular leisure activity was done on holiday, or even replace it. The failure to define the context of leisure participation increases the problems associated with the increasing specificity of the 'aide-memoire': e.g., a woman swimming with her child, or playing cards with her child would probably offer that as *her* leisure activity, but perhaps only after being offered the 'aide-memoire'. Not knowing with whom leisure activity was undertaken is a major omission which prevents British leisure researchers testing fully either American findings on the familial context of much leisure, or feminist findings on the constrained character of much of women's leisure.

Third, the OPCS team themselves indicated three other major problems with the way the data were collected: i) the adoption of a four-week reference period was a compromise between asking for activities over one year (a period subject to much overstatement in their view) and asking respondents to keep time budgets; ii) the GHS sample is balanced over each quarter of the year while leisure activities show shorter seasonal fluctuations; iii) many activities are undertaken by only a small part of the population and lead to large sampling errors. In the GHS leisure report, report ranking procedures are used to overcome this problem.

Some of the problems with the leisure data collected from the GHS may have arisen because the questions were initially designed on behalf of a group of government and non-government agencies interested in the future development of leisure *activities*, rather than the analysis of patterns of leisure behaviour (GHS 1973:73). Paradoxically, such policy and planning considerations may have narrowed the usefulness of the data for policy and planning in leisure! It is, after all, important to know whether a particular leisure activity is undertaken by families as a whole, or with the family in tow, or in quite different social contexts. Despite such problems the General Household Survey remains the best national data set on leisure, and these are simply problems of which the researcher must remain aware.

b) *The GHS80 data set*

In order to isolate the effect of gender, family roles including 'symmetricality' – and stage of family life-cycle on leisure activity, a particular group of GHS respondents have been selected to create a data set for secondary analysis (subsequently referred to as the GHS80 data set). To simplify analysis only those living in nuclear households have been included i.e. those living as couples, as couples with children, or as single parent families. Adults living in households (including multiple households) where there were adult children (16+), or other adults than the couple, have been excluded, as have respondents aged over 60 or non-white.[2] This selection provides a focus only on households where all childcare was the responsibility of either the adult male or female in the household.

The 7376 respondents selected (3882 women and 3494 men) lived in 3726 households: 258 'single parent households' (232 'headed' by women, 26 'headed' by men), 1151 'couple households' (adults aged 16–59 with no children), and 2317 'couple-parent households'. In 1162 couple-parent households there were children under 5, and in 1413, all children were aged between 5 and 15. Two-thirds of households had central heating, four-fifths a colour television, and four-fifths a telephone. Nearly 60 per cent of households had one car available, 16 per cent had two vehicles, but 24 per cent had no access to a car. Whilst 91 per cent of heads of households (it on the OPCS definition, usually male) were in paid employment, 4.2 per cent were unemployed and 2.5 per cent 'keeping house'.

All the subsequent tables report percentage participation rates in leisure activities for this data set *over the entire year*, not for the most active quarter for a particular activity as with many OPCS tables. Three activities are not reported at all, although they are classified as leisure activities by the OPCS team: sewing, do-it-yourself, and gardening. Following Young and Willmott all three of these activities have been viewed as 'mainly work', since in the data set it is impossible to distinguish between those who undertake these activities through social obligation and those who undertake them as leisure.

Although the OPCS team collected data on sixteen specified leisure activities for each respondent, only 4.2 per cent of respondents in the selected GHS8O data set offered more than eight activities. Accordingly the tables presented are based on the first eight activities offered. Only thirty-nine activities (for women) and forty-three activities (for men) had annual participation rates of more than 1 per cent. Rather than aggregating similar types of activities I have preferred to look at the different pattern of participation by men and women for the forty-three activities separately, believing that this would provide a fuller picture of gender differences. Avoiding aggregation of activities will provide a fuller picture of gender, and also occupational, differences.[3]

III Gender, household structure and leisure

a) *Gender differences in leisure activity*

It is necessary first to outline the pattern of leisure activity for the adult men and women in the selected data set. Table 1 shows participation rates for those leisure activities identified by the GHS Leisure questions 1 and 2, Table 2 gives the number of further leisure activities reported by respondents (Question 3), and Table 3 provides the detailed breakdown of these activities.

Five points can be noted from these three tables:

1 The extraordinary pull of the home in leisure activities is confirmed. The only activity that had the same participation rate as watching TV, listening to radio and records, etc. was visiting friends and relatives *in their homes*. The participation rates for these activities were much higher than either drinking or eating out; they were also much higher than participation in other media activities such as going to a film. Leaving aside the world

Table 1: *Use of leisure time by gender*

	All	Males	Females
Had a Holiday	21.6	21.2	22.0
Watched TV	100.0	100.0	100.0
Visited Friends	95.1	94.2	95.9
Listened to Radio	91.5	90.9	92.1
Listened to Records	74.9	74.1	75.5
Gone out for a drink	64.0	71.3	57.5
Read Books	57.7	52.1	62.7
Gone out for a meal	45.3	45.2	45.5
N=	7376	3494	3882

of work, people at this stage of their lives participated in society mainly in their own and in other people's homes.

2 Women were more likely than men to have had no other leisure activities than those prompted, and in general would appear to engage in fewer leisure activities than men. (However, the inclusion of sewing and knitting as leisure activities would alter this picture.)

3 There was a low level of participation in *active* physical pursuits apart from walking, dancing and swimming, *especially* for women.

Table 2: *Number of other activities in previous four weeks, by gender*

	All	Males	Females
None	15.1	11.0	18.8
1	19.0	15.3	22.4
2	19.0	18.4	19.5
3	15.6	17.3	14.0
4	11.1	12.7	9.7
5	7.9	9.8	6.3
6	5.2	5.8	4.6
7	3.0	3.6	2.5
8–16	4.2	5.9	2.3
N=	7376	3494	3882

Table 3: *Leisure activities by gender*

	All	Male	Female
do pools	23.3	32.5	14.9
other walking	21.7	22.0	21.4
chess, indoor games	19.1	22.2	16.4
going dancing	12.8	11.4	14.1
social clubs	11.9	12.5	11.3
visiting historical monument	10.1	10.3	9.9
going to a film	9.3	8.9	9.7
indoor swimming	9.2	9.3	9.0
visiting seaside	9.1	8.5	9.7
voluntary work	8.2	6.8	9.5
darts	8.1	12.9	3.8
bingo	7.8	4.4	10.8
hobbies/crafts	7.1	11.3	3.3
snooker	6.6	12.7	1.1
visiting parks	5.9	5.2	6.5
visiting countryside	5.2	5.1	5.3
going to a theatre	5.0	4.1	5.8
watching soccer	4.6	8.0	1.5
betting	3.9	6.4	1.6
visiting museum	3.7	3.5	3.8
squash	3.5	5.5	1.6
other entertainment	3.4	3.2	3.6
badminton	3.2	3.1	3.3
sing/dance/act	3.1	3.6	2.7
visiting zoo	2.5	2.3	2.8
(visiting safari park	0.6	0.6	0.7)
visiting show	3.0	2.8	3.1
golf	2.9	5.2	0.8
rowing, canoeing	2.7	3.1	2.4
going to fun fair	2.7	2.4	3.0
other local ents.	2.6	2.2	2.9
soccer	2.6	5.4	0.1
fishing	2.5	4.4	0.7
keepfit, yoga	2.4	0.7	4.0
table tennis	2.1	3.0	1.2
evening classes	1.7	0.8	2.4
car, motor-cycle outing	1.6	1.8	1.4
cycling	1.6	1.8	1.4

	All	Male	Female
tennis	1.5	1.8	1.3
camping, caravaning	1.4	1.4	1.4
ten pin bowling	1.4	1.9	0.9
cooking/wine	1.4	1.7	1.2
keeping animals	1.2	1.9	0.6
field athletics	1.2	1.9	0.4
watching indoor swimming	1.1	0.5	1.6
Total N	7376	3494	3882

4 Women apparently attach greater importance to cultural and social pursuits in their leisure: e.g. going to a film, going to a theatre, voluntary work and attending evening classes.
5 'Pub leisure' and active sports are clearly of greater importance for men than for women: e.g. playing darts and snooker.

It is also important to recall (Hobson 1983) that even where women and men nominally participate in the same activities those activities may in fact be very different. This may be true, not only of television watching or radio listening, but also of walking or swimming; women may well undertake such activities, combining walking with shopping and swimming with child-care, in quite different circumstances from men. Certain of the findings of the analysis of GHS8O – such as the increase in *watching* swimming as a 'leisure' activity among mothers with young children would seem to confirm this.

b) *Other influences on leisure behaviour*

Before examining the difference controlling for household structure makes to the relationship between gender and leisure activities, it is also necessary to explore whether other variables should also be controlled for. The 1973 GHS Report concluded that 'six main factors determine participation in leisure activities: age, sex, social class, income, car ownership and education' (GHS 1973:103; see also GHS 1977:135, Table 7.41, and GHS 1983:135). The leisure by gender tables (Tables 1–3) were re-run controlling for each of these variables. Of these variables, controlling for age and occupation produced the most interesting results. First, the distribution of leisure activity by age and gender showed a different pattern than might have been expected. Second, the distribution of leisure activity by gender and occupation appeared to contradict the findings of both Kelly and Young and Willmott.[4]

While most previous leisure research points to a decline in active leisure pursuits with increasing age, for this group of respondents, the most active age group for both men and women was 30–39 years, followed by the under 29s, and then those 40–59. For both men and women many active sports peaked in the second age group, 30–39, rather than the first. Social club involvement and voluntary work both rose with age, but for women voluntary work peaked in the age range 30–39, and for men and women, theatre going and going dancing both peaked in the oldest age group, 40–59. However, women of all age groups remained more likely than men to reply that they had no or only one leisure activity. Two different explanations can be suggested for this pattern. First, higher activity among the under 29s is usually a function of not yet having had children. The significant break in leisure activity is at the point of setting up home and family, rather than age-related per se. Second, for those over 40, when physical activities fall and child-rearing responsibilities have also declined, it would appear that a new pattern of mutual activity is established, more attuned to the pursuits women enjoy – although one cannot know for certain if this is so without information on who did what with whom.

In controlling for occupation women were coded on both their own occupation and on the occupation of their male partners, although the tables reported (Tables 4–6) refer only to women coded on their own occupation. Occupation was coded into four categories: professionals, employers and managers (group 1); ancillary and junior non-manual (group 2); skilled workers and own-account workers (group 3); and semi-skilled, unskilled and personal service workers (group 4).[5]

In the number of activities volunteered by men and women for the previous four weeks (Table 5), gender overrode differences of occupation. Women, in general from whatever occupation, took part in fewer activities than did all men. A manual non-manual divide in leisure activities did appear to exist, however, for both men and for women. As seen from Table 6, a distinctive *semi-skilled/unskilled* male workers' culture is also apparent, based on pub culture (darts and snooker) and betting. (Moreover these men

Table 4: *Use of leisure time by gender by occupation*

OWN OCCUPATION – MEN AND WOMEN

	All	ALL		MALES				FEMALES			
		Males	Females	1	2	3	4	1	2	3	4
Had a Holiday	21.6	21.2	22.0	29.8	22.7	18.3	13.7	30.9	25.7	18.0	16.1
Watched TV	100.0	100.0	100.0	100.0	100.0	100.0	100.0	100.0	100.0	100.0	100.0
Visited Friends	95.1	94.2	95.9	96.0	97.1	93.5	90.4	95.1	97.3	97.4	93.7
Listened to Radio	91.5	90.9	92.1	93.9	93.6	89.2	88.4	91.7	93.5	91.1	90.5
Listened to Records	74.9	74.1	75.5	78.6	76.8	72.1	69.7	80.9	78.7	78.0	69.5
Gone out for drink	64.0	71.3	57.5	65.7	67.6	74.8	73.6	52.5	56.7	61.0	59.9
Read Books	57.7	52.1	62.7	66.0	65.3	43.5	38.7	75.0	69.9	55.7	52.0
Gone out for a meal	45.3	45.2	45.5	62.1	50.4	39.1	28.1	61.8	51.7	42.6	34.9
N=	7376	3494	3882	865	577	1499	519	204	1994	305	1310

1 Professionals, employers and managers
2 Ancillary and junior non-manual
3 Skilled women and own-account workers
4 Semi-skilled, unskilled and personal service workers

Table 5: *Number of other activities in previous four weeks by gender by occupation*

| | All | ALL | | | OWN OCCUPATION – MEN AND WOMEN | | | | | | | |
| | | Male | Female | | MALES | | | | FEMALES | | | |
				1	2	3	4	1	2	3	4
None	15.1	11.0	18.8	8.8	8.7	12.7	13.5	13.7	16.3	21.3	22.1
1	19.0	15.3	22.4	12.8	13.2	17.1	16.4	22.1	19.6	22.3	26.6
2	19.0	18.4	19.5	15.5	18.4	18.2	24.1	12.7	19.7	19.3	20.3
3	15.6	17.3	14.0	18.7	15.8	17.3	15.4	19.1	14.9	13.1	11.9
4	11.1	12.7	9.7	13.3	10.1	13.6	12.5	14.7	10.5	9.5	7.9
5	7.9	9.8	6.3	10.9	14.0	8.8	6.7	6.4	8.0	4.6	4.0
6	5.2	5.8	4.6	7.1	7.3	4.7	5.6	7.4	4.9	6.6	3.4
7	3.0	3.6	2.5	5.1	5.5	2.5	2.5	2.5	3.0	2.0	2.0
8	1.9	2.7	1.2	4.0	3.5	2.1	1.2	1.0	1.6	1.0	0.2
N =	7376	3494	3882	865	577	1499	519	204	1992	305	1310

were least likely to go dancing – a prized leisure activity for women.) The female counterpart to this culture was bingo. To some extent these male and female cultures also exerted influence on all men and women. Men from all four occupational groups were more likely to be part of the pub culture than all women: and all women except 'professionals' were more likely to go to bingo than all men. Important differences between unskilled manual workers and non-manual workers were apparent in the participation rates for activities favoured in general by women, such as film going and theatre going.

One further interesting point is that women in the highest occupational group were the most active in cultural and civic pursuits but not in physical ones. It was women in the second occupational group, i.e. ancillary and junior non-manual workers, who were the most active indoor swimmers, darts players, walkers, rowers, keep-fitters, and visitors to parks and zoos. It is worth noting that these differences are not apparent when women were recoded using head of household's occupation.

Clearly, at odds with Kelly, occupational status remains a generally relevant factor in leisure behaviour. In our subsequent analysis of gender, family life-cycle and leisure activities, occupational classification cannot be made. However, when class is included in subsequent tables, in order to retain sufficient respondents in the cells only a non-manual/manual distinction is feasible.

c) *Family life-cycle and leisure activities*

The subsequent tables are intended to demonstrate clearly the break that occurs in the leisure patterns of adults when young children are in the household, and the differential nature of this break for men and women.

All adults aged 40–59 have been eliminated from the following tables in order to reduce the effect of age on leisure behaviour. This control on age has the advantage of eliminating most couples who have already passed through their child-rearing phase.

From Tables 7–9 it is possible to see the effect on leisure activities of living with small children for all adults aged less than 40.

Several points stand out:

1 From Table 7 it is apparent that while most home based activities stay the same (watching TV, listening to the radio and visiting friends) others, such as listening to records and reading books, decline markedly for both men and women in households with small children in comparison with households without any children. This would reflect an absence of real leisure 'space', or time for oneself.

2 Again from Table 7, while most activities decline for both men and women with small children others do not, e.g. 'going out for a drink'. This activity declines 12 per cent for men with small children under 5 but 27 per cent for women. While some women return to 'going out for a drink' in households with children aged 5–15, differences between male and female drinking habits remain.

3 In Table 8 we find 22.7 per cent of women with children under 5 reporting only 'prompted' leisure activities, compared with 11.4 per cent of men similarly placed, and 12.9 per cent of women in couple only households.

4 In Table 9 further differences in leisure activities between men and women in couple – only and children-couple households are seen. For example, although the proportion of men who played darts and snooker is only slightly reduced for men with young children compared with those without children or with older children, pub-based leisure is common only for women without children (although bingo is a frequent activity for women with small children). Activity rates for going to the theatre, films or

Table 6: Leisure activities by gender, by occupation

| | ALL | | | OWN OCCUPATION – MEN AND WOMEN | | | | | | | |
| | | | | MALES | | | | FEMALES | | | |
	All	Male	Female	1	2	3	4	1	2	3	4
do pools	23.3	32.5	14.9	20.9	28.8	38.2	40.5	9.8	13.1	19.3	17.6
other walking	21.7	22.0	21.4	29.1	25.6	17.5	19.3	23.0	24.0	19.7	17.9
chess, indoor games	19.1	22.2	16.4	22.5	23.6	20.9	23.9	20.6	17.4	18.0	14.2
going dancing	12.8	11.4	14.1	13.2	10.2	12.3	7.9	17.6	14.2	13.8	13.6
social clubs	11.9	12.5	11.3	15.0	14.4	11.3	10.8	12.7	12.3	11.5	9.4
visit his. monument	10.1	10.3	9.9	16.0	13.7	8.1	3.5	11.8	11.8	7.5	7.6
going to a film	9.3	8.9	9.7	9.6	9.2	8.9	7.7	12.3	11.7	6.2	6.9
swimming indoor	9.2	9.3	9.0	12.3	10.6	8.6	5.4	8.3	11.0	6.2	6.9
visiting seaside	9.1	8.5	9.7	9.7	10.1	7.7	6.9	7.4	10.0	10.8	9.4
voluntary work	8.2	6.8	9.5	11.9	7.3	4.3	3.7	12.3	10.9	11.8	6.6
darts	8.1	12.9	3.8	8.3	12.1	14.1	17.5	1.5	3.9	2.6	4.4
bingo	7.8	4.4	10.8	1.3	2.4	5.6	8.1	5.4	6.8	11.8	17.9
hobbies/crafts	7.1	11.3	3.3	11.4	17.3	10.1	7.7	5.4	4.0	4.3	1.9
snooker	6.6	12.7	1.1	9.8	11.6	13.1	17.5	1.5	0.8	1.3	1.5
visiting parks	5.9	5.2	6.5	5.3	6.4	5.4	3.3	3.9	7.6	5.6	5.5
visiting countryside	5.2	5.1	5.3	7.1	6.1	4.4	3.1	3.4	5.9	6.9	4.5
going to theatre	5.0	4.1	5.8	9.8	4.2	2.0	1.2	14.2	7.2	3.3	3.1
watching soccer	4.6	8.0	1.5	7.3	8.1	8.1	8.7	0.0	1.9	1.3	1.4
betting	3.9	6.4	1.6	3.8	4.7	6.8	11.8	0.5	1.6	2.6	1.6
visiting museum	3.7	3.5	3.8	5.2	4.7	2.5	2.1	8.3	3.9	3.6	3.1
squash	3.5	5.5	1.6	10.9	7.6	3.1	1.3	3.9	2.4	0.3	0.5

	7376	3494	3882	865	577	1499	519	204	1994	305	1310
other entertainment	3.4	3.2	3.6	4.3	3.5	2.7	2.3	7.4	3.8	3.3	3.0
badminton	3.2	3.1	3.3	4.9	5.7	1.9	0.8	4.4	4.7	2.0	1.4
sing/dance/act	3.1	3.6	2.7	4.6	7.6	2.1	1.5	5.9	3.7	1.6	0.9
visiting zoo	2.5	2.3	2.8	2.9	2.1	1.9	2.5	2.0	3.6	2.3	1.8
visiting safari park	0.6	0.6	0.7	0.3	0.7	0.6	0.8	0.5	0.8	0.3	0.8
visiting show	3.0	2.8	3.1	5.2	2.8	2.0	1.0	5.4	3.8	2.3	1.8
golf	2.9	5.2	0.8	9.4	7.6	3.1	1.3	2.0	0.9	1.0	0.4
rowing, canoeing	2.7	3.1	2.4	5.0	2.6	2.7	1.5	2.5	2.8	2.0	1.9
going to fun fair	2.7	2.4	3.0	2.9	1.4	2.5	2.5	2.9	2.8	3.9	3.1
other local ents.	2.6	2.2	2.9	2.5	2.4	2.4	1.0	2.9	3.0	3.9	2.5
soccer	2.6	5.4	0.1	3.8	6.4	5.7	5.6	0.0	0.1	0.0	0.2
fishing	2.5	4.4	0.7	3.5	3.6	5.3	1.0	0.0	0.8	1.0	0.8
keepfit, yoga	2.4	0.7	4.0	1.2	0.5	0.5	0.4	4.4	5.1	2.3	3.0
table tennis	2.1	3.0	1.2	3.6	4.9	2.5	1.7	1.5	1.6	1.0	0.6
evening classes	1.7	0.8	2.4	1.5	1.6	0.4	0.2	4.4	3.3	1.6	0.8
car, m-c outing	1.6	1.8	1.4	1.4	1.9	2.2	1.3	1.5	1.5	1.6	1.4
cycling	1.6	1.8	1.4	2.0	3.3	1.3	0.8	2.5	1.7	1.3	1.0
tennis	1.5	1.8	1.3	3.5	1.6	1.4	0.6	1.5	1.6	1.0	0.9
camping, caravaning	1.4	1.4	1.4	1.8	1.6	1.3	1.0	2.5	1.5	2.0	1.1
ten pin bowling	1.4	1.9	0.9	1.3	2.3	1.3	1.3	0.0	0.8	1.6	1.2
cooking/wine	1.4	1.7	1.2	2.2	2.4	1.5	0.8	0.5	1.5	1.0	1.0
keeping animals	1.2	1.9	0.6	1.6	1.9	2.0	2.3	0.5	0.7	1.3	0.5
field athletics	1.2	1.9	0.4	3.0	3.1	1.1	0.6	0.0	0.8	0.0	0.1
watch ind swimming	1.1	0.5	1.6	0.7	0.5	0.4	0.6	2.5	1.7	2.0	1.1
N=	7376	3494	3882	865	577	1499	519	204	1994	305	1310

Table 7: *Use of leisure time by gender adults aged less than 40 by household type*

	All All	All		CH		CPH LT 5		CPH 5–15	
		Males	Fems	Males	Fems	Males	Fems	Males	Fems
Had a Holiday	21.6	21.2	21.0	27.7	29.2	19.9	19.5	18.6	20.1
Watched TV	100.0	100.0	100.0	100.0	100.0	100.0	100.0	100.0	100.0
Visited Friends	95.1	94.2	95.9	97.9	97.4	96.1	97.0	93.4	95.6
Listened to Radio	91.5	90.9	92.1	95.4	96.1	90.1	91.6	90.9	93.5
Listened to Records	74.9	74.1	75.5	87.4	85.8	73.9	76.8	78.3	80.1
Gone out for a drink	64.0	71.3	57.5	85.7	79.8	73.9	52.9	75.5	61.3
Read Books	57.7	52.1	62.7	58.4	72.1	46.9	59.1	50.8	63.3
Gone out for a meal	45.3	45.2	45.5	63.6	64.6	39.1	37.2	44.8	46.8
N=	7376	3494	3882	483	583	1016	1117	723	958

*CH = couple household, CPH LT 5 = couple parent household with children less than five years of age, CPH 5–15 = couple parent household with children aged between 5 and 15 years for this and subsequent tables. A separate analysis of single parent households is not given.

Table 8: *Number of other activities in previous four weeks, adults aged less than 40 years by gender by household type*

	All	Male	Female	CH Male	CH Female	CPH LT 5 Male	CPH LT 5 Female	CPH 5–15 Male	CPH 5–15 Female
None	15.1	11.0	18.8	7.9	12.9	11.4	22.7	8.6	15.0
1	19.0	15.3	22.4	11.6	20.4	16.4	23.8	14.4	19.7
2	19.0	18.4	19.5	14.5	20.6	20.7	18.4	15.9	18.5
3	15.6	17.3	14.0	17.4	16.1	17.2	12.8	17.4	15.9
4	11.1	12.7	9.7	14.9	9.9	12.8	9.7	12.0	10.6
5	7.9	9.8	6.3	13.9	8.4	7.7	5.2	11.5	7.5
6	5.2	5.8	4.6	6.8	6.0	5.1	4.4	7.5	5.0
7	3.0	3.6	2.5	5.0	2.4	3.3	1.5	5.4	4.1
8	1.9	2.7	1.2	3.5	1.7	3.0	1.0	2.9	1.9
N=	7376	3494	3882	483	534	1016	1117	723	958

shows, and for going dancing, also decline for women with young children.

From Tables 7–9 in general there would appear to be a significant break in activity for adults in households with children aged less than 5. This break is apparent for both men and women but it is more dramatic for women. However, it is also apparent that for adult men and women with small children, men's community activity fell while women's rose: for men community activity and family commitments appear in conflict, for women more complementary. In households with children, going to the pub becomes an even more pronounced male activity; bingo became a correspondingly more female one. Women's physical activities – apart from keep fit and dancing – seem increasingly bound up with children's activities in ways that men's activities are not: cycling, golf, tennis, badminton, squash all decline for women, but swimming does not. For men many activities also decline, but less than for women, and some do not decline at all. Although for women as for men, swimming increases as a pastime, this may well be an activity that is undertaken for the benefit of children.

Table 9: *Leisure activities of adults aged less than 40 by gender by household type*

	All	ALL		CH		CPH LT 5		CPH 5–15	
		Male	Female	Male	Female	Male	Female	Male	Female
do pools	23.3	32.5	14.9	28.2	14.8	30.2	10.2	32.8	16.5
other walking	21.7	22.0	21.4	26.3	26.4	19.6	20.7	20.1	19.6
chess, indoor games	19.1	22.2	16.4	24.6	18.2	20.0	14.4	28.2	19.6
going dancing	12.8	11.4	14.1	13.7	17.8	7.8	10.0	12.3	14.5
social clubs	11.9	12.5	11.3	13.7	7.5	9.8	10.6	13.6	12.6
visit hist. monument	10.1	10.3	9.9	14.7	15.4	7.4	7.0	9.3	10.3
going to a film	9.3	8.9	9.7	20.3	21.7	8.4	7.9	7.9	8.9
indoor swimming	9.2	9.3	9.0	7.0	8.4	12.1	12.4	12.9	10.9
visiting seaside	9.1	8.5	9.7	8.1	8.4	9.5	11.3	9.1	11.7
voluntary work	8.2	6.8	9.5	7.7	4.7	4.3	8.6	7.7	13.3
darts	8.1	12.9	3.8	16.8	6.6	13.7	2.1	18.1	4.7
bingo	7.8	4.4	10.8	3.1	6.6	3.1	11.4	4.0	12.7
hobbies/crafts	7.1	11.3	3.3	15.5	4.1	10.9	3.4	10.5	3.2
snooker	6.6	12.7	1.1	17.6	3.0	13.9	0.8	15.4	1.2
visiting parks	5.9	5.2	6.5	3.1	3.2	7.2	10.4	5.4*	6.5
visiting countryside	5.2	5.1	5.3	6.2	6.7	4.5	4.8	4.4	5.3
going to theatre	5.0	4.1	4.8	5.6	7.1	1.8	2.4	4.1	6.9
watching soccer	4.6	8.0	1.5	8.5	2.8	9.1	0.7	10.2	2.0
betting	3.9	6.4	1.6	7.2	2.2	6.0	0.4	6.4	2.2
visiting museum	3.7	3.5	3.8	2.9	3.4	3.0	3.3	3.7	4.9
squash	3.5	5.5	1.6	9.9	3.7	7.0	1.8	6.2	2.1
other entertainment	3.4	3.2	3.6	4.1	3.7	2.7	3.0	3.2	4.2
badminton	3.2	3.1	3.3	5.2	5.4	3.5	3.2	2.6	4.3
sing/dance/act	3.1	3.6	2.7	5.6	5.1	3.2	1.9	2.8	2.0
visiting zoo	2.5	2.3	2.8	1.4	0.9	3.3	4.8	2.9	3.3
(visiting safari park	0.6	0.6	0.7	0.6	0.7	0.5	0.9	0.7	0.7)
visiting show	3.0	2.8	3.1	4.3	5.1	1.7	2.1	3.2	3.9
golf	2.9	5.2	0.8	3.1	0.6	3.8	0.2	6.2	0.8
rowing, canoeing	2.7	3.1	2.4	2.7	2.4	3.0	2.1	4.4	3.5
going to fun fair	2.7	2.4	3.0	2.1	2.1	3.4	4.8	3.2	3.7
other local ents.	2.6	2.2	2.9	1.7	1.9	2.5	3.2	2.5	3.8
soccer	2.6	5.4	0.1	10.8	0.4	7.9	0.0	5.5	0.2
fishing	2.5	4.4	0.7	5.6	0.7	5.5	0.5	4.1	0.9
keepfit, yoga	2.4	0.7	4.0	1.2	5.1	0.6	3.5	0.6	5.4
table tennis	2.1	3.0	1.2	2.9	1.5	3.0	0.9	4.4	1.7
evening classes	1.7	0.8	2.4	1.0	3.2	1.0	1.7	0.8	2.0
car, m-c outing	1.6	1.8	1.4	2.1	1.9	2.1	1.4	1.2	0.8
cycling	1.6	1.8	1.4	1.9	1.7	1.8	0.8	1.7	2.2
tennis	1.5	1.8	1.3	3.5	2.1	1.9	1.1	1.2	1.5
camping, caravaning	1.4	1.4	1.4	1.7	1.7	0.8	0.6	1.4	2.2
ten pin bowling	1.4	1.9	0.9	2.1	1.3	1.1	0.4	2.5	1.1
cooking/wine	1.4	1.7	1.2	3.1	1.5	1.8	1.2	0.6	0.5
keeping animals	1.2	1.9	0.6	2.1	1.7	1.3	0.2	3.3	0.8
field athletics	1.2	1.9	0.4	2.5	0.9	2.0	0.3	2.6	0.4
watch ind swimming	1.1	0.5	1.6	–	–	0.4	1.6	0.7	3.1
Total N	7376	3494	3882	483	534	1016	1117	723	958

d) *Leisure activity, occupational status, and the 'symmetrical family' hypothesis*

Controlling for household type has demonstrated how the presence of small children in the household changes the leisure activity patterns of *both* men and women. But this change is unequal. It might be possible to argue that men and women's domestic lives are *becoming* more symmetrical with respect to leisure patterns, but not that this pattern has been achieved. From the analysis undertaken it appears that men accept some restructuring of their leisure activities when children less than 5 are in the household, but when children are older (5–15) they are more likely to regain their old activities or initiate new patterns. The restructuring of women's leisure activities would seem both more profound and less easily reversed.

Young and Willmott's thesis was in two parts. The argument was both that there was a *tendency* for relationships to become more symmetrical and also that this tendency would become increasingly pronounced in the working-class family as it becomes even more home-centred than the middle-class family (Young and Willmott 1973). Almost a decade after their survey, a decade of the rise of feminism and increase in part-time working women, we can explore this hypothesis by examining the leisure patterns of 'working-class' and 'middle-class' men and women in households of different type.

Tables 10–12 summarise the leisure behaviour of both men and women manual workers, all aged less than 40, controlling for household type, and with women coded on their own occupation.

1 From Table 10 we can note *continuing* gender and occupational differences in the use of leisure time, and little to support the thin hypotheses of 'symmetry'. For example, reading books declines more among female non-manual than male non-manual, albeit from a higher base. 'Going out for a drink' declines much less for both non-manual and manual men than for non-manual and manual women.
2 From Table 11 we can also note that both non-manual and manual women with children under 5 remain much more likely than men to record no 'other leisure activities'.
3 From Table 12, it is also clear that while some activities fell and others rose for both non-manual and manual men with children under 5, pub culture remained extremely strong for manual

Table 10: *Use of leisure time by gender by household structure by occupation, adults aged less than 40*

| | | ALL | | NON-MANUAL | | | | | | MANUAL | | | | | |
| | | | | CH | | CPH LT 5 | | CPH 5-15 | | CH | | CPH LT 5 | | CPH 5-15 | |
	All	Males	Female	Male	Female	Male	Female	Male	Female	Male	Female	Male	Female	Male	Female
Had a holiday	21.6	21.2	22.0	35.2	33.4	25.7	21.9	23.6	23.3	20.3	16.3	16.6	16.0	15.8	16.4
Watched TV	100.0	100.0	100.0	100.0	100.0	100.0	100.0	100.0	100.0	100.0	100.0	100.0	100.0	100.0	100.0
Visited Friends	95.1	94.2	95.9	99.1	98.3	97.6	97.7	96.9	97.5	97.2	94.6	95.2	95.8	91.7	93.9
Listened to Radio	91.5	90.9	92.1	96.9	96.8	94.0	93.1	93.8	93.3	94.0	93.6	87.9	89.8	89.5	93.9
Listened to Records	74.9	74.1	75.5	92.1	87.3	81.2	78.9	79.2	84.7	82.9	81.4	69.9	73.4	77.9	75.3
Gone out for a drink	64.0	71.3	57.5	81.5	79.8	67.8	50.6	72.2	59.5	89.2	79.1	77.5	56.9	77.5	64.2
Read Books	57.7	52.1	62.7	67.8	78.1	62.8	66.5	61.8	70.3	49.4	55.0	37.0	48.4	44.5	55.9
Gone out for a meal	45.3	45.2	45.5	74.4	70.3	51.6	41.2	59.8	53.6	53.4	47.3	31.2	31.0	36.9	40.0
N =	7376	3494	3882	227	401	382	662	259	489	251	129	621	432	458	458

Table 11: *Number of other activities in previous four weeks, by gender, by household structure, and by occupation, adults aged less than 40 years*

| | ALL | | | NON-MANUAL | | | | | | MANUAL | | | | | |
| | | | CH | | CPH LT 5 | | CPH 5-15 | | CH | | CPH LT 5 | | CPH 5-15 | |
	All	Male	Female	Male	Female	Male	Female	Male	Female	Male	Female	Male	Female	Male	Female
None	15.1	11.0	18.8	4.8	11.5	9.9	20.8	5.8	12.5	10.8	17.1	12.4	25.5	10.3	17.5
1	19.0	15.3	22.4	9.7	17.5	16.2	22.4	10.4	17.0	13.1	30.2	16.4	25.9	16.6	22.5
2	19.0	18.4	19.5	11.0	21.4	16.5	18.0	16.2	18.2	17.9	18.6	23.2	18.8	15.9	18.8
3	15.6	17.3	14.0	19.4	16.7	17.5	13.0	17.0	17.6	15.1	14.7	17.1	12.0	17.0	14.2
4	11.1	12.7	9.7	14.5	10.2	12.8	11.8	10.0	11.7	15.1	7.8	12.9	6.7	13.1	9.8
5	7.9	9.8	6.3	13.2	9.5	9.4	6.3	13.1	8.4	14.7	4.7	6.8	3.7	10.7	6.3
6	5.2	5.8	4.6	8.4	7.2	6.0	3.9	9.3	5.7	5.6	2.3	4.5	5.3	6.6	4.4
7	3.0	3.6	2.5	7.0	2.2	4.7	2.1	9.3	4.3	3.2	3.1	2.6	0.7	3.3	3.9
8	1.9	2.7	1.2	4.8	2.0	4.5	1.1	4.6	2.5	2.4	0.8	2.1	0.9	2.0	1.3
N=	7376	3494	3882	227	401	382	662	259	489	251	129	621	432	458	458

Table 12: *Leisure activities by gender, by household structure and by occupation, adults aged less than 40*

| | | ALL | | NON-MANUAL | | | | | | MANUAL | | | | | |
| | | | | CH | | CPH LT 5 | | CPH 5–15 | | CH | | CPH LT 5 | | CPH 5–15 | |
	All	Male	Female	Male	Female	Male	Female	Male	Female	Male	Female	Male	Female	Male	Female
do pools	23.3	32.5	14.9	22.0	14.7	21.5	7.7	24.3	14.7	33.9	15.5	35.7	13.7	37.6	18.6
other walking	21.7	22.0	21.4	33.9	27.4	24.1	22.4	26.3	20.4	18.7	21.7	17.1	18.8	16.8	19.0
chess, indoor games	19.1	22.2	16.4	26.4	19.2	19.9	14.0	10.3	14.0	22.7	14.0	20.0	15.0	27.5	18.1
going dancing	12.8	11.4	14.1	12.8	18.0	9.2	10.6	14.7	15.3	14.7	17.1	6.9	8.8	11.1	14.0
social clubs	11.9	12.5	11.3	18.9	8.5	11.0	11.0	16.2	15.2	9.2	4.7	9.2	9.7	12.2	9.8
visit his, monument	10.1	10.3	9.9	19.8	17.7	11.5	7.9	14.3	10.2	10.0	7.8	4.8	6.0	6.6	10.7
going to a film	9.3	8.9	9.7	23.3	23.7	7.9	9.1	7.3	10.8	17.9	15.5	8.7	6.0	8.1	6.6
swimming indoor	9.2	9.3	9.0	7.5	9.2	16.2	15.1	18.1	11.7	6.8	5.4	9.8	8.8	10.0	10.0
visiting seaside	9.1	8.5	9.7	10.6	7.7	11.3	12.3	13.9	12.1	6.0	10.9	8.5	10.0	6.3	11.4
voluntary work	8.2	6.8	9.5	12.8	5.7	7.1	9.7	10.8	16.0	2.8	1.6	2.3	7.2	5.9	10.7
darts	8.1	12.9	3.8	16.3	7.2	8.1	1.5	12.7	4.3	17.5	4.7	16.7	2.8	21.2	5.2
bingo	7.8	4.4	10.8	0.9	3.5	1.0	7.1	1.5	9.4	2.0	0.0	2.1	0.5	2.0	1.3
hobbies/crafts	7.1	11.3	3.3	15.4	4.5	14.7	4.2	12.7	4.3	15.1	3.1	8.7	2.3	9.4	2.2
snooker	6.6	12.7	1.1	14.5	2.2	7.9	0.2	15.8	1.0	20.7	5.4	17.6	1.6	15.1	1.7
visiting parks	5.9	5.2	6.5	2.2	3.0	8.6	12.5	6.9	7.6	4.0	3.9	6.4	7.4	4.6	5.2
visiting countryside	5.2	5.1	5.3	8.8	6.7	5.2	5.1	6.9	6.3	4.0	6.2	4.0	4.6	3.1	4.4
going to a theatre	5.0	4.1	5.8	10.6	8.5	4.2	3.8	6.6	8.4	1.2	3.1	0.3	0.5	2.8	5.2
watching soccer	4.6	8.0	1.5	7.5	3.2	7.6	0.8	12.4	1.8	9.6	1.6	10.0	0.7	9.2	2.2
betting	3.9	6.4	1.6	4.0	1.7	2.9	0.3	4.6	2.0	10.4	3.9	8.1	0.5	7.4	2.2
visiting museum	3.7	3.5	3.8	4.4	3.7	4.2	3.5	5.8	4.7	1.6	2.3	2.1	3.0	2.6	5.0
squash	3.5	5.5	1.6	4.7	4.7	13.1	2.7	11.6	3.1	4.4	0.8	3.2	0.5	3.3	1.1

other entertainment	3.4	3.2	3.6	5.7	4.2	3.1	3.2	3.5	4.9	2.8	2.3	2.4	2.8	3.1	3.5
badminton	3.2	3.1	3.3	6.6	6.7	6.0	4.5	4.6	5.9	4.0	1.6	2.1	1.4	1.5	2.4
sing/dance/act	3.1	3.6	2.7	9.7	6.7	5.0	2.9	4.2	2.7	5.2	16.3	4.0	17.8	5.2	16.4
visiting zoo	2.5	2.3	2.8	0.9	1.0	4.7	5.9	2.3	4.1	2.0	0.8	2.6	3.5	3.3	2.4
(visiting safari park	0.6	0.6	0.7	1.3	1.0	0.3	1.1	0.4	0.4	–	–	0.6	0.7	0.9	1.1)
visiting show	3.0	2.8	3.1	5.7	5.2	2.4	2.1	6.2	5.3	3.2	4.7	1.1	1.9	1.5	2.0
golf	2.9	5.2	0.8	3.1	0.7	7.3	0.0	11.6	1.4	3.2	0.0	1.8	0.5	3.1	0.2
rowing, canoeing	2.7	3.1	2.4	2.6	2.7	4.2	2.1	5.0	3.9	2.4	0.8	2.3	2.3	4.1	3.3
going to fun fair	2.7	2.4	3.0	2.2	1.7	2.9	4.2	4.2	3.5	2.0	3.1	3.9	5.8	2.6	3.9
other local ents.	2.6	2.2	2.9	2.2	2.2	2.9	3.2	1.5	4.1	1.2	0.8	2.3	3.5	3.1	3.5
soccer	2.6	5.4	0.1	10.1	0.2	7.3	0.0	3.5	0.0	11.6	0.8	7.9	0.0	6.6	0.4
fishing	2.5	4.4	0.7	4.0	0.2	3.0	0.7	2.3	1.1	6.8	1.5	5.6	0.2	5.5	0.5
keepfit, yoga	2.4	0.7	4.0	1.3	6.2	0.8	3.5	0.8	7.0	1.2	1.6	0.5	3.7	0.4	3.9
table tennis	2.1	3.0	1.2	3.1	2.0	3.7	1.2	6.2	1.8	2.8	0.0	2.4	0.5	3.5	1.5
evening classes	1.7	0.8	2.4	2.2	4.0	1.8	2.4	1.2	2.5	0.0	0.8	0.5	0.7	0.7	1.3
car, m-c outing	1.6	1.8	1.4	2.6	1.5	1.8	2.0	1.2	0.8	1.6	3.1	2.3	0.7	1.3	0.9
cycling	1.6	1.8	1.4	2.6	2.0	2.6	1.2	1.9	3.1	1.2	0.8	1.0	0.2	1.5	1.3
tennis	1.5	1.8	1.3	4.4	2.5	2.9	1.4	1.9	1.4	2.8	0.8	1.3	0.7	0.9	1.5
camping, caravaning	1.4	1.4	1.4	1.3	2.2	1.6	0.6	0.8	1.8	2.0	0.0	0.3	0.7	1.7	2.6
ten pin bowling	1.4	1.9	0.9	1.3	1.2	0.5	0.5	3.5	0.6	2.8	1.6	1.4	0.5	2.0	1.7
cooking/wine	1.4	1.7	1.2	3.5	1.5	3.1	1.5	0.4	0.4	2.8	1.6	1.0	0.7	0.7	0.7
keeping animals	1.2	1.9	0.6	2.2	1.0	1.0	0.3	2.3	0.6	2.0	3.9	1.4	0.0	3.9	1.1
field athletics	1.2	1.9	0.4	4.0	1.2	3.4	0.5	3.5	0.6	0.8	0.0	1.1	0.0	1.7	0.0
watch ind swimming	1.1	0.5	1.6	–	–	0.8	1.7	0.8	4.1	–	–	0.2	1.4	0.7	2.0
Total N	7376	3494	3882	227	401	382	662	259	489	251	129	621	432	458	458

men, whether or not there were children in the household and whatever the age of those children. This was not the case for non-manual men, but for this group playing golf rose dramatically when there were children in the household, and the golf club, and activities like it, may be the non-manual equivalent of pub culture. For both non-manual and manual women pub culture collapsed completely when there were children under 5, but for manual women darts playing, for example, recovered when children are older. Bingo, however, stayed at the same high rate for manual women whether or not there were children and whatever the age, as did social club activity. For non-manual men and women most physical activities show some decline with children in the household. For some manual women many physical activities increase with children 5–15, reaching levels comparable with those for non-manual women. This rise in manual women's activities, however, seems likely to be associated with the obligations of parenting and suggests the strength of these obligations for all women.

Conclusions

The obvious limitations of the GHS leisure data must temper any general conclusions. Nevertheless, in a way which can be seen as complementary to more limited case studies, our reanalysis of the GHS data does strongly suggest that gender and stage of life/household type are highly significant variables in the explanation of leisure behaviour. Therefore controlling for household structure is crucial in the analysis of women's leisure activity. Household structure is also an important control for the analysis of men's leisure activity but less so than for women. From this analysis leisure activities could not be said to be symmetrical in the modern British family. Moreover the importance of the 'pub' in continuing to construct a separate male culture, especially for manual workers, is clearly demonstrated. The existence of the pub as an important leisure institution in Britain may *create* an alternative focus for leisure activity outside of the family which is different from the American context. We cannot, however, fully test Kelly's argument on the family-centredness of leisure in the British context without more information on who did what with whom.

This article started with the problem of defining an appropriate sociological approach to the field of leisure. What indications are there that British sociologists of leisure should take seriously definitions of leisure which see leisure as the 'liberation of the individual', and as important a field as the study of work and family? In 1977 Roberts argued that there were no *minimum* recreational needs, of a similar order to the minimum needs for food and shelter (Roberts 1977), but increasingly research into women's lives raises the question of whether this is true. Wimbush's work on leisure and well-being may well lead in very new directions and establish such minimum needs. These minimum needs may well be two-fold: both the need for the leisure space in which to construct ongoing close relationships, and also the need for the leisure space to renew individual energy and potential. Research into depression amongst women has begun to look into the relationship between leisure and depression. In their classic study Brown and Harris have argued that the lack of a confiding relationship with their domestic partner was a factor which increased women's vulnerability to depression (Brown and Harris 1978). Given Kelly's argument that leisure activity is a crucial area for the construction of such confiding relationships (Kelly 1983), Roberts may be wrong in rejecting the concept of leisure needs. Furthermore, the quite different leisure need, the need for time on one's own may also be a fundamental. It may well be that present research into the leisure needs of women with young children, where those needs are not met, may answer questions about the centrality of 'leisure' to the lives of both men and women, paving the way for a more adequate sociological definition of leisure.

The General Household Survey can only address such questions by implication, but secondary analysis of the General Household Survey leisure data is a useful initial testing ground for conflicting theses on leisure behaviour.

Notes

1 This article originated in a post-doctoral master's dissertation: 'Women, Family and Leisure 1980' (MSc Surrey 1985). The analysis used the SPSS files of the GHS generated at the University of Surrey and Sara Arber, Angela Dale and Jane Fielding were all very helpful in overcoming problems with using the GHS leisure data. Angela Dale originally created the Household Structure variable used in the final runs for this article. Sara Arber, Mike Proctor, Rosemary Deem and Muriel Nissell all discussed the problem of women's leisure with me.
2 Selection was also made for completeness of interview. It is also important to emphasise that the GHS data files used (those prepared by the University of

Surrey for running with SPSS) selected *individual* adults. The subsequent analysis is of individual men and individual women living in particular household structures.

3 In the 1983 General Household Survey Report the OPCS team also report selected individual activities by gender and occupation but in contrast with the analysis here, gender is not controlled for before occupation is controlled for.

4 The findings on age, further education, total family income, the problems in using the car access variable, and relationship of women's employment to leisure can all be found in my M.Sc. dissertation.

5 Occupation was coded into four occupational categories using the Registrar General's socio-economic groups: professionals, employers and managers, coded occupational group 1 (which equals socio-economic groups 1, 2, 3, 4, 5, 6, 16), ancillary and junior non-manual coded occupational group 2 (socio-economic groups 7, 8, 9), skilled workers and own-account workers, coded occupation group 3 (socio-economic groups 11, 12, 15, 17) and semi-skilled, unskilled and personal service workers, coded occupation group 4 (socio-economic group 10, 13, 14, 18).

References

Brown, G. and Harris, T. (1978), *The Social Origins of Depression*, London, Tavistock Publications.

Cheek, N. and Burch, W. (1976), *The Social Organisation of Leisure in Human Society*, New York, Harper and Row.

Collins, M. (1982), *Leisure Research*. The Sports Council, The SSRC, The Leisure Studies Association.

Comer, L. (1974), *Wedlocked Women*, Leeds, Feminist Books.

Deem, R. (1982), 'Women, leisure and inequality', *Leisure Studies*, Vol. 1, No. 1.

Deem, R. (1984a), 'Paid work, leisure and non-employment: shifting boundaries and gender differences', unpublished paper presented to the BSA, April 1984.

Deem, R. (1984b), 'Education for family and leisure', Block 7, *Conflict and Change in Education*, Open University Course E205.

Deem, R. (1986), 'The politics of women's leisure', this volume.

Dixey, R. (1983), 'The playing of Bingo: industry, market and working class culture', in A. Tomlinson (ed.) *Leisure and Popular Cultural Forms*, Brighton Polytechnic, Chelsea School of Human Movement.

Dixey, R. and Talbot, M. (1982), *Women, Leisure and Bingo*, Leeds, Trinity and All Saints College.

Dumazedier, J. (1967), *Towards a Society of Leisure*, London, Collier-Macmillan.

GHS (1973), *The General Household Survey 1973*, London, HMSO.

GHS (1977), *The General Household Survey 1977*, London, HMSO.

GHS (1983), *The General Household Survey 1983*, London, HMSO.

Gilbert, G.N., Dale, A. and Arber, S. (1983), 'The General Household Survey as a source for secondary analysis', *Sociology*, 17,2.

Green, E., Hebron, S. and Woodward, D. (1985), 'Women and leisure: ideologies of domesticity and processes of social control', Paper given to the LSA/BSA Study Group of Leisure and Recreation, North Staffs Polytechnic.

Hobson, D. (1981), 'Working class women, the family and leisure', in Strelitz (ed.).

Hobson, D. (1983), 'Watching television – viewing with the audience', in A. Tomlinson (ed.), *Leisure and Popular Cultural Forms*, Brighton Polytechnic, Chelsea School of Human Movement.

Kaplan, M. (1960), *Leisure in America*, New York, Wiley.

Kelly, J. (1978), 'Family leisure in three communities', *Journal of Leisure Research*, no. 10.

Kelly, J. (1981), 'Leisure adaptation to family variety' in Strelitz (ed.).

Kelly, J. (1983), *Leisure Identities and Interactions*, London, Allen and Unwin.

Oakley, A. (1974), *The Sociology of Housework*, London, Martin Robertson.

Rapoport, R., Fogarty, M.P. and Rapoport, R. (1982), *Families in Britain*, London, Routledge & Kegan Paul.

Rapoport, R., Rapoport, R. and Strelitz, Z. (1975), *Leisure and the Family Life Cycle*, London, Routledge & Kegan Paul.

Roberts, K. (1977), 'Leisure and life styles under welfare capitalism' in Smith M. (ed.).

Sillitoe, K. (1969), *Planning for Leisure*, London, HMSO.

Smith, M. (ed.) (1977), *Leisure and Urban Society*, Leisure Studies Association.

Smith, M. (1980), *Leisure in the '80s*, Centre for Leisure Studies, Salford University.

Strelitz, Z. (ed.) (1981), *Leisure and Family Diversity*, Leisure Studies Association, Conference Paper No. 9.

Szalai, A. et al. (1972), *The Use of Time*, The Hague, Mouton.

Talbot, M. (1979), *Women and Leisure*: A State of The Art Review, The Sports Council/SSRC.

Wimbush, E. (1985), *Women, Leisure and Well being: Phase 1 Interim Report*, Centre for Leisure Research, Dunfermline College of Physical Education, Edinburgh.

Young, M. and Willmott, P. (1973), *The Symmetrical Family*, London, Routledge & Kegan Paul.

The Figurational Sociology of sport and leisure of Elias and Dunning: an exposition and a critique

John Horne and David Jary

Introduction

The aim of this article is to outline and appraise the strengths and weaknesses of the Figurational Sociology of Sport of Norbert Elias and Eric Dunning. With its 'distinctive' focus on the 'civilising process' (Elias, 1978b and 1982a) and on the 'sociogenesis' and complex 'structural determination' of shifting 'social (con)figurations' (Elias, 1978a). This approach has been strongly advanced not only as offering the best of all possible bases for a sociology of sport but also as able to make a contribution to the mainstream of sociology, by throwing new light on aspects of cultural and social change previously neglected by the discipline. As well as the seminal work of Elias and Dunning (especially see Dunning, 1971a and Elias and Dunning, 1969), a number of significant monographs have appeared, on rugby (Dunning and Sheard, 1979), soccer (Dunning, 1979; Wagg, 1984) and cricket (Brookes, 1978). Under the influence of Dunning, sociologists based at the University of Leicester have also become a force in research and public debate on 'soccer hooliganism' (see Dunning et al., 1982; Williams et al., 1984). A Figurationist 'paradigm' in the sociology of sport and leisure would appear to be well established, and a theoretical text on the sociology of leisure written from the point of view of Figurational Sociology has recently appeared. As its author puts it: 'Figurational Sociology is now a force to be reckoned with in the sociology of leisure' (Rojek, 1985:95).

If the objective of a sociology of sport is now widely recognised as the provision of a theoretically adequate and historically grounded analysis of changing patterns of sport, then Figurational Sociology has contributed strongly to this recognition. Its study of sport's role in the long-term transformation of culture and manners, and of the changes in class and power associated with this 'civilizing process', marked a major step forward in the sociological analysis of sport and leisure. Its thoroughgoing and uncompromising theoretical and empirical sociological focus on the interrelations of social structure and individual 'affects', and its bringing into view aspects of the process of social development previously 'hidden from history', has clearly achieved much more than most earlier approaches. These had been usually characterised either by narrowness of empirical focus or by speculative theory, with little connection between the two. Among the latter approaches rightly criticised by Dunning (especially see Dunning, 1971a and 1975 and also Dunning and Sheard, 1979) we can note the work of Huizinga (1955), who sees 'play' as the 'creative' element in social life now being overwhelmed by the 'overseriousness' of leisure, and Stone (1955), for whom the massification of society and the reduction of much modern participation in leisure to a spectator role – a concentration on 'spectacle and display' – constitutes a 'destruction of play', a literal '*dis*-play'. While the Figurational Sociology of Sport incorporates elements of such theories, their limitations are seen to lie in 'Romanticism' and 'elitism', and a yearning for a mythical *Gemeinschaft*, with little grounding in either sociological or historical study. They are seen as failing to come to terms with the real world complexities of historical or modern sport.

The contribution of Figurational Sociology in achieving a reorientation of the sociology of sport is outlined in the first part of this article. For all its strengths, however, a key question about Figurational Sociology to be addressed in the latter part of the article is: How far its contribution has been the outcome of a 'unique' methodological position – as the Figurationists would have us believe – or how far it has resulted simply from the raising of classical sociological questions, and from recourse to conventional sociological 'best practice', in an area where these had hitherto been conspicuously absent? The latter view will be taken here. In so far as there are methods advocated by the Elias school which can be seen as differing from conventional sociological 'best practice', our argument will be that these methods should not be adopted and are likely to restrict the development of the sociology of sport. Prominent among such methodological orientations are the Figurationists' over-drawn hostility to other, including Marxian, forms of analysis, and also the restrictiveness of their methodological stance on 'involvement and detachment' (see Elias, 1956 and 1978a). In more substantive terms, significant reservations will also be expressed about the theoretical adequacy and empirical fit of the thesis of a 'civilizing process'. Once these criticisms have been made, the way will be clear to underline the rival merits of other approaches to the sociology of sport and leisure (e.g. neo-marxian approaches), general approaches which tend to be merely caricatured and summarily dismissed by the Elias-Dunning school.

Our overall objective then is to acknowledge the achievements of the Figurational Sociology of Sport, but in a way which leaves space for alternatives to it, for approaches which, we will argue, would be best regarded as complementary to the Figurationists' own view and research programme.

The central concepts of Figurational Sociology

The effectiveness of the Elias–Dunning perspective in achieving a reorientation of the sociology of sport can be seen as arising above all from the use in combination of two main concepts:

  i) the concept of 'human (con)figuration', and
  ii) the concept of the 'civilizing process'.

While the former of these ensures a focus on sport and leisure within a strong sociological frame of reference, the latter provides a general historical model in terms of which sport and leisure can receive systematic analysis. Added to this, there is also the 'accident' of Elias's fondness for presenting the general conception of the human figuration in terms of the metaphor of the 'dance' and the 'game'. Arguably a recourse to such metaphors helps to legitimise a 'serious' sociological concern with sport and leisure, and the acceptability of Elias's theoretical and substantive perspectives in this area.

The concept of the 'social figuration'

What the concept of 'human figuration' refers to is the 'nexus of interdependencies between people', the 'chains of functions' and 'axes of tensions' – both cooperation and conflict – which can be identified for any social context. It should be noted here that the concept of 'function' is presented as altogether different from that of conventional functionalism in that no necessary reference to the 'maintenance and reproduction' of social systems is involved. This said, however, Figurational Sociology retains roots in functionalist sociology, particularly the functionalism of Durkheim.

The primary strength of the concept of figuration from the point of view of its influence on the sociology of sport is that it allows the strong assertion of the 'autonomy of sociology': the rejection of any model of Man as *homo clausus* – the closed or discrete individual – and the rejection of any suggestion that social explanations can be achieved satisfactorily by any reduction to purely 'individual' agency. So much is made clear in Elias's use of the metaphor of the dance and the game in illustrating his concept of the 'figuration':

> The image of the mobile figurations of independent people on a dance floor (or playing sport) . . . makes it easier to imagine states, cities, families and also entire (social) systems as figurations. (But) it would be absurd to say that dances (or games) are mental constructions abstracted from observations of individuals considered separately. (Elias, 1978b:262)

On the other hand, any out-and-out assertion of purely structuralist forms of explanation is equally clearly rejected by Elias. The general position advanced involves the repudiation of any form of analysis which views the 'individual' and 'society' as separate entities. A further related central position of particular value for the sociology of sport is an insistence on a recognition of the historical specificity of social figurations, their 'processual' character and their essential openness to change. The adoption of a 'four-dimensional' framework in sociological analysis is seen as essential: the provision within sociological models of a place for both 'structural' dimensions and the 'flow of social time'. The overriding view of the Figurationist is that satisfactory explanations in sociology, of a phenomenon such as modern sport, can only come from the painstaking historical and sociological analysis of the specific as well as the general features of figurations. Such explanations cannot be simply read-off – 'atomistically' – from the universal, psychological characteristics of individuals, nor can they be forthcoming from conceptions of sociology which trade on rigid conceptions of structural and historical necessity.

John Horne and David Jary

The 'civilizing process'

The formulation of Elias's conception of a 'civilizing process' is couched in terms of these general requirements of Figurational Sociology. As Abrams succinctly puts it, what the concept of the 'civilizing process' draws attention to are the:

> profound redefinitions of 'normal' and 'proper' behaviour, the building of powerful psychological and institutional barriers to the old indiscriminate enactment of feeling (both enthusiasm and aggression) and, as a concomitant of that, the establishment of increasing . . . distance between the civilised and uncivilised members of society. (Abrams, 1982:231)

Thus, farting and spitting, the carrying out in public of all manner of unseemly bodily functions, are increasingly prohibited. Previously popular pastimes like bear-baiting or the ceremonial burning of cats become restricted by law as well as by 'internalised' feelings of revulsion. In his formulation of this process Elias was strongly influenced by Freud's *Civilisation and its Discontents*, which 'presupposes precisely the non-satisfaction (by suppression, repression or some other means) of powerful instincts' (Freud, cited in Bauman, 1979:122).

Elias's view of the 'civilizing process' as outlined in rich detail in his general historical studies (Elias, 1978b and 1982a) is that it constitutes an historical secular tendency in human societies to increasing external and internalised control over individual 'affects' and social behaviour, a tendency for the control of violence and the gradual transformation of manners, and a general distancing from nature. This process is also presented as bound up with increasing social differentiation: the creation of both increased 'individuality' and new bases for social hierarchy, as well as increasing levels of social interdependence ('mutually attuned functions') and increased social density. In general the process is connected with a strengthening in the monopoly of violence and power (and the capacity to enforce laws and standards) possessed by state formations. Along with this Elias also recognises a tendency to 'democratisation' which also brings an intensification of individual and class competition in manners, and which means that competition in terms of standards of behaviour, previously confined to members of 'court society', becomes diffused in the long run to society at large.

The ramifying implications of such a 'civilizing process' constitute the most general of figurational tendencies with which all more specific social figurations, including the forms of sport and leisure, must be seen as bound up.

The Figurational Sociology of Sport

As Dunning sees it, what Elias's general framework achieves is 'to prepare the way for the sociology of sport' (Dunning, 1971a). What Figurational Sociology ultimately succeeds in providing is an account of the origins, codification, diffusion and consolidation, and general character of modern sport.

The historical evolution of sports and games

The phenomenon of modern sport is located by Elias in terms of his general model of the civilising process. Pre-modern sports such as the original Olympic Games or the 'folk games' – the 'semi-institutionalised fights' – which are a significant source of 'tension-release' in pre-industrial societies, are characterised as involving much greater levels of violence than typical of modern sports (Elias, 1971b). This level of violence is directly related to the overall social figurations within which these games were located. The original Olympic games, for instance, were bound up with the military character of Greek society; they also involved pre-modern conceptions of 'honour', which are seen by Elias as far removed from our modern conceptions of 'fairness' and sport. In general in the Ancient World the outcome of games and sporting events could often be bodily mutilation or even death. It is such levels of violence which, according to Elias, were progressively brought under control as a consequence of the 'civilizing process'; aspects of this same process are seen as leading to the new standards of 'fairness' and correct sporting behaviour which modern forms of sport introduce.

For Elias and for Dunning modern sport is 'a specific type of pleasurable excitement' which is markedly different from the less than pleasurable type of excitement that people experience in serious critical situations. Sports along with many other forms of leisure in modern society take on a 'mimetic' quality. In the modern forms of 'combat sports', for example, deeply rooted

John Horne and David Jary

emotions are socially channelled into relatively controlled contexts. Modern forms of football – both soccer and rugby – are identified by Elias and Dunning as civilised versions of earlier forms of traditional folk games in which levels of violence are carefully controlled. As games, they must continue to meet the need for excitement in what Elias and Dunning portray as 'inherently unexciting societies'; but they must do so without threatening the requirement for new standards of social and self-control (Elias and Dunning, 1969).

The internal dynamics of sports games

It is the number and subtlety of the new perspectives on sport and society which Elias and Dunning are able to achieve which give their analysis its strong interest. Exemplification of this is seen in the variety of levels at which their analysis operates. As well as the analysis of the wider social forces impinging on sports and games, the internal – 'figurational' – features of particular games which give these games their distinctive appeal also receive analysis. Drawing on Elias's more general recourse to an abstract, 'formal' figurational analysis of games (Elias, 1978a), the capacity of modern football to sustain a controlled 'excitement' is analysed in these terms (Elias and Dunning, 1969). Among mimetic 'combat sports', soccer in particular is portrayed as notably effective in maintaining a rule governed 'controlled tension' while at the same time confining this conflict to those levels acceptable within civilised society.

The social origins of modern soccer and rugby

This initial analysis of football and rugby by Elias and Dunning receives further impressive elaboration in the later work of Dunning, in conjunction with Sheard. Particularly fruitful, both as specific studies and as models of general sociological inquiry, are their studies of Rugby Football (Dunning and Sheard, 1979) and Soccer (Dunning, 1979).

The central questions addressed in both these studies, as summarised by Dunning and Sheard (1979:6), are:

i) 'the reasons why Britain was the first country to develop modern forms of sport',

92

ii) the role of the civilising process in the shaping of modern forms of football,

iii) the 'novel angles' which the study of sport can throw 'on the development of the British class structure',

iv) the way in which the character of modern sports is still changing in line with the major social and economic forces in modern society.

In each of these areas Dunning and Sheard are able to demonstrate how the development of both soccer and rugby can be interpreted as involving complex responses to industrialisation and to changes in class relations and social power. Their work can be regarded as providing the well grounded account of the rise of modern sports for which Elias (1971b) had called to replace the more speculative histories which hitherto had typified the historical and 'sociological' study of sport.

An account of the main phases in the development of modern football as identified by Dunning and Sheard will be indicative of the overall character of their analysis. It is the efforts from the 1830s onwards of influential Public School headmasters like Arnold at Rugby to limit the incidence of pupil-power and unruly behaviour within these schools which Dunning and Sheard see as leading to the introduction of new forms of football. The replacement of disorderly premodern forms of football in the Public Schools by new forms of football more compatible with changing conceptions of 'proper' behaviour and the 'gentlemanly ideal' is shown as linked with conflicts which are clearly class-related. The drive for change came from schoolmasters, themselves often drawn from relatively humble middle class backgrounds, who were anxious to undermine the ethos and influence of the traditional gentry within these schools, while increasing their own authority. At the same time, they aimed also to increase the appeal of these institutions to a rising urban industrial middle class by providing forms of schooling which would equip its offspring in the intensifying contest over status in modern society.

At every stage leading up to the modern forms of football, class and status considerations continued to exert a profound influence: in the period in which the newly introduced games were gradually codified between 1830 and 1863, at the point of bifurcation between soccer and rugby with the formation of the Football Association in 1863 and the Rugby Football Union in 1871, and in the later bifurcation of Rugby into its amateur and professional forms of 1895.

In general terms, Dunning and Sheard see modern sports, including soccer and rugby, as first emerging in the context of a conflict between traditional agrarian mores and the competitive ideology and new social controls of modern society. Traditional folk-games had flourished in a social context 'characterised simultaneously by massive inequality and patterns of intimate social mixing in spheres such as sports' (Dunning, 1979:13). In these circumstances social mixing could occur without this posing a threat to the preservation of social distance in other spheres. In contrast, in an era of greater social democratisation, the development of modern football occurs in a climate of pervasive class and status competition, status emulation and increasing class conflict.

In this manner, the initial division of football into two codes is convincingly demonstrated by Dunning and Sheard to be the outcome of a class competition between two schools: the 'aristocratic' Eton and the more 'bourgeois' Rugby. Thus the initial trend to the codification of sporting rules arose from a competitive drive to social respectability within the Public Schools, a process also carried forward in the ancient Universities. Subsequently, in a continuation of the process of social emulation, the new sports were adopted by the middle class at large. Finally, in a more general process of intra- and inter-class diffusion, which Dunning and Sheard say still needs to be better studied, the game spread to the working class.

When the professionalisation of soccer occurs this is associated not so much with the outright possession of the game by the working class (cf. Taylor, 1971) but with the game's capture and control by a wider entrepreneurial and commercial middle class than had been responsible for its initial codification. Because of this, the social conflicts which surround the professionalisation of soccer, while also involving differences of view about the amateur ideal, were heavily overlain with the language and strategies of class competition and class conflict. For as long as it remains the dominant ideology in modern sport the amateur ideal acts to preserve for socially privileged groups a sporting advantage over those less privileged and unable to compete as effectively at the highest levels. When overthrown as the dominant mode, the amateur ideal nevertheless lives on as a basis of social closure and social exclusion in leisure pursuits, and also as a basis of wider social differentiation. Illustration of this is seen in the way in which the introduction of professional soccer leads to a switch from soccer to rugby in public schools and grammar schools, ostensibly to escape the 'tainting' of amateur sport by the values of professionalism but also achieving a social class differentiation of sporting pursuits. Rugby's elevation as the socially superior game, which had occurred only after soccer's professionalisation and its increasing adoption by the working class, is secured by this process. It is further assisted by the hiving off from the Rugby Union of the professional Rugby League in 1895.

This split between the two codes of rugby football is again explained by Dunning and Sheard in class terms. Their suggestion is that the leadership of the game of rugby in the 1890s was less socially secure and in closer competition with rising classes than had earlier been so when plainly elite groups had been able to retain overall control of soccer through the Football Association – preserving a single code, while at the same time allowing space for formation of the professional Football League. Battles over professionalisation in rugby, coming somewhat later than in soccer, take place at a time when class competition and conflicts had intensified. Rugby, with its peculiar sharpness of institutional separation into amateur and professional and middle and working class forms, and its division also from soccer, is regarded by Dunning and Sheard as a Durkheimian 'crucial case' allowing clear visibility of the decisive forces underlying the development of modern sport.

'Football hooliganism'

On the face of it, the apparent growth of 'football hooliganism' is a phenomenon which would seem to contradict the thesis of a 'civilizing process'. But to accept such a simple view would be to fail to appreciate the nature of the Elias hypothesis, which refers to a long-run and essentially erratic tendency. This leaves open to the Figurationists a number of possible arguments. Partly it can be suggested that football hooliganism attracts attention precisely because violence is now more exceptional and less acceptable than previously, and generally at odds with the civilising process. Nevertheless, contrary to some views, the Figurationists do not dispute the 'reality' of football violence, although they do dispute that it is an entirely new phenomenon. The thesis of the Oxford school (e.g., Marsh et al., 1978) who suggest that football 'violence' can be seen as mainly 'ritualised aggression' and, if left alone, as 'self-regulatory', is rejected. The arguments of this school, a 'theoretical melange' of phenomenological idealism and structural linguistics' according to Dunning (1983) are regarded as 'ahistorical' and flawed by 'individualism'. Instead, an analysis of historical figurations shows clearly (see Dunning, 1981) that the incidence of football violence is broadly related to shifting levels of class frustration and class conflict, although affluence and mobility, as well as media construction and amplification, are also acknowledged as playing a part in recent increases in football violence (also see Williams et al., 1984).

An attempt to explain football violence in terms of class conflict is, of course, not new. Taylor (1971) in particular had suggested so much in seeking to trace football violence to frustrations arising from a greater social distance between players and working-class supporters which he saw as the result of increasing commercialisation and general loss of working class involvement in the workings of football clubs. However, Taylor's general thesis is found unacceptable by Dunning and his co-researchers on a number of counts, not least the absence of any evidence that football ever had been substantially under working-class control. The alternative class analysis which the Leicester team themselves present to explain the resurgence of football violence derives from the work of the urban sociologist Graham Suttles (1972) as well as Elias, depending on a Durkheimian ideal type distinction between 'functional' and 'segmental' bonding. While 'functional bonding' is seen as the characteristic form of bonding in modern 'civilised' societies, segmental bonding is nevertheless still present, notably in the important representation through sport of concepts of locality and nation. Moreover this latter form of bonding is seen as possessing particular potency within working class localities, especially so in those areas where economic recession has fuelled class frustrations and has helped to bring a reversion of 'rough' and relatively 'uncivilised' patterns of social behaviour, including football violence.

Contemporary sport

As seen from its account of 'soccer hooliganism', and for all its emphasis on the historical role of class conflict in the evolution of sport, it is a relatively orderly picture of contemporary sport which finally emerges from Figurational Sociology. There is a recognition of variations between societies in the pace and the forms of development (e.g., notable differences between Britain and America arising from a different balance in the strengths of the amateur ideal and commercialism – Dunning and Sheard, 1979). But contemporary sport is presented as on the whole well matched to the needs of modern society, and moving ultimately in line with the requirements of the 'civilizing process', including the onward march of commercialised leisure and professional sport, now occurring even in such previously sacrosanct spheres as rugby union.

Strengths and weaknesses of Figurational Sociology

Our sketch of the contribution of the Elias–Dunning school to the sociology of sport now completed, it will be useful to summarise what we see as its main achievements:

i) an account of the rule-governed character of modern sport in which 'mock fights' on the whole replace true violence,

ii) an analysis and historical account of sport and society in which changes in the division of labour and class relations are shown to be central to the development and institutionalisation of modern sports and games,

iii) a neo-Durkheimian account of the important 'symbolic' role of sport in providing significant 'representations' of nation and community in modern society, and a source also of 'personal identities' (for further indication of these aspects see Dunning and Sheard, 1979, and Sheard and Dunning, 1973).

In all of this, it is not only the generality but the historical detail and the considerable subtlety of the Figurational Sociology of Sport which stands out compared with most previous approaches.

We now wish to move, however, to the substantial reservations we have about the claims made in association with Figurational Sociology. As well as questions about the claims made for its 'uniqueness' of methodology compared with alternatives, there are also major questions to raise about the concept of the 'civilizing process', including its, in some respects, apparently contradictory relation to many of Figurational Sociology's main methodological precepts.

The success of the Figurational Sociology of Sport, in our view, has had most to do with its being first in the field – armed with its notion of the 'figuration' – in providing a general historical sociology which could effectively interrelate the internal dynamics of sport with the wider dynamics of society. That it was in general able to do this while also avoiding either 'methodological individualism' or a 'reifying structuralism' was a further strength (cf. Turner, 1985). However, any thesis of the distinctiveness or the indispensability of the concept of 'figuration' in making Figurational Sociology's contribution possible must be challenged. What needs to be asserted is that there are other approaches within general sociology which could have achieved the same outcome; or put another way, the same approaches exist elsewhere under other umbrellas within the discipline. As pointed out by Bauman, there exists a clear affinity between 'the idea of figuration and such rather household sociological notions as "pattern" or "situation"' (Bauman, 1979:118–19). Bauman and also Abrams (1982) are examples of numerous recent commentators (also see Wolf, 1977; Bourdieu, 1977; and Smith, 1984) who, while finding much to praise in Elias's general sociology, firmly reject the claims of its supporters that it constitutes an 'alternative sociology' – Bauman refers to Figurational Sociology as a 'credo'. Among those sociological commentators particularly persuaded by or centrally involved in voicing Figurational Sociology's more strident claims to special status we can note Wilson, (1977), Mennell (1982) and especially Goudsblom (1977a and b) – at times, a near 'charismatic movement', according to Bauman (1979:112). The fact is, however, that what is valuable in the general approach within Figurational Sociology need not be seen as other than the classical approach in general sociology; it is not now distinctive in the sociology of sport. In addition to this, the Figurational approach seriously underestimates the importance and viability of central approaches in general sociology – especially but not only the marxian – where 'relational' conceptions of structure and agency are found which, although remaining sensitive to problems of reification, make possible a fuller elaboration of the structural forces impinging on sport.

In part, the special pleading for Figurational Sociology can be explained as the outcome of the fact that Elias stood somewhat off the main track of academic sociology at the time he was writing *The Civilizing Process*. This, along with the book's apparent marginality of subject-matter, engendered an isolation for his sociology, compounded also by the irony of the volume's publication in German in the context of war in 1939. Claims for distinctiveness were fostered in this context of exclusion. They were further fired by the search by Elias supporters for explanations for the neglect of his work, so that Elias's reception became interpreted in terms of a blindness induced by central weaknesses of method and perspective in modern sociology, which Elias presented as dominated by 'pseudo dichotomies' (Elias 1978a) – e.g., 'individual versus society', 'order versus change'. However, it can be strongly argued that this picture of modern sociology itself provides a distorted view of the discipline. Whilst the substantive focus of Eliasian sociology was certainly neglected, Elias admits that his own general approach to sociology has been constructed as a continuation of nineteenth-century classical sociology. However, it is simply not true that mainstream sociology has ever lost contact with this tradition; rather it has continuously sought to grapple with the necessity of combining structure and individual agency, and order and change, within one sociology. This lack of distinctiveness may perhaps explain the relative absence of direct use of Elias's work – as well as some criticism of his work – by a number of leading sociologists who studied under or worked with Elias at Leicester (e.g., Giddens, 1984). Rather than mainstream sociology losing reality in a pursuit of 'pseudo dichotomies' it can be suggested that it is Elias and his supporters who have themselves constructed such dichotomies – and most 'unfigurationally' – in caricaturing the work of others.[1] These stereotypes can be seen as preventing any open 'dialogue' between Elias's general sociology and the mainstream, and a clear view of alternative sociologies of sport.

Rather than any methodological 'distinctiveness', then, the 'marginality' of Elias's sociology would seem to be best explained as bound up with the context of the initial publication of his *magnum opus* and with its focus on apparently 'marginal' cultural phenomena. In this context Dunning in particular is to be congratulated on exploiting the possibilities of the focus for the sociology of sport and leisure. This does not mean, however, that the focus on cultural and sporting phenomena embodied in Elias's concept of the 'civilizing process', whatever its productiveness in some respects, can itself escape criticism. It can be seen as an amalgam of fruitful notions and those whose utility is more questionable, including the apparent contradictions in the central methodological prescriptions of Figurational Sociology, especially a tendency to 'latent evolutionism'. On the positive side, as seen above, the concept of the 'civilizing process' is responsible for the focus on 'combat sports' and the codification and domestication of these in their modern forms. It provides a systematic – if only one – rationale for focus on class, class emulation and class conflict. Against this, however, and variously at odds with some elements of Figurational Sociology's own methodological self-definitions, functionalist, evolutionary and related assumptions associated with the concept of the 'civilizing process' have been rightly questioned, for example: 'the apparent irreversibility of the process' (Lasch, 1985), its 'irrefutability' (Smith, 1984), its explicit or implicit reference to 'societal needs' and 'functional requirements'. Of course, there need be no outright objections to functional analysis or the use of 'untestable' general frameworks in sociology – indeed the productiveness of the concept of the 'civilizing process' in these respects is apparent. But there are aspects of the concept of the 'civilizing process' and its implicit functionalism and evolutionism which are one-sided in the questions raised (despite the best intentions of Figurational Sociologists).

Noting this, some observers have wanted to locate Figurational Sociology clearly in the ranks of the 'social order' and 'social control' sociologies, as presenting leisure as performing 'compensatory' functions (Stedman Jones, 1977). Others also note the Figurationists' relative neglect of countertendencies to the civilising process (e.g., public displays of sexuality, the 'barbarism' of modern warfare – Buck–Morss, 1977 – and some modern sports) and their tendency to overlook more 'negative' aspects of modern social control (e.g., attacks on privacy, pervasive surveillance – Lasch, 1985), including the 'social control' goals of some modern sports administrators. This also can be seen as leading to a relative neglect of forms of leisure potentially more socially transformative in their implications (e.g., the rise of new uncompetitive sports, especially among women). It is an 'oversocialised' and 'one-dimensional' conception of the person and society that emerges in Elias and Dunning's work – with only part of the tradition of Freud apparent. In general, there is a neglect of the overall 'hegemonic' and contested functions of sport within a capitalist society (e.g., the role of sport in fostering competitiveness and possessive individualism). Instead, a focus on 'affect control' and the new 'domestication' of sport holds the centre stage: an emphasis on 'evolutionary' adjustments or on regressions in terms of this process. Dunning's use of Suttles's model in accounting for 'football hooliganism' is revealingly symptomatic of this aspect of the Figurational approach.

The 'functionalism' and 'latent evolutionism' of Figurational Sociology – tending always to override its methodological emphasis on the necessity for detailed historical research – can also be seen in an obvious weakness of the Figurationists' discussion of gender and sport. Both Elias (1971b) and Sheard and Dunning (1973) rightly stress the general role of modern sport in the social construction of 'personal identities', and are in many ways perceptive on the implications for specifically 'male identity' of the continuation of sports like rugby as a 'male preserve'. However, the background assumptions of this analysis – e.g., changes in the significance of rugby as a male preserve arising from new pressures for increasing gender equality in society (especially also see Dunning, 1986) – are 'evolutionary' ones which short-circuit any great dependence on historical and empirical study. Jennifer Hargreaves (1986), for instance, is critical of both the 'ahistorical' assumption about 'patriarchy' and the 'inevitability' of equality found in this analysis. She also notes the failure of Figurationists to relate fully to alternative feminist research and theory.

If one-sidedness and a degree of implicit theoretical overclosure can be seen as a problem in Figurational Sociology, at odds with its own explicit stress on the open-endedness of social situations, a source of this apparent paradox can be traced to the ultimately 'empiricist' epistemological position adopted by Figurationists. Smith (1984) as well as Bauman (1979) see this as a significant problem: the expressed intent of Figurationists to 'surrender only to the intrinsic logic of the object' of analysis, the attempt never to import into an analysis general frameworks which 'the figurations themselves do not dictate', leads to a failure to achieve a sufficient coverage and range in theories, especially in relation to possible transformations of society. Significantly Elias's approach is praised by Bendix (1978), a sociologist who in recent years has grown noticeably suspicious of theoretical ambition in sociology. For Smith (1984), however, Eliasian historical sociology must be compared adversely with other historical sociologies – e.g., Barrington Moore – which are more willing to take on board explicit theorising about alternative futures. The problems of Eliasian 'empiricism' are also evident in a different form in the recent monographs produced by students working within the Figurationist frame of reference. The studies by Wagg, *The*

Football World (1984), and Brookes, *English Cricket* (1978), are examples here, possessing limitations which can perhaps be laid at the door of a too literal acceptance of Eliasian precepts of empiricism, leading these studies to get bogged down in minor details of the sports form, without always engaging fully with general issues.

The co-existence of the problems of speculative functionalism/ evolutionism and descriptivism in Figurational Sociology would appear to point to unsatisfactory elements of incoherence and incompleteness in its overall framework. The general difficulties here are also exacerbated by the further central doctrines of Figurational Sociology on 'neutrality and involvement' articulated by Elias (1956) and endorsed by Dunning (e.g., Dunning, 1983). Elias supports the general goal of 'neutrality' in sociology, which along with the 'descriptivist' emphasis above, he sees as achieved by avoiding philosophical speculation and involvement with values in the research phase of sociology. The failure to do this is seen as a weakness particularly of marxian sociology.[2] This leads some observers (e.g., Smith, 1984) to see Elias and Dunning as foregoing all evaluations, but in fact this is only apparently the problem. In actuality, Elias remains heir to the classical Comtean tradition in sociology, with its criticism of purely speculative philosophy but also its continued goal of reaching well-founded evaluation on a scientific basis. The problem then is not that Elias and Dunning fail to provide social evaluations, but that they do so on the basis of their own allegedly 'neutral' findings – while trying to withhold this possibility from other more 'committed' – e.g., neo-marxian and feminist – sociologies (e.g., Dunning, 1983 and 1986). As an alternative to this view of knowledge, it would seem more conducive to the pursuit of 'objectivity' (see Gouldner, 1976; Becker, 1967) to view sociology of all types as necessarily involving evaluations while always seeking to ground these adequately in sound knowledge and open 'unconstrained' discourse between theories.[3] Here, as elsewhere, as long as the Figurationists persist in special pleading and the differentiation and self-distantiation of their own sociology from other forms, this will only be damaging to the development of the sociology of sport.

Alternative sociologies of sport

Since in our view there now exist several major alternatives to

Figurational Sociology within the sociology of sport – all of them embodying good general sociological practice, sensitivity to history, and a concern to avoid individualist or structuralist traps – we want to round off this article by examining examples of these. These alternative approaches, we want to suggest, possess the same general capacity to focus on the important themes raised by the Figurational approach, but do so in a far broader way. This makes them, if not necessarily a replacement for this approach, very much complementary to it, in ways either ignored by the Figurationists or misunderstood or misrepresented by them.

The approaches we want briefly to outline are Richard Gruneau's critical sociology of sport (especially Gruneau, 1983) and research carried out at the Centre for Contemporary Cultural Studies (CCCS) into youth and sport and recreation (see Hall and Jefferson, 1976; Clarke, 1978; Clarke et al., 1979; Hall et al., 1980; Clarke and Critcher, 1985). These represent respectively a critical sports sociology derived from cultural and historical studies and the work of Giddens, and a cultural studies marxism influenced by Gramsci.[4]

Class, sports and social development – the work of Gruneau

As an amalgam of several strands of thinking in recent social theory, including Gramscian Marxism, English Cultural Studies, and also the work of Wright Mills and Anthony Giddens, Gruneau's explicit objective has been to remedy what he sees as the failing of the conventional approach to sports history, the downplaying of social conflict and division, in favour of a stress on the integrative and smooth evolution of games and sport.

Two emphases can be seen as uppermost in his developmental sociology of sport: i) the ever present 'duality' of 'liberating' and 'constraining' developments and ii) the limitations increasingly placed on sport and recreation, especially those constraints seen as arising specifically from *capitalist* society. While neither of these emphases is entirely absent in the perspective of the Figurationists, it is the latter in particular which remains understated in their work, and both of these elements receive a more rounded treatment in the work of Gruneau and those like him, which also allows a far greater integration with more general work on class and state power. In contrast with the restrictive doctrines of 'ethical neutrality' of Elias and Dunning, a further advantage is that the evaluative position of Gruneau is also far more 'up front' and undisguised by epistemology.

Like Dunning and Sheard in their study of English sport Gruneau isolates critical phases in the development of Canadian sport (see Gruneau, 1983:93). In discussing these phases Gruneau engages directly with the work of the Figurationists, explaining how in the case of Canada 'the formal organisation of football . . . lagged behind such developments in England until well into the late nineteenth century' (Gruneau, 1983:103–4). In mid-nineteenth-century Canadian society the predominance of mercantile capital and the absence of a strong industrial bourgeoisie are seen by Gruneau as making cricket, instead, the greater attraction: for Canada's colonial merchants and aristocrats

> it combined an excellent and enjoyable forum for learning discipline, civility, and the principles of fair play with a body of traditions and rules offering a ritual dramatisation of the traditional power of the colonial metropolis and the class interests associated with it'. (p. 104)

Gruneau largely accepts the Dunning and Sheard thesis that 'the concept of amateurism seems to have evolved in a dialectical fashion as a conscious strategy of exclusion in class relations' (Gruneau, 1983:109). It became a major factor in the establishment of Canadian national governing bodies of sport in the last three decades of the nineteenth century and in the rearguard action against both commercialisation of sport and new conceptions of 'scientific play'. However, in the long run 'a petty bourgeois mobilisation of bias' in favour of commercialisation replaced the earlier amateur ideal. As Gruneau expresses it, 'greater freedom revealed itself, paradoxically, also to be an abstract symbolisation of constraining commodity relations' (p. 121).

It is here and in his treatment of the decisive 'critical' phase in Canadian sports development that the greatest contrast is apparent between the approach of Gruneau and the Elias school. The transition from colonial society to industrial capitalism is seen as bringing in its wake a commodity-like form for 'spectacular game-contests' in which workers became consumers of a product within what Braverman (1974) has called the 'universal market'. Gruneau dates modern corporate sport in Canada as emerging finally during the 1920s and 1930s, and becoming manifest particularly in the 'cartelisation' of ice hockey. Trends established then, such as the 'embourgeoisement' of professional players, and interlocking patterns of team ownership, have since been supported and reinforced by the influence of the mass media and sports sponsorship. In summary, Gruneau argues that:

> close cultural ties between working-class recreation and commercial gaming and sporting activities were generated and solidified at a time when such activities were somewhat oppositional features within the hegemony of the late nineteenth century. However, the full-scale incorporation of commercial sports into Canadian capitalism has (now) created a situation where this long-standing cultural attachment appears to have reproductive consequences. (Gruneau, 1983:127–8)

Sport and recreation in twentieth century Canada are thus seen as often indistinguishable from commodity relations, aiding the incorporation of the working class into capitalist relations.

Plainly, although he shares with Dunning an obvious concern to develop a historical sociology in which social processes and class relations are paramount, for Gruneau the history of sports developments explores dimensions which are weakly present or simply absent in the approach of the Figurationists. For Gruneau sport is always an arena where hegemony can be seen at work (or perhaps more aptly 'in play'). Furthermore, although he recognises in sport certain of the symbolic qualities ascribed to it by the figurationists at their most Durkheimian, for Gruneau sports as symbols are important not only as incorporatively hegemonic or because they are 'texts which tell us stories and provide an excitement rarely found in other areas of life' (Gruneau, 1983:149) but also because sports can sometimes act as 'metaphoric' statements with a capacity to 'dramatize utopian aspirations for human freedom, heroic actions and equality' (ibid., p. 147). As such, sports are also seen by Gruneau as 'expressions of agency'. Whether or not one would wish to accept all its elements, what Gruneau's analysis obviously achieves is an openness of emphases on both structure and agency (including more explicit consideration of alternative futures, as well as a different order of 'evaluation') which are largely missing from the approach of the Figurations. In general, then, Gruneau can be said to offer the greater coverage and wider range in the theoretical analysis of sport and leisure that critics of Figurational Sociology have called for, and he does so without loss of credibility as a genuinely sociological imagination.

John Horne and David Jary

Resistance through rituals – the work of the CCCS

The perspective of students and researchers from the CCCS – even if not to be accepted uncritically – provides a final indication of the kinds of absences to be weighed against the strengths of Figurational Sociology. First, the CCCS emphasis on ritualistic aspects of leisure ('resistance through ritual', e.g., via a 'bricolage' of commercial styles) provides a particularly valuable model of the 'hegemonic' and the 'oppositional' import of sport and leisure. Second, whereas the role of the state in contemporary society receives little systematic elaboration in the work of the Figurationists, the theoretical framework for analysing state power provided by the CCCS is potentially highly fruitful.[5]

Essentially, what the CCCS research directs attention to is the post-war 'social construction' of youth and leisure through media and state intervention. They see this issue as a 'uniquely modern problematic'. In particular, CCCS researchers have revealed working class youth culture as facing changes in the neighbourhood and the local labour market, and seeking through leisure 'magical solutions' to class predicaments (see Hall and Jefferson, 1976; Cohen, 1980) – the source of plainly different and more 'open-ended' accounts of working-class behaviour than, for example, the 'functionalist' accounts of 'football hooliganism' – as regression to earlier patterns of social solidarity – offered by Dunning et al. (1982).

It is of interest to note in detail the markedly different treatment of 'football hooliganism' provided by CCCS researchers (see Critcher, 1979, and Clarke, 1978). The figurationists suggest that CCCS researchers and others, neglecting history, view football hooliganism as an 'entirely new phenomenon'. But this is not so. As Clarke (1978) sees it: 'Types of behaviour which were once perfectly normal and commonplace in football crowds . . . (become) . . . seen as deviant and hooligan behaviour' (Clarke, 1978:57). For Clarke, violence as such is 'not the centre of the difficulty, for football's history has always been marked by forms of violence both on the pitch and off it' (p. 55). The central problem, is that since the sixties the controllers of the game have sought to reshape the sport to make it a more respectable and, in Gruneau's general phrase, a more 'marketable and consumable video product' (Gruneau, 1983). Ian Taylor's (1985) counter to the Dunning thesis is also of note, suggesting that it is easy to see why the project to play down the distinctive recent levels of football

106

violence is 'helpful' to an 'evolutionary' and idealist theory such as the thesis of a civilising process, but denying that this is helpful in understanding contemporary working class youth in Britain.

What these features of the CCCS approach, and of Gruneau, underline is that, contrary to the suggestions of Figurational Sociologists, 'ahistoricity' or 'determinism' are not the problem in neo-marxist sociologies of this sort. On the contrary, theoretical analysis and empirical research on relations between cultural forms and state, class, and economy are handled – actually or potentially – more fully than in Figurational Sociology, reflecting what, following Gramsci, CCCS researchers recognise as the need to capture the 'current moment' of hegemony – the specific state of 'negotiations' over authority and meanings between dominant and subordinate class groupings. CCCS researchers have demonstrated in their historical case studies of youth and recreation an awareness of the need to provide full elaborations of the historical context as well as analysis in general terms. In contrast, Dunning et al.'s (1982) analysis of 'football hooliganism' is pitched at too high a level of generality, resulting from its over-reliance on the 'evolutionism' of the concept of the 'civilising process'. Thus, the idea of a 'curvilinear pattern' of football related violence, somehow connected to shifting levels of class frustration and class conflict (Dunning et al, 1982:147), whilst attractive, is never fully explicated or entirely historically grounded. The CCCS approach can be seen as allowing more space for open agency and a more adequate account of structural factors and ideological influences in modern society than usual in Figurational Sociology. Arguably, a history relating the cultural spheres of society with changes in the economy and state formation, to which the CCCS researchers and theorists like Gruneau, are beginning to point the way, provides a more satisfactory basis for developing a general sociology of sport, and one complementary to, but potentially transcendent of Figurational Sociology.

Conclusions

Our argument has been that there should be clear recognition of the part played by Figurational Sociology in helping to bring major improvements in the sociological analysis of sport and leisure, but that its exclusive claims and restrictive epistemology – especially when combined with a caricaturing of alternative positions – have served to limit its focus. Our contention is that alternative approaches to Figurational Sociology, while retaining an emphasis on historical sociological analysis and on 'structure and agency', can now provide a fuller elaboration of the 'duality' of structure and agency than Figurational Sociology has typically managed.[6] It must be underlined that we have not sought to argue for the outright superiority of the 'alternative' approaches to Figurational Sociology examined. Nor would we wish in any way to suggest that all is well with these alternatives. A good deal remains contentious in these approaches. But the questions raised by alternative theories are vital ones, with which the Figurational Sociology of sport fails to engage fully, and which need to be raised. It is in this respect that the two sets of approaches can be seen as complementary.

Although there are some signs that Dunning is growing more open to the ideas of others (e.g, his welcome for Gruneau's volume – Gruneau, 1983), his inclination nevertheless is still to seek to emasculate alternative theories – e.g., 'framing' even those neo-marxian theories he finds acceptable as 'abandoning marxism' (Dunning, 1983) – and he remains critical of their continuing lack of 'value neutrality'. In his view any 'synthesis' in the sociology of sport would require a 'distance and detachment from the cold war and the class struggle' (Dunning, 1983:141) as well as from feminism – clear evidence of his continued attachment to a restrictive methodology and a tendency to relapse into unhelpful caricature of alternative, but potentially complementary, approaches.

Notes

1 Elias (1978a) abounds with generally caricatured accounts of alternative approaches to his own. Although he acknowledges that at the time of his first formulation of the Figurational approach and its alternatives his familiarity with much of sociology was limited, central elements of these accounts have changed little, and there is only limited evidence of any genuine openness to other views.
2 Uncharitable, caricatured presentation of alternative sociologies are again in evidence here. Marxism is portrayed as presenting itself as a science only for reasons of prestige.
3 We would make recourse here to a 'discourse' theory of truth (c.f. Habermas, 1970; Feyerabend, 1978) which although it does not require a 'synthesis' of approaches does require an openness to issues between sides which is unconstrained by restrictive epistemology. In general Elias's own conception of science, while it anticipates something of the Kuhnian view, is not systematically

worked through or consistently applied. His own entry into the field of epistemological debate shows a characteristic disregard for the true position of others (see Elias, 1971a, and 1974). One looks in vain for a more truly figurationist sensitivity to the real world context – and value involvements – of the social construction of science.

4 Although we have long had mixed feelings about Figurational Sociology, it was a member of the CCCS group, Chas Critcher (1985) who stimulated our resolve to consider its role in the study of sport more fully. In an appraisal of Dunning and Sheard (1979), Gruneau (1983) and Allan Guttman's *From Ritual to Record* (1978) Critcher typified the second and third as 'Marxist' and 'Weberian', but the first as 'Functionalist'. It should be obvious our view would be that Dunning and Sheard are much better understood as 'Figurational Sociologists'. At the same time, we share many of Critcher's arguments with respect to all three texts – that all three approaches make a strong contribution to a historically grounded and sociologically sophisticated analysis of sport. In this way Critcher's view also supports our criticisms of Figurational Sociology's claims to exclusivity in the sociological study of sport.

5 While Elias's analysis of the evolution of the modern state is clearly of major interest, Figurationists have not directed their attention to contemporary state forms in the same way. Furthermore, whatever its acknowledged strengths, the Elias developmental analysis of the state can itself be criticised as lacking in adequate conceptualisation of radical 'discontinuities' and revolutionary shifts in state power – e.g., see Buck-Morss (1977).

6 Bramham (1984), in a useful article, explores the utility of Giddens's notions of 'duality of structure' and 'dialectic of power' to the sociology of sport, regarding Elias and Dunning's work as best exemplifying the required emphasis on 'agency and structure'. However, we cannot agree that either Giddens's highly abstract formulations (cf. Archer, 1985) or Figurational Sociology now represents the best basis for the sociology of sport.

References

Abrams, P. (1982), *Historical Sociology*, Open Books, Shepton Mallet.
Archer, M. (1985), 'Structuration versus morphogenesis', in Eisenstadt, S. and Helle, H. (eds), *Macrosociological Theory: Perspectives in Sociological Theory*, Sage, London, pp. 58–88.
Bauman, Z. (1979), 'The phenomenon of Norbert Elias', *Sociology*, 13:117–35.
Becker, H. (1967), 'Whose side are we on?', *Social Problems*, 14:239–47.
Bendix, R. (1978), Foreword to Elias, N. (1978a), pp. 11–12.
Bourdieu, P. (1977), cited p. 72 in Gleichman (1977) – from a note: 'Post-scriptum' to Norbert Elias, 'Sport et Violence', *Actes de Recherche en Sciences Sociales*, 2:20–1.
Bramham, P. (1984), 'Giddens in goal: reconstructing the social theory of sport', in Bramham, P. et al. (1984), *New Directions in Leisure Studies*, Department of Applied and Community Studies, Bradford and Ilkley Community College.
Braverman, H. (1974), *Labour and Monopoly Capital*, Monthly Review Press, New York.
Brookes, C. (1978), *English Cricket*, Weidenfeld and Nicolson, London.

Buck-Morss, S. (1977), Review of 'The Civilising Process', *Telos*, 37:181–98.

Clarke, J. (1978), 'Football and working class fans', in Ingham et al., *Football Hooliganism: the Wider Context*, Interaction Inprint, London.

Clarke, J. and Critcher, C. (1985), *The Devil Makes Work*, Macmillan, London.

Clarke, J., Critcher, C. and Johnson, R. (eds) (1979), *Working Class Culture*, Hutchinson, London.

Cohen, P. (1980), 'Subcultural conflict and working class community' in Hall, S. et al. (1980), pp. 78–87.

Critcher, C. (1979), 'Football since the war', in Clarke et al. (1979), pp. 161–84.

Critcher, C. (1985), 'Sport and social development', paper to the BSA/LSA Leisure and Recreation Study Group, North Staffs Polytechnic, May.

Dunning, E. (ed.) (1971a), *The Sociology of Sport*, Frank Cass, London.

Dunning, E. (1971b), 'The development of modern football', in Dunning (1971a), pp. 116–32.

Dunning, E. (1975), 'Theoretical perspectives on sport: a development critique', in Parker, S. et al. (1975).

Dunning, E. (1979), *Soccer. The Social Origins of the Sport and its Development as a Spectacle and a Profession*, Sports Council/SSRC, London.

Dunning, E. (1981), 'Social bonding and the sociogenesis of violence: a theoretical and empirical analysis with special reference to combat sports', in Tomlinson, A. (ed.) (1981).

Dunning, E. (1983), 'Notes on some recent contributions to the sociology of sport', *Theory, Culture and Society*, 2:135–42.

Dunning, E. (1986), 'Sport as a male preserve: notes on the social sources of masculine identity and its transformations', *Theory, Culture and Society*, 3:79–90.

Dunning, E., Maguire, J., Murphy, P. and Williams, J. (1982), 'The social roots of football hooligan violence', *Leisure Studies*, 1:139–56.

Dunning, E., Maguire, J., Murphy, P. and Williams, J. (1983), 'Football hooligan violence before the First World War: preliminary sociological reflections on some recent findings', in Tomlinson, A. (ed.) (1983).

Dunning, E. and Sheard, K. (1979), *Barbarians, Gentlemen and Players: Sociological Study of the Development of Rugby Football*, Martin Robertson, Oxford.

Elias, N. (1956), 'Problems of involvement and detachment', *British Journal of Sociology*, 7:226–52.

Elias, N. (1971a), 'Sociology of knowledge: new perspectives', *Sociology*, 5:149–68 and 355–70.

Elias, N. (1971b), 'The genesis of sport as a sociological problem', in Dunning, E. (ed.) (1971), pp. 88–115 (also see 'Foreword' ibid., pp. xi-xii).

Elias, N. (1974), 'The sciences: towards a theory', in Whitley, R. (ed.), *Social Processes of Scientific Development*, Blackwell, Oxford, pp. 21–42.

Elias, N. (1978a ⟨1970⟩) *What is Sociology?*, Hutchinson, London.

Elias, N. (1978b ⟨1939⟩), *The Civilizing Process, vol. 1: The History of Manners*, Blackwell, Oxford.

Elias, N. (1982a ⟨1939⟩), *The Civilizing Process, vol. 2: State and Civilization*, Blackwell, Oxford.

Elias, N. (1982b), 'Scientific establishments', in Elias, N. et al. (eds), *Scientific Establishments and Hierarchies: Sociology of the Sciences*, vol. 6, Reidel, Dortrecht, pp. 3–69.

Elias, N. and Dunning, E. (1966), 'Dynamics of sport groups with special reference to football', *British Journal of Sociology*, 17:388–402 – also reprinted in Dunning, E. (ed.) (1971a).

Elias, N. and Dunning, E. (1969), 'The quest for excitement in leisure', *Society and Leisure*, 2:50–85.

Elias, N. and Dunning, E. (1971), 'Folk football and medieval and early modern Britain', in Dunning, E. (ed.) (1971a), pp. 116–32.

Feyerabend, P. (1978), *Science in a Free Society*, New Left Books, London.

Giddens, A. (1984), *The Constitution of Society: Outline of the Theory of Structuration*, Polity Press, Oxford.

Gleichman, P. et al. (1977), *Human Figurations*, Amsterdams Sociologisch Tijdschift.

Goudsblom, J. (1977a), *Sociology in the Balance*, Blackwell, Oxford.

Goudsblom, J. (1977b), 'Responses to Norbert Elias's work in England, Germany, and the Netherlands and France', in Gleichman (1977), pp. 37–97.

Gouldner, A. (1976), *The Dialectic of Ideology and Technology*, Macmillan, London.

Gruneau, R. (1983), *Class, Sports and Social Development*, University of Massachusetts Press.

Guttman, A. (1978), *From Ritual to Record: The Nature of Modern Sports*, Columbia University Press, New York.

Habermas, J. (1970), 'Towards a theory of communicative competence', *Inquiry*, 13:360–75.

Hall, S. and Jefferson, T. (eds) (1976), *Resistance through Rituals*, Hutchinson, London.

Hall, S. et al. (1980), *Culture, Media, Language*, Hutchinson, London.

Hargreaves, Jennifer (1986), 'Where's the virtue? Where's the grace? A discussion of the social production of gender relations in and through sport', *Theory, Culture and Society*, 3:109–21.

Hargreaves, John (1975), 'Toward a political economy of sport', in Parker et al. (eds) (1975).

Hargreaves, John (1982), 'Sport, culture and ideology', in Hargreaves, Jennifer (ed.), *Sport, Culture and Ideology*, Routledge & Kegan Paul, London.

Huizinga, J. (1955), *Homo Ludens*, Beacon Press, Boston.

Lasch, C. (1985), 'Historical sociology and the myth of maturity – Norbert Elias's "very simple formula"', *Theory and Society*, 14:705–20.

Marsh, P., Rosser, E. and Harre, R. (1978), *The Rules of Disorder*, Routledge & Kegan Paul, London.

Mennell, S. (1982), 'From social constraint to self-restraint', *THES*, 2 July (also see ch. by Mennell in Gleichman et al., 1977, pp. 99–109).

Parker, S. et al. (eds) (1975), *Sport and Leisure in Contemporary Society*, Polytechnic of Central London.

Rojek, C. (1985), *Capitalism and Leisure Theory*, Tavistock, London.

Sheard, K. and Dunning, E. (1973), 'The rugby football club as a type of "male preserve": some sociological notes', *International Review of Sport Sociology*, 8:117–24.

Smith, D. (1984), 'Established or outsider', *Sociological Review*, 32:367–89.

Stedman Jones, G. (1977), 'Class expressions versus social control? A critique of recent trends in the sociology of leisure', *History Workshop Journal*, 4:162–70.

Stone, G. (1955), 'American sports: play and display', *Chicago Review*, 9:83–100, reprinted in Dunning (1971a).

Suttles, G. (1972), *The Social Construction of Communities*, University of Chicago Press (also see Suttles, 1968, *The Social Order of the Slum*, Chicago University Press).

Taylor, I. (1971), 'Football mad' in Dunning (1971a), pp. 352–79 (also see his 'Soccer consciousness and soccer hooliganism', in Cohen, S. (ed.) (1971), *Images of Deviance*, Penguin, Harmondsworth).

Taylor, I. (1985), 'Putting the boot into a working class sport: British soccer after Bradford and Brussels', Paper to the North American Society for the Sociology of Sport, Boston, Mass.

Tomlinson, A. (ed.) (1981), *The Sociological Study of Sport: Configurational and Interpretive Studies*, Brighton Polytechnic.

Tomlinson, A. (ed.) (1983), *Explorations in Football Culture*, Brighton Polytechnic.

Turner, B. (1985), 'Review of The Civilising Process and The Court Society', *Theory, Culture and Society*, 2:158–61.

Wagg, S. (1984), *The Football World: A Contemporary Social History*, Harvester Press, Hassocks.

Williams, J., Dunning, E. and Murphy, P. (1984), *Hooligans Abroad: The Behaviour and Control of English Fans in Continental Europe*, Routledge & Kegan Paul, London.

Wilson, B. (1977), 'A tribute to Elias', *New Society*, 7 July, pp. 15–16.

Wolf, E. (1977), 'Encounters with Norbert Elias', in Gleichman (1977), pp. 28–35.

Leisure, symbolic power and the life course

Mike Featherstone

Introduction

Sociologists of leisure constantly draw attention to the problems involved in providing an adequate definition of leisure. Often it is defined residually in relation to paid work, leisure being non-work time, or free time. This raises the question of those who do not do paid work, children, the old, housewives, the retired, the unemployed – do they have leisure? It also raises questions about the nature and significance of non-work activities. Should leisure be confined to rational recreation (organised sport, etc.) or include more mundane activities such as the 'big five' described by Roberts (1978): television, drinking, smoking, betting and making love? The term leisure also suggests fun, distraction, pleasure, but non-work time can include routinised maintenance pursuits, do-it-yourself, housework, etc. and the fact that such activities themselves are sometimes regarded as a source of pleasure and personal transformation should not be ignored (Martin 1984). Individuals may therefore find varying degrees of expressivity and self-control, in effect *leisure*, while engaged in routine work.

A further problem with the emphasis upon leisure as 'relatively self-determined activity' (Roberts 1978, p. 5) is that it is in danger of drifting towards a consumer sovereignty model, where the freedom of individuals to choose leisure pursuits is presented as a progressive feature of modern industrial societies in contrast to the alleged integration and bonded constraints of the traditional communal order. Such approaches neglect the way in which choices may be reduced effectively to the choices of necessity for certain groups and strata, at the bottom of the class structure. Furthermore it is equally flawed to focus upon the freedom, self-realisation and authenticity other groups (e.g. the new middle class) perceive in the active construction of leisure life-styles. This orientation may not only occur at a restricted point in the class structure, but represent a set of choices which equally can be coded. In effect taste which is often naturalised or individualised can be classified: taste which acts as the locus of an individual's classificatory practices also classifies the classifier (Bourdieu 1984).

Leisure pursuits like other consumption practices (tastes in food, drink, newspapers, films, cars etc) can therefore be mapped onto the social space and related to class, occupational, gender- and age- divisions. From this perspective leisure is merely one indicator of a more general class-, gender-, generation- or age-related orientation towards life which is manifest in the adoption of a particular way of life, a life-style. Here life-style reflects the cultural genesis of tastes from the specific point within the social space from which individuals originate and is manifest not only in leisure and consumption practices but the underlying dispositions which form individuals' general sense of tastes, life priorities, time and space. Such dispositions are not merely cognitive frameworks but are also materialised in possessions and unconsciously inscribed onto bodies in terms of differentials in shape, weight, or deportment, demeanour, stance, expression etc. Hence the cultural formation of the tastes which classify the individual will be manifest in work and non-work activities alike.

This paper will therefore argue that leisure tastes like other life-style tastes can be related to the class structure. It argues that differences in taste must be understood relationally, with the significance of a particular seemingly individual choice only being made intelligible when it is mapped onto the social field and placed in relation to other tastes within the universe of class tastes which operate within a particular society. Bourdieu, for example, argues that the distinctiveness of pure taste celebrated by the intellectuals – high culture – can only be understood in relation to, and in its differentiation from, the vulgarity of working-class culture. Likewise preferences for 'serious' or intellectualised leisure – avant-garde theatre, 'difficult' modernist music or gourmet cooking involve capital investment and accumulation of knowledge, a cultivation of taste, which contrasts with the frivolity, unreflexiveness of more simple direct, sensuous, and therefore deemed less civilised, pleasures which the working class find in popular forms of association, music and eating.

Here we seek to generate a perspective which goes beyond a familiar debate within the sociology of leisure concerning the

114

freedom/constraint, expressive/instrumental, autonomy/determinism polarities. This entails treating with suspicion statements such as 'Leisure is expressive culture, interactional more than organisational, and a matter of choice as well as determinism' (Kelly 1983, p. 24). What is important here is not to deny that individuals have a sense of choice and freedom in their leisure practices, but to inquire into:

1 The socially constructed boundaries to individual choices which should sensitise us to the fact that individuals of different social classes carrying out the 'same' activity may do so in wholly different ways which can be related back to their different formation within specific class culture (e.g., rugby, golf, squash, dancing, drinking, eating, have different significance, are stylised in different ways and occupy a different position within the lifestyle universe of the particular class or class fraction).

2 The very notion of choice – the expectation and duty to construct one's life in a projective way with an expectation of development and changes in taste and life-style – may, far from being universal, relate to the cultural expectations of particular class fractions.

3 The significance and meaning of a particular set of leisure choices must therefore not be understood as expressively chosen, or even as haphazard, idiosyncratic market behaviour, but can only be made intelligible by inscribing them on a map of the class-defined social field of leisure and life-style practices in which their meaning and significance is relationally defined with reference to structured oppositions and differences.

This is not to suggest that the approach to be followed here is based upon structuralism. Given our interest in a class-based, relational theory of leisure practices, it is evident that if we want to relate this to the life course, we should ultimately direct our attention to investigating the way in which the relations between life-style and leisure practices change over time as cohorts of individuals move through life. While life can therefore be understood as a process it is important to emphasise that the life course is a socially structured process. This suggests we should also comprehend the relationally or positionally generated differences and oppositions between the elements within it. We therefore need to look at the relational differences between childhood, adolescence, early adulthood, middle age and old age and the ways in which historical shifts in the boundaries between these phases, and the redefinition of the meaning of one phase, will necessarily alter the others within the field. Clearly here we are putting forward an argument for a complex approach to leisure and the life course, an argument which we are only too well aware is based upon theoretical premises which can only be substantiated by detailed empirical research into the generation of lifestyle and leisure tastes (see Bourdieu 1984). This should be coupled with a longitudinal approach to detect changes in taste which take place *within* the same generational cohort over time if we are to isolate the age specific changes. We have, however, been referring to a particular approach to the *life course*. Our first task is therefore to clarify the meaning of this term by way of a discussion of previous conceptions of the life cycle, life course or lifespan and the changes in taste that it is held to generate through life.

The life course

The conventional wisdom is that individuals change their tastes, dispositions, and leisure activities and political attitudes as they move through life. This has been buttressed by some social science research which has adopted the term life cycle from biology where it is used to refer to the regenerative cycle of birth, immaturity, maturity, reproduction, degeneration and death which the various species follow. At times it is used to imply similar biologically-rooted assumptions about the nature of the human life course. The Rapoports (1975, p. 14) in their study of *Leisure and the Family Life Cycle*, for example, argue that the human life cycle is based on 'psycho-biological maturational processes' which underlie class and subcultural differences. A similar psycho-biological emphasis lies behind the influential theories of lifespan development of Erikson, Bühler, Levinson and others who emphasise that life entails a one-way development through a series of stages whose negotiation involves the completion of a series of age-structured tasks which are crucial for successful growth.

Recently a greater scepticism has emerged about the psycho-genetic type of logic and the claims for universality of such theories. (Baltes et al. 1980; Freeman 1984; Harris 1986). A major drawback is that lifespan development theories are speculative and are often based upon inter-cohort data, using contrasts from individuals living at the same time who have different historically formed experiences of childhood, old age, etc. Where the changes occurring within an individual's life have been studied there is the danger that significant events have been constructed in collusion with the researcher stimulating retrospectively-generated data via a biographical approach. The harmonising narrative structure may be imposed *a posteriori*. There has been little systematic empirical research to back up the normative assumptions of development and normalcy. The problem remains that what may be claimed to be developmentally normal may be empirically rare and hence a curious inversion of the normal and pathological occurs (for a discussion in relation to Levinson's work see Featherstone 1979). Such approaches therefore tend to play down class, gender and cultural variations which point to differences in age norms, important life events and directional changes, which structure and code the life course.

Neugarten and Datan (1974), for example, suggest that different classes have a different notion of social time which points to a social clock superimposed upon the biological clock. Chronological or lived time may therefore not be crucial because the institutional expectations and density of life events, which create the perception of closure and openness, of an upward or a downward trajectory to life, differ significantly between classes. The working class regard young adulthood (20–30) as a phase of responsibilities, coping with the real problem of married life with young children; for the middle class it is a time of identity exploration, a prolonged adolescence. For the upper middle class middle age (40–60) is truly the prime of life, they are the command generation, whereas for the working class it is a time of decline, of coming to terms with being a 'has been'. Likewise it has been suggested that there is a different rhythm to the 'life courses' of men and women with men moving from an *active* approach to the first half of life to a *passive* orientation in the second half. Women move in the opposite direction and leave behind their early passivity to become more active, aggressive, instrumental and dominant in the second phase (Guttman 1977; Lowenthal et al. 1975).

These points suggest that we should be cautious about assuming that there is a universal human life cycle involving psychological development which is the basis for changes in leisure lifestyles. The different class, gender and cultural variations suggest that chronological age is a weak explanatory variable (Neugarten 1985). Rather, we need to look at the social institutions and practices which differentially structure social ageing. A shared ontogenic process conceived as a cycle or a development must therefore be rejected in favour of the more neutral term, life course, which is devoid of teleological overtones.

A social constructionist approach emphasises the variety of ways in which the temporal span of the life course has been conceived and accorded significance through notions of development, maturation and decay. It points to the variety of ways in which the life course can be divided up into stages or phases, the variations in temporal span accorded to these stages, and the different prioritization and meaning accorded to stages in different eras and cultures. We have, for example, been made aware that childhood is a recent social construction 'invented' since the eighteenth century (Ariès 1962). Against this rather romantic view which regards children, prior to this stage, as free 'adults' in charge of their lives, we note that Norbert Elias's (1978) work on the civilising process suggests that adults in the Middle Ages lived in a world in which the constraints were external, they therefore generally lacked strong internal restraints on the emotions. Effectively adults could give vent to the full range of emotions like children without shame or guilt: the distance between adults and children was therefore not so great. Modernity has not just seen the construction of childhood as a phase of dependence but the construction of adulthood as a phase of independence, of alleged psychological maturity and authorised citizenship. The important point suggested here is that childhood cannot be understood in itself but must be compared to adulthood, in effect the meaning of a particular phase of the life course is defined relationally by its similarities to and differences from the other phases.

The various phases or stages of the life course are not fixed but undergo historical change. The emergence and institutionalization of new phases of the life course can be linked to the interests and struggles of social groups (childhood with the eighteenth-century aristocracy, adolescence with the growth of psychology and the helping professions in the late nineteenth and early twentieth centuries). A 'developmental' view of adult personality has resulted, with the demarcation of adult life into specific phases namely early adulthood, middle age, young old age, deep old age – each with their own distinctive tasks and problems. The investigation of this process whereby new growth models and critical transitions are created to redraw the map of adult life has only just begun (for a discussion of the colonisation of middle age and the discovery of new crises such as the midlife crisis see Featherstone and

Hepworth 1982). The preconditions for these changes, for example, increase in life expectancy (from age 50 in 1900 to over 70 today) and the relative internal pacification of societies which means increasing numbers of citizens will have their deaths in old age also require investigation, as do the entrepreneurial activities of social groups to create and legitimate new life stages.

Th. construction of new stages within the field of the life course alters the relationship between formerly existing elements. It is no longer sufficient (if it ever was) to conceive of the generational struggle as between the young and the old. With increasing numbers of men and women living into their 70s and 80s those in their 50s and 60s can no longer be defined as the old. A one-way generational struggle becomes a two-way one with the middle aged assuming the role of the old for the young, and the role of young in relation to the old. The relationship is further complicated by the power differential which means that each generation has a different developmental stake in the other (cf. Bengston and Cutler 1977). The older may deny intergenerational differences because they want good social heirs while the younger may be concerned with developing their own distinctiveness and individuality, their own values and institutions. Part of the upsurge of academic and popular interest in the middle aged, the generation which has to look both ways, can be attributed to the problems involved in coping with these two power-balances.

A further problem with using generation in this sense, which sensitises us to the danger of externalising the characteristics attributed to a particular phase of life, is that the vast majority of the descriptions of the young, the middle aged and the old have been gleaned from surveys of inter cohort differences. In effect one is not able to compare like with like because only rarely have individuals been followed through the life course. There is therefore the danger that characteristics which appear to document different stages of the life course may be cohort, or period-specific. Here we use the term generation in a historically specific sense to point to the uniqueness of the cultural values which generations embody (e.g. 'the generation of 1914' (Wohl 1980), the 1920s generation (Fass 1977), the 1960s generation (Feuer 1969). Generational research suggests that the values which are developed and inculcated in a person's formative years (15–25) will be carried with them through the rest of their lives (Bengston and Cutler 1977). This applies as much to political views (Butler and Stokes 1969) as to tastes in leisure pursuits (Dumazedier 1967).

119

We therefore have moved from a discussion of the psycho-biological genesis of the life cycle to a preference for the social construction of the life course, to the view that the latter itself must be contextualised in terms of historical generations, remembering that both should also be understood in relation to class and gender differences. Before concluding our discussion of the life course and looking more closely at the social structuration of differences in leisure tastes we need to introduce one further complicating factor in the relational theory of the life course we are developing. If generations carry their values and tastes with them through life, then in certain circumstances one might expect the subsequent generation to develop their values and tastes in opposition to the prior one. Here we could expect a youth generation such as the 1960s generation which extolled irre-sponsibility, romanticism and permissiveness (values which contrast with the austerity of their 1930s Depression generation parents) to carry their values with them into middle age when they would be opposed by the new young generation, sections of which may be forced to reject *youthfulness* and adopt a more mature, responsible conservative life-style to maintain an oppositional stance. A relevant example is the emergence in Britain in the 1980s of 'young fogies' as a section of middle-class youth culture. Likewise the heroicism and asceticism of the 'generation of 1914' (born in the 1880s) can be regarded as oppositionally related to the decadence of the *fin-de-siècle* 1890s generation. Of course such broad generalisations must be approached with caution and require detailed investigations of the specific historical circumstances, the tensions between different classes within a generational cohort and the role of the intellectuals in catalysing a generational conscious-ness.

The boundaries between generations and the capacity to define the meaning of other generations in relation to one's own is always the source of struggle. This in part explains the difficulties in defining when old age begins, which is similar to the problem of defining where the rich start: both frontiers are stakes in a struggle (Bourdieu 1980b). To allow middle age, for example, to be redefined as middle youth from one perspective is to suggest an appropriation of youthfulness, a desired quality, from the young. Yet from the perspective of the young-old this may be a label they willingly foster on the middle aged, because youth (here associated with irresponsibility and frivolity) is a quality opposed to the maturity and wisdom necessary for power holders, which the old seek to preserve for themselves. Likewise the middle aged may seek to send the young-old into old age as they in their turn seek to maximise their choice to either retain command or retire on their own terms. At the same time they distance themselves from the old-old, who possess few resources in the game to combat institutionalisation and the repelling properties of deep old age. It is legitimate here to talk about the generations in terms of a power struggle over resources (some of which are symbolic and include the capacity to define the meanings and frontiers of generations). It is generally assumed that the movement through life entails a life course trajectory which ultimately involves a shedding of resources and capital of all kinds (economic, symbolic and cultural). This social unity needs to be deconstructed and the generational and life stage leisure differences discussed in terms of class and gender (an approach which accepts that one must speak of at least two youths or two old ages each possessing different resources and subjected to different social clocks). First it is necessary to spell out the rudiments of an approach to the relation between leisure, lifestyle and class based upon the work of Pierre Bourdieu.

The social space of life-styles

Bourdieu suggests that if we seek to understand a particular set of social practices, such as leisure, we can do so in a way which recognises the autonomy of the particular field in question by focusing upon the specific internal dynamic, structuring principles and process which operate there in a way analogous to the economy. This is not to argue for a reduction of cultural practices to the economy, rather one can detect the distinct processes of market competition, the principles of supply and demand, the tendency towards monopolisation which operate *within* specific social fields at particular points in time. In effect one can analyse 'the economy of cultural goods' (Bourdieu 1980a), the specific economies whose principles are generally misrecognised or denied which operate within a variety of social practices. Some of those analysed by Bourdieu and his colleagues include sport, photography, linguistic exchanges, education, marriage, art, science and religion. Particular sets of social practices can be regarded as economies which operate to restrict access to culturally valued goods and prestigious symbols and determine the power chances of particular classes of individuals whose position within the field and capacity to move upwards or downwards is structured in relation to the volume of capital they possess. Here it is important to emphasise that by capital Bourdieu is referring to the operation of cultural and symbolic capital not just economic capital. Within many fields money or income may not guarantee access to positions of power, rather we have to talk about cultural capital with its own structure of value, (usually misrecognised or disguised) and rates of convertibility into social power. Despite the misrecognition and denial of the market in cultural goods by the specialists in symbol production such as intellectuals and artists, there is a definite market with an exchange rate whereby prestigious cultural goods (usually presented as the products of natural talents – the ideology of charisma – which will have no truck with the material world) are convertible into money.

Classes and class fractions, for example the intellectuals, are involved in a constant struggle to turn the market principle in operation in a particular field to their advantage. The intellectuals will always seek to increase the autonomy of the cultural field and enhance the scarcity of cultural capital in relation to economic capital. They, like other groups will seek to monopolise access to the production of goods within their particular field, to re-name and legitimate the structuration of the field to their advantage. The production of cultural symbols, be they high culture, popular culture or consumer goods, are therefore the subject of an endless process of struggle on the part of classes, class fractions and groups to rename and legitimate the particular set of tastes which reflect their interests. Those classes which possess a high volume of economic capital (the bourgeoisie) and cultural capital (the intellectuals) are clearly in a stronger position to define what is legitimate, valid and 'pure' taste. The appreciation of legitimate taste depends on the accumulation or investment of a high volume of cultural capital (e.g., education, knowledge of high culture and the arts) symbolic capital (presentation of self, demeanour) and economic capital (money) which contrasts to the non-legitimate common, vulgar tastes of the working class who possess little capital of any kind and are disinclined to invest. It should be emphasised here that society is not conceived as being held together by a dominant ideology which produces a common culture. On the contrary while legitimate taste achieves hegemony and recognition, different classes and class fractions pursue tastes which are a reflection of their particular position (determined by type and volume of capital) within the social space. In effect their own tastes are naturalised, being a set of classificatory practices unconsciously assimilated by virtue of their common occupancy of a specific point in the social field, and a certain antipathy and hostility developed towards the 'strange' tastes of other fractions.

Bourdieu terms this set of classificatory schemes, unconscious dispositions and taken-for-granted preferences *habitus*. The differential formation of habitus for different groups and classes will result in a 'natural' disposition to produce certain practices and to classify and judge the practices of others. In effect habitus is the generative principle of taste differences. It systematically produces a set of distinctive preferences which form the basis of different lifestyles. This set of taken-for-granted preferences is evident in the agent's sense of the appropriateness and validity of his taste for cultural goods and practices – art, food, drink, sport, hobbies etc. Habitus does not, however, simply operate on the level of everyday knowledgeability, but is *embodied* being inscribed onto the body and made apparent in body size, volume, demeanour, ways of eating, drinking, walking, sitting, speaking, making gestures, etc. Tastes and lifestyle preferences, which in our society are frequently individualised, are therefore a product of a specific habitus which in turn can be related to the volume of economic and cultural capital possessed and hence the position a particular occupation, age or gender category, class or class fraction occupies can be mapped onto the social space. Bourdieu conceives a set of homologies whereby the grid of different habituses can be related to the grid of capital volume (which is the basis of the occupational structure) and the grid of lifestyle choices.

For example, in *Distinction* Bourdieu sets out to show how taste functions as a marker of class by mapping onto the social field the different tastes in 'high' culture practices (museum visiting, concert-going, reading, art, theatre, etc.) as well as tastes in consumption and life-styles (food, drink, clothes, furniture, cars, newspapers, magazines, sport, holidays, hobbies and leisure pursuits). The relational determination of taste becomes clear when we consider the oppositions which are generated between different occupational categories and classifications. Bourdieu's analysis is based upon detailed survey data which allows him to demonstrate the correlations between occupational categories (based upon a given volume and composition of cultural or economic capital) and lifestyle tastes. For example, according to

Bourdieu (1984, pp. 128–9), those who have a high volume of economic capital and low cultural capital (industrialists, commercial employees) have a taste for auctions, second homes, hotel holidays, sport, hunting, business meals, foreign cars, tennis, water-skiing, right-bank galleries. Those who possess a high volume of cultural capital and a low volume of economic capital (higher education teachers, artistic producers, secondary teachers, cultural intermediaries) have a taste for left-bank galleries, avant-garde festivals, foreign languages, foreign food, chess, flea markets, country walking, camping, mountains, swimming, hang-gliding, ecology, etc.). Those low in both economic and cultural capital (unskilled workers), Bourdieu argues, are faced with 'the tastes of necessity' (cheap simple food: potatoes, bread, pasta, ordinary red wine, watching sports, football, public dances). Such examples do not do justice to the complexities of the social space and the richness of Bourdieu's anthropological description of each particular class habitus and set of life-style practices.

It is therefore clear from Bourdieu's approach that it is pointless to seek to detach the analysis of leisure practices from the way in which more general life-style tastes are structured by their relationship to the habitus of particular class fractions and groups. The set of distinctive preferences and classificatory schemes, which operate as the habitus, generates perceptions and practices which encompass a wide range of aspects of life-style and the same principles of structuring taste and meaning, in effect the *modus operandi* of a class fraction or group, are to be found in housing patterns, dietary patterns, style of dress, artistic, leisure tastes, etc. It is useful to outline briefly some of the differences and discuss the ways in which they, in turn, are modified and structured by ageing and the life course.

In the first place the life-style differences are evident in the type and volume of material possessions and the relative amount of cultural capital which dictates the appropriateness and legitimacy of the practices different classes and class fractions build around their property. For sectors of the traditional working class and the unemployed working class there is a taste (dictated by necessity) for essential, clean, practical goods, which contrasts with the middle-class preference for more fashionable goods given that they possess both the economic capital (financial resources) and cultural capital (knowledge of fashions and style) to withdraw from the outmoded. The bourgeoisie or the established upper class have a preference for luxury goods, and high fashion, which effectively act as emblems of class not just by their possession, but in the way they are used. Bourdieu (1984, p. 281) remarks, for example, that owning a chateau or manor house is not just a question of money, it must be appropriated – cultural capital is necessary to appropriate the cellar and learn the art of bottling, to appropriate the landscape via landscape design, to appropriate the interior via the art of interior design and develop knowledge of art objects, entertaining, gastronomy etc. The art of conspicuous consumption must also be mastered which depends upon a gradual and imperceptible accumulation of cultural and symbolic capital from childhood onwards which puts a person at ease with the 'naturalness' and appropriateness of his or her taste. This contrasts with the unease, over-restraint or over-compensation of autodidacts, evident in the new bourgeoisie and the new middle class. Of course the distaste of the upper classes for the parvenu, who lacks their ease and mastery of the art of conspicuous consumption, should not hide the investment returns in social capital (connections) which such apparent squandering provides (cf. Elias 1983). For Bourdieu there is no disinterested natural or cultural sphere beyond the reach of social interests and he is fond of pointing out the recondite capital-investment strategies of those who reject the world, the interest in lack of interest. While in general terms the life course involves an accumulation of capital of all types, which peaks in middle age, the movement into old age necessarily involves a shedding, a reduction of the capacity to accumulate economic capital and a devaluation of particular types of cultural capital (by dint of attachment to forms of knowledge and styles which have become deemed as outmoded). At the same time certain types of symbolic capital, manifest in demeanour, way of speaking and attitude towards the body, may retain their distinction and value into deep old age, for example amongst the aristocracy or royalty.

Movement through the life course, after physical maturity is reached in early adulthood, involves a gradual bodily decline, but this decline is managed differently by different classes through the different habituses which result in differences in the meaning, use and significance ascribed to the body. We can, therefore, following Bourdieu speak of a universe of class bodies in which differences, resulting from type and volume of capital, mediated by class habitus, become visibly inscribed onto the body and are accompanied by different dispositions towards the body (aesthetic, instrumental, functional, etc.) and different investments of leisure time into bodily practices. With regard to food and drink the working class habitus produces a taste for heavier, cheaper fatty foods and the 'eat well and let yourself go' philosophy, which can be contrasted to the middle class valuation of restraint and slimness. Dispositions become literally incorporated into different body shapes and tolerances of the 'naturalness' of the alterations accompanying ageing (i.e. middle-aged spread). These differences in dispositions are evident markers of class. In the working class there is a struggle to resist the entrepreneurial efforts of health educationalists to produce a uniform acceptance of the middle class definition of the healthy bodily form. The working class are disposed more to accept and naturalise bodily difference in height, weight and shape, and to accept bodily decline as inevitable with age rather than seek to maintain or improve their bodies. This is not to suggest that the working class do not go in for bodily improvement – body building is a clear example. But working-class body building on the part of young men to enhance masculine virility, contrasts with the more health-directed, middle-class jogging and aerobics which is increasingly acceptable for older age groups.

The working-class disposition towards the body can be contrasted to that of the new middle class, those engaged in occupations involving representational and presentational skills (the media, advertising, marketing, public relations, fashion, the helping professions) whose habitus provides a sense of unease, alienation and embarassment towards the body. In contrast to the upper classes' assurance, restraint, and sense of ease with the body which involves an indifference to the gaze of others, the new middle class who are pretenders, aspiring to be more than they are, to move upwards in the social space, betray the insecurity of their investment orientation to life in the way that they watch, check and correct the body, self-consciously aware of the gaze of others.

The popularity of practices such as body-maintenance techniques within the new middle class, (jogging, aerobics, new gymnastics, Californian outdoor sports) can be related to their occupational concern with self-presentation; with exercise for 'looking good and feeling great' as the advertising slogan runs (Featherstone 1982). For the new middle class the body is a sign for others and while the cosmetic benefits of body maintenance can be regarded as a means towards an end (which also reflects the disproportionate number of women employed in the occupations of this class fraction), the activities themselves are frequently glamourised and presented as expressive leisure, as fun, as providing opportunity for stylistic display and distinction. This can be related to the habitus of the new middle class (whom Bourdieu refers to as the perfect consumers) who, unlike the working class who inherit a ready-made life-style are actively concerned to foreground style, to become absorbed in the conscious stylisation of life, to make life a work of art, to search for individuality and self-expression via their possessions, practices and body-for-others (Featherstone 1985). They are crucially positioned as a numerically increasing fraction with a rising trajectory in the social space. They also occupy a key role as cultural intermediaries, symbol creators and transmitters, able to legitimate and purvey lifestyle information, to promote the stylisation of life in fashion, design, leisure, sport, the new arts, popular culture. A stylisation which we hasten to add should not be taken to amount to a coherent new ideology, for their role as intermediaries sensitises them to a constant re-cycling of old styles and a modernist search for the 'new'. At the same time their role as cultural intermediaries should not disguise their activity as cultural entrepreneurs. Their predilections for an active, totalising, experiencing, maximising orientation to life involves them in many struggles (e.g. health education) in which they can present themselves as progressively promoting a better, healthier life-style in which the traditional attitudes towards the body 'natural', and reticence towards exercise on the part of the working classes, must be exorcised.

For the new middle class, who are keen to generalise, through the media, their own bodily dispositions, the ageing body is a source of anxiety: the capital investment in it may let the owner down before the expected returns are realised. Body maintenance is therefore regarded as a means of combating ageing and eventually avoiding the repulsive properties associated with old age (wrinkled flesh, frailty, unpleasant odours, incontinence, etc.). While, following Norbert Elias (1978), we can acknowledge in modernity a gradual rise in the shame threshold with regard to bodily functions and a growth in the disgust function (Elias 1985) which make it difficult for individuals to identify with the elderly, the reaction to the aversive properties of old age will be different in different classes. The embarrassment, and lack of ease with the body, characteristic of the new middle class habitus may therefore make them over-sensitive to the repulsive properties of old age and dispose them to utilise their economic resources to manipulate their appearance and image for as long as possible. While they are however inclined to legitimate their particular set of dispositions to the wider population by way of the media, different class fractions may resist the message in various ways. Not only do the traditional working class react against the message, but the upper class habitus with its incorporation of symbolic capital into the body (distinguished demeanour, presence, ways of speaking, etc.) equips the individual with a set of dispositions which allow him/her to distance him/herself from the repulsive properties of old age. In effect the embodied symbolic power facilitates a presentation and disposition to overlay the negative traits with those which reinforce the bearer's status. The repulsive properties are effectively denied and their social significance misrecognised by the individual whose symbolic power enables him to manage and impose this misrecognition on others (e.g., the heroes of ageing such as the Queen Mother; see Featherstone and Hepworth 1986).

When we discuss the non-work or leisure practices that surround the body as it moves through the life course, we have therefore to talk about a number of middle ages, or old ages. It is not enough to refer to the expansion of the leisure market, or to talk about the enforced dependence on home life, and the problems of old age, as leading to a blanket deprivation response. The different resources groups possess in terms of economic, cultural and symbolic capital and subsequent dispositions generated through habitus ensure differential responses. Enforced dependence on home life and isolation may be a perceived problem for working-class men and women born into a generation brought up in large extended families or more dense kinship networks and is rightly recognised as such by statutory and voluntary agencies. Yet whether this will be a perceived problem to the same extent for the working-class middle-aged generation is problematic, and whether we can generalise this disposition to, for example, the new middle class, is more problematic still. This last class fraction, which tends to be young in generational terms, and which has a higher proportion of post-Second World War born men and women, may be disposed to regard the loss of family ties differently, having chosen a life-style in which family ties have been regarded as dispensable. A retirement in a seaside old-age community may therefore not just be chosen for purely economic reasons with a sense of loss, but may be chosen because of an active cultural preference for a more independent life-style in a predominantly one-age one-class community.

Just as it is possible to speak of a universe of class bodies and bodily practices, we can also talk about a universe of sporting bodies which can also be mapped onto the social space (Bourdieu 1978). Different classes derive different types of profit from sport in terms of health, slimness, relaxation, social relationships, etc.

The dominant class engages in sports such as golf, tennis, sailing, riding, skiing, water-skiing, hunting, etc. These sports require early training and special clothes, in effect a previous investment in time and money. Such sports are frequently practised in exclusive places (private clubs) in which the possession of symbolic capital, not just economic and cultural capital, may be important and yield a return of social profit. This is not to suggest that these sports are exclusive to the upper class. Golf, for example is practised across the class scale, in certain countries like Scotland, and even in England working-class men have long been involved in golf driving (Tomlinson 1985). Rather it is to emphasise that different classes practise sports in different ways, from the point of view of different bodily dispositions and expectations of returns on type and volume of capital. To take a further example there is a deal of difference between tennis played with proper dress and equipment at a private club and tennis played in trainers and running shorts on a municipal court. The consequences of the dynamic of inflation whereby previously scarce and exclusive goods and practices become popularised will be discussed below.

We have already noted the affinity that the new middle class has for body maintenance. Whereas the working-class men may engage in gymnastics to develop a *strong* body, the new middle class seek to produce a *healthy* or slim body. The new middle class is disposed towards a health-orientated hedonism in the new Californian solitary, non-team sports: trekking, wind-surfing, hang-gliding, orienteering etc. in which style and individualism are foregrounded. There is also an important generational factor at work here since these sports are largely the province of the 1960s generation with their cultivation of the natural, the pure and the authentic, which have been carried with them through the life course from youth into middle age, in contrast to the traditional middle class (especially the old petite-bourgeoisie) who tended to abandon participation in sport after youth. As a general rule, participation in sport declines with age, and watching sport increases as one moves down the social hierarchy. For the working class (despite the entrepreneurial attempts of the new middle class with their 'sport for all' campaigns) sport after youth means watching the popular sports of football, rugby, horse-racing, snooker, etc. For the upper class the disposition is for sports which are less dependent on physical strength and endurance (golf, sailing, hunting) which may be pursued well into retirement and continue to yield greater returns in social capital than in actual changes in bodily form and functioning (health, strength, aesthetics, etc.)

The different class dispositions are also evident in other practices which are usually more strictly defined as leisure: hobbies, pastimes, holidays, etc. For example, the working class display a realistic hedonism in leisure, they are at home with noise and crowds, whereas the middle class seek to distinguish themselves by withdrawing from the common and popular. Yet this distaste for the popular and intolerance of noise and crowds is different in the middle class and the upper class; the former tend to 'overdo it', their autodidacticism, the eager learning-mode towards life, betrays their own insecurity, whereas the latter do not have to worry about their distinction and can show discretion, a refusal of the showy, flashy and pretentious (cf. Bourdieu 1984, p. 249). For those sections of the middle classes whose position in the social space is dependent on the acquisition of cultural capital as they move through life (by way of certification, autodidacticism — here we think of secondary school teachers in particular) their habitus orientates them towards the least expensive and most austere leisure activities (country holidays, walking, camping, mountains) and towards serious cultural practices such as visiting museums. Here they share with the intellectuals an ascetic aesthetic with a distaste for material interests and luxury goods. Like the new intellectuals and new middle class they are disposed towards the new minor forms of legitimate culture (photography, cinema, jazz) which, unlike traditional high culture, do not involve a high investment in economic and symbolic capital to appreciate them (opera, ballet, etc.). The middle class and upper class thus withdraw from the common, vulgar and popular pursuits of the working class in different ways. For the upper class a more hedonistic aesthetic is permissible, real luxury, expensive and prestigious activities can be enjoyed: reading expensive glossy magazines, visiting antique dealers, galleries, concert halls, hotel holidays in spa towns, skiing, golf, riding, hunting, water-skiing, social gatherings. Activities in which they can display, without the anxiety of the parvenu the symbolic capital, sense of ease and confidence in bodily demeanour, language, and legitimate taste which have been acquired 'naturally', effortlessly as they move through life; activities which are not threatened by the ageing process, rather participation in such activities provides them with increased opportunities to accumulate and display confidence.

For purposes of analytic clarity we have talked about the relationship between class tastes in life-styles so far in a relatively static manner, but it is important to emphasise that if we are to continue to follow Bourdieu we must pay attention to process and consider the dynamics of the field once the time dimension is introduced. The first point to note about the relational dynamic is that goods and practices which were the exclusive property of either the upper class or the intellectuals become popularised and passed down the social space, thus prompting higher groups to seek new distinctive symbolic goods and practices with which to re-establish the original distance and combat inflation.

Within consumer capitalism the market dynamic to sell new commodities leads to a constant search for new images, symbols, fashions and lifestyles. Here the role of the new middle class discussed earlier is important, for as cultural intermediaries they have an interest in searching for new cultural goods, re-discovering old fashions, de-stabilising existing symbolic hierarchies to make the social space more fluid. They have an interest in discouraging tendencies in the intellectuals, the prime specialists in symbolic production, towards closure and monopolisation, by seeking to popularise not only new intellectual fashions but also the lifestyles of the intellectuals and artists as well. Encouraging avant-gardeism, the modernist and postmodernist search for the new and the different, they are on the side of the new outsider intellectuals in their power struggles against the old established intellectuals. The economic market dynamic of capitalism, and the power struggles internal to the producers of symbolic goods, therefore, ensure a constant supply of new goods, tastes and practices which contrasts to the monopolisation symbol producers usually achieve in maintaining the stable, sealed-off symbolic hierarchies which are characteristic of traditional societies (Featherstone 1985).

As we mentioned earlier in our discussion of generations, individuals tend to take their tastes with them as they move through life. This loyalty to the tastes which were in fashion in their youth, when they were apparently more in control of their lives, is evident in the retention of tastes for types of music, songs (Roll Out the Barrel), drinks (port and lemon), brands of cigarettes (Woodbines), clothes, hairstyle and in turns of phrase, ways of speaking, smiling, laughing, pitch of voice, demeanour (the military upright stance) which date individuals. The out-modedness of the particular set of tastes becomes more obvious as the particular class fraction moves from the position of 'command generation' (40–60) to the position of 'survivors' (60 plus). As the 'survivors' economic and cultural capital with which to defend their set of tastes diminish, along with the total numbers in the cohort, the minority and passé qualities of their life-style become more pronounced.

Particular class fractions manage the obsolescence of their tastes, which is generated by the market, historical and generational dynamics, in different ways. For those fractions in the traditional working class, whose tastes are restricted to the choices of necessity, there may be neither the economic or cultural capital resources nor the inclination to distance themselves from certain long-held aspects of lifestyle tastes (for example, style of personal appearance, furniture, decoration of the home). Likewise the upper class or aristocracy who are not moving in the social space, having already arrived, may be at ease with long established tastes, which are more substantial and acceptable in their eyes than is following superficial change in fashion. This loyalty to a longer tradition coupled with the symbolic capital incorporated in bodily presence, which can make a virtue out of being outmoded, contrasts with the new upper class, and the new middle class whose alternation between vulgar fashionability and hyper-correctness, betrays the anxiety of the self made who has just arrived, or is still moving through the social space. The concern with presentation and re-presentation on the part of these groups is evident in the way in which active life-styles and fashionable body-maintenance techniques are embraced in middle age, retirement and old age.

The sense of the appropriateness of one's set of tastes as one moves through the life course may also depend upon the age-composition of one's particular class fraction and whether or not they are increasing numerically. Small farmers and peasants are part of a numerically declining class fraction with a downward trajectory in the social space. The historical sense of decline, the growing inappropriateness of their tastes and lifestyle may lead to a 'I hate progress' stance. Not only has the individual's power declined over time, but also that of the group. These long-term changes in the division of labour which underpin the trajectory of an occupational group, and therefore the legitimacy and relative social power of its habitus, can therefore determine a group's sense of historical destiny. In Britain the current North-South divide, which has brought mass unemployment amongst the traditional, northern, declining (heavy industry), working class, also leads to a sense of defensiveness in support of a set of tastes, which become perceived as increasingly aged as the balance of power regionally (north v. south) and on the intra-class level (traditional or unemployed v. privatised or new working class) changes.

The sense that one's tastes are prematurely ageing may also be hastened by the changes in the conditions of entry to occupational groups whereby the educational system becomes increasingly central in providing the necessary credentials. The already incumbent members of the group who gained entry on different criteria, may be defined as obsolete hangers-on by the new cadres. Where different types of capital clash in this way (e.g., educational v. social capital) the difference between generations is increased, as is the basis for generational conflicts. This may occur not just within an occupational category but within a class fraction: for example the petite-bourgeoisie. Here the old petite-bourgeoisie (small shopkeepers, businessmen) are on a declining trajectory (although their habitus has enjoyed a revival in British political culture in recent years) in the social space, whereas the new petite-bourgeoisie or new middle class (cultural intermediaries in advertising, media, helping professions, etc.) are on an upward trajectory in which their positive modernist outlook is generalised to society as a whole through consumer culture. They occupy relatively new occupations, or those which have been redefined in terms of greater inputs of educational and cultural capital (credentials, training, etc.) and therefore they tend to be younger in actual age terms, and have a different habitus and a taste for modernist younger life-styles.

As mentioned earlier, groups will tend to take their tastes with them through the life course. It should therefore be expected that the new middle class and the new rich (new bourgeoisie) will retain their youth-oriented, fashion-oriented set of tastes. However, the new middle class in their role as culture intermediaries will seek to present and represent to a wider audience their set of life-style tastes as *the* set of life-style tastes. From the perspective of any group which aspires to move upwards in the social space (including the new working class as well as the above groups) there is a fascination in the representational problems of the newly-arrived, or almost-arrived – with their learning-mode orientation to a new universe of stylistic possibilities. Here we can cite the widespread popularity of the television sagas of the US sunbelt new rich – Dallas, Dynasty, The Colbys, etc.

The cultural intermediaries may also be involved more directly as cultural entrepreneurs in educating the wider public into health education and consumer culture with respect to their efforts to re-define middle age as middle youth (an extended active, expressive consumption phase) which also extends into retirement. Pre-retirement planning today is presented as the management of life-style and consumption opportunities to enable retirement to be a progressive set of options and choices – a phase in which the individual is presented as still moving within the social space, still learning, investing in cultural capital and putting off the inevitable disengagement of deep old age (Featherstone and Hepworth 1985). The appropriateness of such a strategy on the part of the middle classes should also be related to the demographic changes and changes in the division of labour which will produce greater numbers of old people, the expected duration of whose state retirement pensions cannot be financed from the existing state funds. Hence we should not assume that the construction of retirement in the twentieth century and the current popularisation of retirement lifestyles is an inevitable feature of contemporary capitalism. The predicted incapacity of the state to fund retirement may lead to a deconstruction of retirement with a range of diverse strategies proposed (continued employment, part-time employment, sabbaticals, small-scale/state/local employment schemes, etc.). These changes would clearly affect different class fractions in different ways and be mediated by the habitus which does not automatically change in response to changes in the division of labour (Bourdieu talks of a possible lag of as much as three generations).

In a similar manner it is possible to look at the changes taking place in youth. Changes in the division of labour and employment possibilities have heightened the differences between youth class fractions. It has always been possible to detect differences in taste (music, fashion, etc.) between middle-class and working-class youth in school (see Frith 1983; Roberts 1983). In the same way unemployment is experienced differently. Here we think of the working class boys who hang around shopping centres and learn the art of doing nothing, whereas the middle class have the use of a heated bedroom, computer, music centre, a room which is their own and not shared with brothers or sisters (Willis 1985). With regard to youth we should also be aware of the constant attempt to redefine the leisure practices of certain fractions of working class young males. Football hooliganism which is firmly grounded in the habitus of a class fraction's dispositions towards masculinity, the body and fighting (Dunning 1986) is contested by the dominant class, cultural intermediaries and helping professionals etc. New versions of 'rational recreation', proposals to domesticate and re-channel the violence into sport, campaigns to institute sports centres for the unemployed, these are all examples of the attempted re-definition of leisure practices.

Youth and old age have been highly studied phases of the life course when compared to early adulthood and middle age, which points to the 'social problems' framework which has dominated much of the research in these areas. To understand lifestyle and leisure practices within these phases we need to consider the different youths and old ages which different class fractions experience, and map these onto the social space in terms of the volume and type of capital fractions possess at each particular stage in life.

To ask for such a three-dimensional picture incorporating class and the life course is to contest the notion of an homogeneous set of tastes and life-styles for youth or the old, and to point to the need to integrate time/age analysis with class. In this context we should also refer to gender, for as we have mentioned below it is clear that certain class fractions and occupational groups have greater proportions of women (e.g., the cultural intermediaries, the helping professions). Gender too must be inscribed onto the social space and while it is tempting to assume an homogeneous response based upon limited economic and cultural capital which means that women have no leisure of their own, only domestic labour ('men's leisure is women's work'), we need to tease out the differential class lifestyles here, and to add a further complication, relate it to age/time in our three dimensional space. Many studies of leisure (e.g., Clarke and Critcher 1985), which acknowledge the importance of class, then proceed to talk about gender without any reference to the different class specific genders.

Here an analysis of the changing balance of power between the sexes which occurs in different classes is important. In effect we need to look at the way in which different class habituses form gender specific life-style tastes and acknowledge that the power balance between women and men is structured in different ways. It would be interesting, for example, to examine the life-style of the new middle class women, the cultural intermediaries who are celebrated as the hard-working, home-making 'you can have it all' superwoman in magazines like *Cosmopolitan* and *Options* (see Winship 1983). Such women may have the economic and cultural capital to construct a habitus which defines a legitimate space for their own life-style and leisure pursuits in relation to men, where they have their own time and are able to draw men into their re-definition of appropriate joint leisure pursuits. Such a class fraction is numerically small, but entrepreneurially active and in many cases committed to thematising gender differences for their 'sisters' in the working class. There is not the space here to discuss gender in relation to the life course, but it can be said that for this particular class fraction middle age may prove to be a time of greater independence and self-control despite the continued prevalence of what Sontag (1978) has called the 'double standard of ageing' with reference to women's appearance. This is because married or divorced women from this strata, freed from family responsibilities now the nest is emptied, are in a stronger position to re-enter the labour market, to accumulate economic and cultural capital, to explore leisure and lifestyle possibilities. We should not exclude a discussion of the upper class women here, for in contrast to the working class for whom leisure is defined very much in subordination to men, within marriage, upper class women who possess large amounts of economic, cultural and symbolic capital, have much greater power in defining appropriate leisure activities.

I have argued in this paper for a relational theory of the life course and leisure life-styles. Class, age and gender must be inscribed onto the same social space. Biological ageing, lived time, clearly produces changes in bodily growth and decline. Yet these changes (which are most noticeable in the dependence phases of early childhood and deep old age) are, however, mediated by the amounts and type of capital, different class fractions possess, which are evident in the habitus, the locus of lifestyle tastes. The sense of legitimacy, appropriateness and distinction of a set of life-style tastes depends upon the relative power of different class fractions and their ability to sustain their position within a field in which the relative value of different life-style tastes is changing as individuals move through the intersection of historical time and the lived time of the life course. The intention of this paper has been to make a theoretical argument for such an approach. Its success can only be judged on the basis of detailed empirical research into particular societies.

References

Ariès, P. (1962), *Centuries of Childhood*, London, Cape.

Baltes, P.B. et al. (1980), 'Life span developmental psychology', *American Review of Psychology*, 31.

Bengston, V.L. and Cutler, N.E. (1977), 'Generational and intergenerational relations' in R. H. Binstock and E. Shamas (eds), *Handbook of Ageing and the Social Sciences*, New York, Van Nostrand.

Bourdieu, P. (1978), 'Sport and social class', *Social Science Information*, 17, 6.

Bourdieu, P. (1980a), 'The production of belief: contribution to an economy of symbolic goods', *Media, Culture and Society*, 2,3.

Bourdieu, P. (1980b), 'La "jeunesse" n'est qu'un mot', in *Questions de Sociologie*, Paris, Minuit.

Bourdieu, P. (1984), *Distinction: A Social Critique of the Judgement of Taste*, London, Routledge & Kegan Paul.

Butler, D. and Stokes, D. (1969), *Political Change in Britain*, London, Macmillan.

Clarke, J. and Critcher, C. (1985), *The Devil Makes Work: Leisure in Capitalist Britain*, London, Macmillan.

Dumazedier, J. (1967), *Towards a Society of Leisure*, London, Collier Macmillan.

Dunning, E. (1986), 'Sport as a male preserve', *Theory, Culture and Society*, 3,1.

Elias, N. (1978), *The Civilizing Process, Vol. I: The History of Manners*, Oxford, Blackwell.

Elias, N. (1983), *The Court Society*, Oxford, Blackwell.

Elias, N. (1985), *The Loneliness of the Dying*, Oxford, Blackwell.

Fass, P. S. (1977), *The Damned and the Beautiful: American Youth in the 1920's*, New York, Oxford University Press.

Featherstone, M. (1979), Review of D. Levinson et al. 'The seasons of a man's life', *Journal of Biosocial Science*.

Featherstone, M. (1982), 'The body in consumer culture', *Theory, Culture and Society*, 1,2.

Featherstone, M. (1985), 'Lifestyle and consumer culture', paper presented to Conference on Everyday Life, Leisure and Culture, University of Tilburg, Netherlands.

Featherstone, M. and Hepworth M. (1982), 'Ageing and inequality: consumer culture and the new middle age' in D. Robins et al. (eds), *Rethinking Social Inequality*, Aldershot, Gower.

Featherstone, M. and Hepworth, M. (1985), 'Changing images of retirement', in D. Bromley (ed.), *Gerontology: Social and Behavioural Perspectives*, London, Croom Helm.

Featherstone, M. and Hepworth, M. (1986), 'New lifestyles for old age' in C. Phillipson (ed.), *Dependency and Independency in Old Age*, London, Croom Helm.

Feuer, L. (1969), *The Conflict of Generations*, London, Heinemann.

137

Freeman, M. (1984), History, narrative and life-span developmental knowledge', *Human Development*, 27.

Frith, S. (1983), *Sound Effects: Youth, Leisure and the Politics of Rock 'n' Roll*, London, Constable.

Guttman, D. (1977), 'The cross-cultural perspective: notes towards a comparative psychology of ageing' in J. E. Birren and K. E. Schaie (eds), *Handbook of Psychology of Ageing*, New York, Van Nostrand.

Harris, C. (1986), 'Individual and Society: a processual approach', paper presented to British Sociological Association Conference, Loughborough University.

Kelly, J. R. (1983), *Leisure Identities and Interactions*, London, Allen and Unwin.

Lowenthal, M. Fiske et al. (1975), *Four Stages of Life: A Comparative Study of Women and Men Facing Transitions*, San Francisco, Jossey-Bass.

Martin, B. (1984), 'Mother wouldn't like it! housework as magic', *Theory, Culture and Society*, 2, 1.

Neugarten, B.L. (1985), 'Interpretive social science and research on ageing', in A. Rossi (ed.), *Gender and the Life Course*, New York.

Neugarten, B. and Datan, N. (1974), 'The middle years', in S. Arieti (ed.), *American Handbook of Psychiatry*, 2nd edn. Vol. I, New York, Basic Books.

Rapaport, R. and Rapaport, R. (1975), *Leisure and the Family Life Cycle*, London, Routledge & Kegan Paul.

Roberts, K. (1978), *Contemporary Society and the Growth of Leisure*, London, Longmans.

Roberts, K. (1983), *Youth and Leisure*, London, Allen and Unwin.

Sontag, S. (1978), 'The double standard of ageing', in V. Carver and L. Liddiard (eds), *An Ageing Population*, London, Hodder and Stoughton.

Tomlinson, A. (1985), 'Working class culture and regional consciousness: the case of poor man's golf', paper presented to the Conference on Everyday Life, Leisure and Culture, University of Tilburg.

Willis, P. (1985), 'Youth unemployment and the new poverty', paper presented to the Conference on Everyday Life, Leisure and Culture, University of Tilburg.

Winship, J. (1983), '*Options* for the way you live now – or a magazine for superwomen', *Theory, Culture and Society*, 1, 3.

Wohl, R. (1980), *The Generation of 1914*, London, Weidenfeld.

The body, sport and power relations

John Hargreaves

I

It is extraordinarily difficult to think of the body and its functions
in any other terms than as a natural phenomenon. The rationalist
bias in Western culture entails a radical separation of body and
mind that accords primacy to the mind. The latter is the province
of 'civilization'. In contrast, the body belongs to nature, the
kingdom of desire, the source of threatening, irrational impulses
and dangerous appetites; and it must be disciplined if civilization is
to survive. Since the beginning of the modern era the image of the
body as a machine which only functions properly under the control
of the rational faculty has expressed such assumptions with
profound effects. Accordingly, until quite recently, the body has
been almost entirely evacuated from social and political theory: a
built-in resistance prevents its role in the constitution of power
relations from being analysed. Sociology, for example, in attempting
to map the field of social relations as a domain *sui generis*, met
competition from other disciplines, which would reduce the social
to the biological and psychological levels, by shying away from
attributing social significance to the body. Similarly, the silence of
the marxist tradition on the body, and its tendency to dismiss those
who attach significance to it, reflects an aversion to irrationalist
ideologies which reduce history and society to a universal,
unchanging human nature. Theoretically and practically the body
has become the property of the natural sciences – pre-eminent
among them medical science and technology – while the relations
between body and mind have been consigned largely to philosophy
and reductionist psychologies. Scientific discourse and common
sense combine to naturalize the 'truth' about the body so that its
historicity and its significance in the constitution of social relations
is obscured.

Yet control over the appearance, treatment and functioning of the body is a universally important aspect of social order, and elaboration and refinement of such forms of control has been critical in the emergence and development of modern social formations (Elias, 1978). Bodily colour, texture, posture, movement, gesture, facial expression, adornment, smell, and so on, constitute a language structuring social action. The body then, is an emblem of society, and the ritual practices governing its usage symbolize and uphold fundamental social relationships and bind individuals to the social order (Douglas, 1973). Furthermore, power is incorporated or invested in the body through meticulous, insistent work on people's bodies – on children in families and schools; on soldiers, prisoners and hospital patients; in the gym, at the dinner table, and in the bathroom (Foucault, 1976). Such work produces the social body through material operations on the bodies of individuals, which are carried out on the basis of and elaborate, articulated economy and technology of control[1] – medical / hygienist / therapeutic; athleticist / physical; exercise / recreationist; fashion / advertising; culinary / nutritionist; etc. – and in accordance with programmes designed to form 'normal' individuals. Body image is the foundation of personal identity: nothing is more personally real than one's body; one lives in and through one's body. At this site individual identities and social relations are constructed together. Changes in bodily ritual and general bodily usages indicate fundamental changes in social relationships; and interference with them has serious implications for social and cultural reproduction. The more the social situation exerts pressure on individuals the more the demand for conformity tends to be expressed by demands for physical control. The greater the conceptual distancing between social and physical bodies the more threatening is the loss of control over the body and bodily processes to the social order.

The body then, constitutes a major site of social struggles and it is in the battle for control over the body that types of social relation of particular significance for the way power is structured – class, gender, age, and race – are to a great extent constituted. Is it accidental then, that with the collapse of consensus politics in Britain, the kind of issues that exercised, preoccupied, and in a sense, diverted Victorian Britain, once again tend to be the ones that arouse most emotion and demands for control, namely those concerning the use and abuse of bodies? Sexually transmitted diseases, rape, pornography, homosexuality, incest, male violence to women, sexual harassment, 'child-abuse', 'drug-abuse', 'alcohol-abuse', smoking, 'mugging', environmental pollution, overeating, and so on, constitute the compost in which moral panic flourishes and on which the forces of law and order thrive.

The course of the struggle over the body and its relationship to power in the modern era can be charted in broad outline. Ponderous, repressive forms of control characteristic of respectable everyday life and work discipline during the emergence and subsequent development of industrial capitalism, are no longer dominant (Bauman, 1983). Negative forms of constraint are becoming recessive: the dominant form of control now is an expansive system of discipline and surveillance based on stimulation and satisfaction of desire (Foucault, 1980). The trend is most evident in the way the body is deployed in consumer culture, a culture which, above all, thematizes the primacy of the personal and satisfaction of individual desires (Featherstone, 1983). The leisure, advertising, fashion, and entertainment industries, not without the complicity of their clientèle, are engaged in a constantly elaborating programme whose objective is the constitution of the modern 'normal' individual. Consumer culture discourse/practice structures and satisfies individual desire so that individuals enthusiastically discipline themselves.

We want to show how the body, deployed in sporting activity and physical recreation, relates to this transformation (Hargreaves, 1986). The extent to which any given cultural formation feeds the power network depends on its distinctive character. Although the degree of physical input varies from sport to sport, the primary focus of attention in sport overall, is the body and its attributes – strength, skill, endurance, speed, grace, style, shape, general appearance, and so on, are tested and displayed. Judgement, motivation, and aesthetic awareness are integral to physical performance, of course; but it is the body that constitutes the most striking symbol, as well as constituting the material core of sporting activity. The latter encompasses a bewildering diversity of activities defying watertight definition, of which a good proportion have little to do with power. However, sporting activity tends to display sufficient distinguishing features to enable us to analyse how, in specific conditions, the sport-body-power relation is constituted. First, play is the *raison d'être* of sport. Thus, while it is true that commercialized and politicized sport is highly instrumental, without the ludic element they could not function at all. Second, sports are governed by formal rules and in this sense sports play is not spontaneous and flexible – it constitutes a 'regimen'. Nevertheless, like all play, sports in a sense 'suspend reality', in that they occupy a social space reserved for 'unserious' activity, set aside from the rest of life. This feature becomes clearer if we note thirdly, that sports involve some element of contest between participants. However, the rules which structure sporting contests, unlike those that regulate competition and conflict in non-sporting space, deliberately set out to equalize participants' chances of winning, that is, their aim is to ensure no party to the contest has an advantage over the others. This makes the outcome inherently uncertain. It creates a tension and an excitement unique to sports, which is one of the main reasons they become the object of such intense interest and emotional commitment. Fourthly, the play-acting, competitive, and un-predictable character of sports mean that sports are also inherently dramatic affairs. Indeed, when an audience is present, in effect, they constitute a form of popular theatre. The theatre of sport is a form of display providing players and audience with rich oppor-tunities to invest meaning in it, for the dramatic element is reinforced by the ritual nature of sporting activity. Ritual activity is rule-governed behaviour of a symbolic character which draws the attention of participants and onlookers to objects of thought and feeling held to be of special significance (Lukes, 1977). The significance of sports in relation to the way power is structured then, is that they are uniquely endowed with the capacity for deploy-ing the body in such a way as to represent and reproduce social relationships in a preferred manner. The most obvious examples are when the body of an athlete, victorious in international competition, becomes the emblem of the nation; or when the FA Cup Final is made to function as a ritual celebrating national unity. Sporting activity is a deeply embedded central component of the culture and it has made a significant contribution to the strategic elaboration of power in societies like Britain. In what follows we focus on this particular case.

II

In the mid-nineteenth century an equation was made between mental powers and moral rectitude on the one hand, and physical well-being on the other hand. It soon became an established part of mid-Victorian sensibility and practice (Haley, 1978). The doctrine of 'mens sana in corpore sano', nourished by Muscular Christianity and evolutionary theory, expressed a profound change, not only in bodily imagery and practice, but also in social relations. A new regimen of the body emerged governing 'correct' shape, health, diet, appearance, work and rest, sexuality, and so on, and one of its main sites was the public schools. In these institutions a new programme was implemented for normalizing the male progeny of emergent dominant groups as 'gentlemen'; and a new technology was discovered and developed to accomplish it – athleticism (Simon and Bradley, 1975; Mangan, 1981; Gathorne-Hardy, 1977). Popular physical pursuits and pastimes, in particular games like cricket and football, were appropriated and where necessary, reformed and reconstructed to distinguish them from their plebian origins and then were made the linchpin of the curriculum (Dunning and Sheard, 1979). That what the Victorians called a 'moral education', that is, a training in how the individual was to relate to the social order, could be programmed in athleticism, was a truly original discovery with profound consequences. The strategy was to extend the gaze of authority beyond normal school work as it had been previously conceived, into the playlike activity of their charges. By making the body uninterruptedly visible in this process authority extended control over the 'soul' of the individual (over the 'character' in athleticist parlance). Under this Spartan regimen the many hours per week devoted to the sporting ritual and physical exercise taught pupils the need for sustained effort and spirited determination in the face of adversity, for self-denial and control over one's egoistic impulses, the acceptance of authority, how to fit in with one's peers, how to take decisions and confidently to lead subordinates, and to accept responsibility. Gentlemen were constituted irrationally in the sense that such ritual activity engaged individuals in their bodies and in their emotions; it appealed to their sense of 'good form', rather than their intellectual faculties (Wilkinson, 1964). Shrouded in mystique, the social relations constructed in athleticist ritual were virtually impenetrable to rational appraisal, indeed, athleticism literally denigrated the intellect. The social relations inscribed in public schoolboys' bodies were at the same time reproduced in work carried out on the bodies of adult males, throughout the network of voluntary sports organizations that had spread at local and national level over the country.

Athleticist discourse/practice was absolutely crucial in the formation of the dominant class in Britain. Unlike elsewhere in the major European societies and in the United States, the older and newer dominant classes were able to accommodate peaceably in a power bloc, and in this process culture played a very important part (Johnson, 1976). It would scarcely be an exaggeration to say that athleticism and the cult of the amateur which lay at its heart, in the main, provided the meaning of life for 'gentlemen' destined to rule the nation and an empire. Put into practice as a way of life, gentlemanly amateurism limited the potential damage the rationalizing, utilitarian, democratizing forces could do to the power of the older ruling group, and vindicated the latter's sense of being naturally fitted to rule. At the same time it taught the latter to understand that the price of stability, privilege and power was a willingness to compromise and accept change; and in particular it taught the need for a principled commitment to duty, to conducting oneself responsibly and with a modicum of efficiency (James, 1976). It is no accident that team games, which emphasize collective effort and responsibility, rather than individual sports events, which run the risk of egoism, were the favoured vehicle for this form of normalization. Also, sports fulfilled the growing need among dominant groups for a form of leisure and sociability that contrasted with, while being complementary to, work (Bailey, 1978). By the same token athleticism served to demarcate dominant from subordinate groups.

Among dominant groups, athleticism became one of the main ways in which the subordinate position of women was reproduced, for this was an exclusively male culture. Since athleticism was considered unsuitable for the inferior female constitution, it was, therefore, inappropriate for 'ladies'. The sense of male identity among dominant groups was, in fact, largely formed through athleticism. Apart from war, with which it was increasingly associated, athleticism was considered the epitome of 'manliness'. Later in the century the girls' public schools challenged these assumptions and managed to modify somewhat the equation between sporting activity and manliness, by successfully demonstrating that, when suitably deployed, sports were also functional for the production of 'ladies' (Atkinson, 1978). Their major innovation was to harness medical/therapeutic technology and hygienism to athleticism in a new scientific regime of the body, by instituting regular medical inspections to monitor health, growth and development; through rigorous control over diet and sleep; and by doing remedial work on 'defective' bodies.

Among dominant groups also, athleticism was one of the chief means of reproducing a sense of 'Englishness'. Cricket, especially, was thought to reveal the essentially English qualities which made us superior to Continental foreigners, like the over-intellectual, somewhat effete French, and the studious, over-serious Germans (Brookes, 1974). The public schools also, of course, had an imperial mission to perform: their products were destined to rule an empire consisting, in the main, of non-white peoples scattered over a considerable proportion of the globe. Athleticist principles followed the flag as part of this 'civilizing' mission and cricket and other sports accordingly accompanied the gun, trade and Christianity.

The second major way the body, sport and power are related is through the important place sport has come to occupy in the culture of subordinate groups, in particular, the role it plays in working class culture. This came about through the deployment of athleticism by dominant groups with the objective of 'improving' the working classes; through the commercialization and popularization of reconstructed sports like football; and through the existence and further development, again aided by commercialization, of an independent, plebian, 'disreputable' sporting tradition. Although early and mid-Victorian Britain witnessed much activity on the part of dominant groups to ensure that working class people spent their free time in 'rational', 'improving' pursuits (Bailey, 1978), it was not until a more independent, combative, organized working class re-emerged in the last two decades of the nineteenth century, and growing economic and military competition at the beginning of the new century raised the question of national efficiency, that a recognizable programme for disciplining the working class was set in motion. Under the patronage and leadership of the 'urban gentry' a philanthropic strategy was adopted with the objective of bridging the perceived dangerous gap that had developed between the classes (Gray, 1977). A variety of organizations, mostly of a socio-religious character, and some of which ante-dated the period, unified by their common objective, set up shop in working class communities, where they missionized and monitored the inhabitants' use of free time. The missions, institutes, working men's clubs, youth clubs, YMCA, the uniformed youth organizations, such as the Boy Scouts, the Volunteers, the Band of Hope, Sunday Schools, and such like, extended a helping hand in one way or other from dominant groups, in return for which the recipients were to submit themselves to supervision and normalization (Bailey, 1978; Cunningham, 1980; Meller, 1976). One of the most common instruments deployed in this exercise in class fraternization and

145

discipline was athleticism. Most of the organizations involved were heavily reliant on sporting activity and physical recreation to establish contacts with working class people through which they exerted their influence.

The model normal individual knew his place and was positively committed to the established social order. Body imagery, discourse and practices figured prominently in the grand design for improvement. An upright posture with no hands in pockets, short hair, a clean well-washed body, a simple neat and tidy appearance, teetotalism, no smoking, no 'self-abuse', no sex outside marriage, active participation in organized sport, frequent and regular physical exercise, fitness and good health, and above all, a 'hard' body – constituted the God-fearing, obedient, hard-working, respectable individual (Gillis, 1975). Team games were not considered so appropriate for those who were required to follow rather than to lead, so there was a greater stress on physical exercise and fitness. The state's contribution to this programme was by way of the elementary schools where physical exercise technology was deployed on the bodies of working class children, initially in the crude form of military-style drill. As anxiety grew in ruling circles about the population's fitness for modern industry and war, there was a turn towards developing a more scientifically-based form of body management, and a modified form of Swedish gymnastics was introduced (Smith, 1974; McIntosh, 1968). Athleticism was promoted, nevertheless, in these schools in extra-curricular activities voluntarily organized by the teachers, again with the 'improvement' of their charges in mind, a practice which articulated extremely well with the philanthropic programme.

The strategy exerted a significant effect on class relations, not because it succeeded in disciplining the majority of the working class – which it conspicuously failed to do – but because it helped to involve a key section of the class in a pattern of 'rational recreation' which detached it from the remainder of the class during its leisure time (Gray, 1976). This section comprised male manual workers in relatively stable economic circumstances, who were inclined to self-improvement, and were more organized in their daily lives. Above all, it was among those involved in religious culture and among skilled manual workers that athleticism made its deepest impression. The effects were mediated, of course, by the nature of this group's culture. Organized sports were not simply imposed. Often independently of philanthropy, skilled workers, when they had the opportunity, would affiliate to voluntary sports bodies catering for the middle classes, and they were capable of forming their own clubs and organizations which they affiliated to the network established and controlled by dominant groups.

A substantial proportion of working-class people were, however, untouched by athleticism and remained outside the rational recreation orbit. Some were involved in exclusively working-class recreational activities regarded as outside the pale by their 'betters'. And a large number were involved in a quasi-disreputable popular sporting tradition, strongly associated with drinking and gambling, which was patronized by certain elements amongst the dominant groups and supported by commercial interests, especially by the brewers. In this tradition sporting activity was over-whelmingly entertainment-oriented as opposed to 'improving' (Bailey, 1978; Cunningham, 1980).

The entry of the working class into athleticized sports as active participants, their growing popularity as public spectacles, and the convergence with more commercialized sport as a form of popular entertainment, threatened to undermine the orderly production of gentlemen and respectable workers. The latter gave the mystique of athleticism, the veneration of rules, and gentlemanly conduct short shrift. Their object was to defeat the opponent unequivocally, and to be defeated oneself was looked upon as absolute disaster. Victory commanded material rewards in the shape of careers as professional sportsmen, cash and other prizes, and gambling winnings. Disciplining the body is also in the interest of collective victory and expresses communal solidarity in relation to other similar communities (Walvin, 1975; Metcalfe, 1979). Secondly, sporting activity is a celebration of 'manliness', hence the premium on toughness which discounts effeminacy at almost all costs. The preferred body shape is as far removed from the feminine as possible: it is one more suited to physical combat, heavy physical work and the 'blow-out' style of conviviality. This body was not so much 'well-proportioned' as thick-set – too heavy and likely to run to fat by the more ascetic standards of the middle class. Body imagery, discourse and practice are here at one with the popular, more disreputable sporting tradition, a tradition in which the 'sporting man' is down-to-earth, sociable, enjoys a drink and a smoke and a good time. The body may be subjected to rigorous discipline in the interests of efficient performance and of being a 'proper man', but the regimen may be relaxed and the body may be even considerably abused in the interests of enjoyment.

Working-class people certainly affected the development of sport at this time, but although it became an important part of their culture, their actual control over sport as a cultural form was rather limited. The voluntary sector, that is, the network of organizations catering for sport and physical recreation needs that was not run for profit, remained under the control of amateur gentlemen. This was accomplished, first by excluding professionalism and money-making from sport altogether – as in the case of rugby union and athletics – or by accommodating them within a structure hegemonized by amateur gentlemen – as in the case of football and cricket (Delaney, 1984; Scott, 1984; Brookes, 1974; Mason, 1980). Second, spectator sports, whether they were hegemonized by amateurism or by commercial interests, involved their clientèle as consumers, that is, the relationship between controllers and clientèle was primarily an impersonal market relationship. So, whether working class people were actively involved, or involved as spectators and followers, sport as a central component of working class culture which crystallized in the period 1880–1914, was hegemonized by dominant groups.

This pattern of involvement made an input to the power network in various ways. First, it reproduced the division between the upper, better-off, respectable working class, which was more involved in athleticised sport and the rational recreation tradition, and the lower working class whose members were more interested in sport as a form of entertainment. It thus contributed at the cultural level to the fragmentation of the class. Second, rather than uniting working-class communities, it further fragmented the class by encouraging localism and even rivalry between communities. Thirdly, involvement in sport of whatever kind became a major source of a working class version of masculinity entailing a discourse and practice which strongly reproduced working-class women's subordination. Fourthly, unlike its Continental counterparts, the British working class movement produced no independent sports culture of its own (Lidtke, 1985; Holt, 1981). Involvement in sport was an element in the remaking of the working class at this time in a corporatist mode. It represented at the cultural level an accommodation on the part of working-class people to the social order which reproduced their subordination at the economic and political levels (Stedman Jones, 1973; Joyce, 1980; Hobsbawm, 1967).

III

As a result of the continued expansion of sporting activity of all kinds since the First World War, which has brought sports within the reach of the majority of the nation, sport is now a major component of the national popular culture. However the manner in which body-sport-power relations are constituted has undergone significant changes. The developing tension between deploying the body in an essentially repressive disciplinary mode epitomized by athleticism, the philanthropic strategy, and respectable sporting activity on the one hand, and the hedonistic, disorderly deployment of the body epitomized by 'disreputable' sports and sport as commercialized entertainment, has been resolved in favour of deploying the body in sport as a means of individual expression. The main way in which this change has been accomplished is through the progressive articulation of sporting activity on consumer culture. The opposing traditions still function as elements of this cultural form, but they have been re-articulated to form part of a broader programme aimed at constituting a new, 'liberated' individual.

Consumer culture is the way of life in the modern era which is organized around the consumption of goods and services for the mass market. Commercialized sport is not new – it dates at least from the eighteenth century (Plumb, 1978). What is new is the way sporting activity articulates with a particular pattern of consumption, to which amateur athleticism was an impediment. Since the early 1960s social forces have undermined and finally toppled amateur athleticism in all but a few sectors of sport. The financial crisis of sports caused by inflation and changes in the pattern of public demand for leisure pursuits have forced them to adapt in order to survive. In the absence of a sufficient level of philanthropic support and state aid, organized sport has come to rely increasingly on capital and on modern capitalist management and marketing techniques. Hegemonized now by business-efficiency oriented interests, sport now functions increasingly as a specialized branch of the entertainment industry. Advertising/public relations/business sponsorship, the media, and the interests of the sports elite provide the main driving force for the transformation. The state too plays a part.

Before the Second World War the physical training ritual in schools stressing alertness, precision, the soundness of bodily parts and their harmonious functioning, symbolized the organic solidarity

149

of the social body. After the war a 'progressive', 'child-centred' regimen of physical education loosened the time and space framework of lessons, introduced a greater informality, and a problem-solving approach to body management, which symbolized a social order founded on individual merit and responsibility (Hughes, 1975). Further steps, taken to break down consumer resistance in the secondary school, as it were, widened the scope of physical education by including a greater variety of recreational activities; it was made an optional subject in the upper school; and sport was also encouraged as a voluntary extra-curricular activity. In effect, physical education has come to function as a form of training and preparation for orderly, healthy leisure consumption (Hendry, 1978).

Similarly, the Sports Council's promotion of 'Sport for All', via a variety of programmes, attempts to fill the gaps in target groups' leisure time with sport and physical recreation as a means of reviving the community, integrating deprived and alienated groups, and promoting family life (Sports Council, 1982). The strategy is to co-ordinate the private and public sectors so that they complement each other, rather than function as competing alternatives. In effect the strategy assimilates public provision of sport and recreation to consumer culture since the techniques of leisure management and marketing, developed in the private sector, serve as the model for the way sport overall should function. Furthermore, this process of assimilation has been strongly reinforced through the Sports Council's policy of promoting business sponsorship of sport.

Consumer culture constitutes a specifically modern version of the good life. The dominant discourse/practice is hedonistic – the main orchestrating themes are youth, beauty, sexual liberation, movement/variety/change, excitement, luxury, fun and entertainment, individual choice fulfilment and freedom. Its dominant icons are the young, attractive, healthy person and the happy family. Above all, this culture valorizes self-expression through the meticulous attention that is paid to aspects of their lives that are deeply personal to people. This can be seen in the importance given to personal appearance (hair, shape, skin colour, teeth, etc.), how one feels (health, confidence, tension, etc.), how one smells (deodorants, toothpaste, perfumes, etc.) and so on. The discourse selects from the range of experience certain ways in which we are affected personally and offers personal solutions. Collective concerns and collective, as opposed to individual, consumption as the solution to problems, are largely absent from this discourse. The collective is displaced to the level of personal reality, and it is the individual, as such, who is made solely responsible for it. It is not that this systematically produced imbalance displaces what is important with what is trivial: it is that this culture is hegemonized through the thematization of concerns which are absolutely central to peoples' sense of identity on the one hand, and the suppression of the relationship between these and public issues or collective concerns on the other hand.

What links consumer culture with sports culture so economically then, is their common concern with, and capacity to accommodate the body meaningfully in the constitution of the normal individual. The body is clearly one of the major focuses of consumer culture: a good deal of its strength resides in its ability to harness and channel personal needs and desires – for health, longevity, sexual fulfilment, sociability, and so on, to the political order and the production system. Sports culture's stress on play, contest, strength, energy, movement, speed, skill, etc., allows such themes to be given a particularly vivid, dramatic, aesthetically-pleasing and emotionally-gratifying expression, so that almost by definition to be sportive is to be desirable, fit, young and happy. The significance of the progressive commodification of sport is that athleticist and physical recreation discourse/practice are now unified with a heterogeneous array of elements in an emergent programme of discipline and surveillance. Control by meticulous, restrictive and repressive work on the body, which constrains the individual's capacity for expression, is giving way to control through the ordered stimulation and satisfaction of desire. The redeployment of sexuality, age, and health are key elements in the way consumer culture and the sporting forms are articulated in the power network. The cultural imperative to all alike, irrespective of age, appearance and sex is to look, act and feel in conformity with the dominant icons. The strategy of repressive discipline and surveillance is to normalize individuals by extending the gaze of authority from the centre so that the subject of surveillance is perfectly visible to it, while authority itself remains invisible. In contrast, the strategy elaborated under a system of expansive discipline and surveillance produces normal persons by making each individual as visible as possible to each other, and by meticulous work on person's bodies at the instigation of subjects themselves. The successful achievement of this programme is dependent particularly upon the 'liberation' of the sexual and youth apparatuses. Hence consumer culture is replete with symbols and slogans which appropriate women's and youth's voices and project them in preferred ways (Coward, 1985; Hebdige, 1978). Our increased visibility to each other in public space – on the street, in open-plan buildings, work spaces and stores, at school and college, in the media, the swimming pool, the beach, the health club, and so on, constitutes a comprehensive system of mutual discipline and surveillance, a relentless authority diffused throughout social space. Consider the disciplined enjoyment of freely-chosen activities like jogging, dieting, dressing fashionably and displaying, cleansing oneself, applying cosmetics, playing sports, and so on; and the volume of associated goods and services that go into the production of oneself as a normal man or woman. Now, in the 1980s sport and physical recreation – especially in the current form of the health and fitness boom – are emerging in many ways as the foci of a regimen for producing sexually attractive, young, healthy and fit persons, which combines several advanced technologies – athleticist/fitness, medical/pharmaceutical, nutritionist/culinary, and beautician/sartorial. The notion that to do something about one's body is to be doing something about oneself is profoundly true. At the same time, it represents a response which individualizes social relations, which from an alternative perspective can be seen as problematic and as requiring collective, rather than purely individual action.

IV

The image of the body in sport does not coincide in every respect with those circulating in consumer culture. Sports culture is enabled to articulate with consumer culture precisely because as an autonomous cultural formation it has a unique contribution to make to cultural reproduction. For example, the predominant image of the female body circulating in sport and physical recreation is of the trained, 'attractive' rather than 'erotic', clean and healthy, young, firm, mesomorphic body – an image which contrasts with the women's fashionwear ideal of an eroticized, thin, long, languid body. Sports culture and consumer culture are wholly united however, in regarding old, weak, handicapped, ill, and unhealthy bodies as an anathema. When age and physical handicap are the focus of attention, in BBC TV coverage of the London Marathon, for example, the rather patronizing attitude towards older competitors and the almost voyeuristic treatment of wheelchaired competitors, signifies the presence of undesirable bodies, threats to the ideal, deviations from the norm. But images of the body deviating from the latter do, nevertheless, circulate in sports, some of which may even challenge it by encoding alternative meanings. Around the more sedentary sports popular with many working-class people, particularly those requiring good timing, hand-eye co-ordination, and light touch, such as snooker, darts and bowls, body image possesses more hedonistic connotations of the good life and social relations – of over-indulgence in food and drink (displays of pot bellies) of indulgence in unhealthy practices like smoking, and as well, of being older. A variety of images, in fact, coexist in sports culture, differentially drawing attention to the nature of the social body. Snooker can project an image of relaxed sociability, but also of cool, ruthless, aggressive competition. Weight-lifting projects an image of immense strength, a quality much admired in working-class culture, one which denies the middle class ideal of the balanced, proportioned aesthetically-pleasing body. Body-building, on the other hand, caricatures the mesomorphic ideal and carries 'unhealthy' connotations of narcissism and homosexuality. The longer-distance athletic events depict an ascetic, courageous individual. In body contact sports like football the body image powerfully signifies the importance of work rate, skill, and competitive team spirit. Cricket and tennis pit individuals against each other in a concentrated display of self-control, 'nerve', grace, and determination.

The articulation of sport and consumer culture makes an input to the power network not only as an individualizing force but as a stratifying/differentiating force as well. It is a significant factor in the constitution of class, gender and race relations, and in constituting the population as a nation. Despite the fact that sporting activity, as a major component of the national popular culture, provides a common reference point for diverse groups, it nevertheless reproduces class divisions. Dominant groups are more involved in terms of active participation (Veal, 1979) and have greater control over the sports apparatus. Their higher levels of income and membership of wider and more exclusive social networks provides them with far more opportunities to participate and to demarcate themselves from subordinate groups. The *petite bourgeoisie* are also more involved, especially in the current health and fitness boom. The trained, fit, punished-into-shape, slim body marks this group out, distinguishing it from others through the special attention paid to the aesthetic dimension (Bourdieu, 1984).

Sports activity continues to fragment the working class by reproducing the division between the upper and lower strata. Skilled manual workers, together with routine non-manual workers exhibit a far higher propensity to participate actively, especially in the more achievement-oriented athleticised sports. In this respect they have more in common with the *petite bourgeoisie* (Veal, 1979, 1982). Whereas semi- and unskilled workers tend to be more passively involved in the kind of sporting activity associated with drinking and gambling as well as being more reliant on media sport. Also, sporting activity still encourages localism and rivalry between working-class communities, rather than class solidarity which extends over the nation.

In working-class culture involvement in sporting activity unequivocally differentiates men from women in a way which reproduces the latter's subordination. To be involved in sporting activity as a matter of course confirms male identity; whereas when women are involved in anything other than a peripheral fashion, their identity as women is brought into question. Amongst dominant groups and the *petite bourgeoisie*, on the other hand, the division is not nearly as acute. While women have more opportunity to participate on equal terms with men without jeopardizing their femininity, sports nevertheless, provide a major input into the constitution of the 'normal women'. In fact, at every level sports culture is one of the strongest bastions of traditional gender differentiation.

In schools physical education and sport are still the only sex-specific subject on the curriculum. Girls are given less opportunity and are given less encouragement to participate than are boys (King, 1973). In the course of their school careers the sexes are progressively channelled into different patterns of sporting activity, despite attempts at changing traditional school practices. Neither have the efforts of the Sports Council been successful in changing patterns of inequality among adults outside the school. The articulation of consumer culture and sport, represented by media sport, ensures that sportswomen are standardly presented in terms of their 'attractiveness', and by whether they are wives, girl friends or mothers. Deviations from the stereotype tend to be unsympathetically portrayed, and deviants may be subjected to a considerable degree of pressure to conform, in particular, by a sensation-hungry press. This is not wholly surprising when positions in media sport, unlike most other aspects of the media, are virtually monopolized by men. In contrast, male identity is routinely confirmed in media sport, which is indicated also by the fact that advertisements for deodorants and perfumes for men use sports stars and sports images to ward off possible association of this type of product with effeminacy.

The articulation represented by the health and fitness movement manifests some interesting elaborations of the sport-body-power relation. Sports fashionwear, for example, which is an extremely important aspect of the movement, goes considerably beyond enhancing female attractiveness and into the production of 'liberated', glamorous, erotic-looking women. Certain aspects of the movement do challenge somewhat the traditional gender imagery. For example, women now routinely run distances, lift weights in training, and perform at martial arts, all of which, not long ago, exclusively conferred male status. With women weight-training and now entering body-building, the 'correct' body shape has become more negotiable; and androgyny has become more acceptable. Homosexuality is now no longer so strongly associated with an aversion to 'manly' sports. Now that homosexuals manifest a greater, overt presence in these types of activities, sports are no longer the automatic badge of masculinity they once were.

One of the most enduring myths about race and sport is that sport promotes racial harmony and equality. Schools evidently are persuaded so, when they sponsor black pupils' sporting achievement as compensation for low academic achievement (Carrington and Wood, 1983; Cashmore, 1982). The unintended effect however, is to sponsor black pupils as 'non-academic', which reduces their employment opportunities and thus reproduces their subordinate position. Schools here operate on the basis of the notion widespread in the culture that blacks are somehow 'naturally' better at physical pursuits and are accordingly less intellectually capable than whites.

Routine practice here encodes the message that blacks are closer to nature and are therefore less civilized than whites. Perhaps this is the reason why black bodies are so often perceived in the culture as threatening. Working-class enthnocentrism is strongly underpinned by such notions, and as well, by localist sentiment generated around certain sports, such as football, which defines ethnic minorities as non-British 'outsiders'. Hence the considerable degree of difficulty experienced by ethnic minorities in integrating into working-class, community-based sport, and of which racist abuse of black Football League players is one

155

symptom. Hence also the tendency for local sport to be organized more on ethnic lines with the appearance of black football teams, Asian cricket teams, and black street hockey teams. Media sport, while formally free of such influences and while registering strong approval of the entry of blacks into the sports elite, for example, in effect reinforces them in a number of unintended ways. Media coverage of international events like the World Cup is permeated with ethnic stereotyping practices in which skin colour, hair type and colour, etc., are important elements (Nowell-Smith, 1979). Although black sportsmen and women are very prominent in British sport, very few media sports reporters and commentators are themselves black, which means that it is whites who mostly depict race relations where sport is concerned. When media sport routinely shows blacks like Daley Thompson and Tessa Sanderson successfully achieving in sport and becoming celebrities, what is being signalled is racial harmony and progress. Quite inadvertently inequality and conflict occurring elsewhere is written off the agenda. The Sports Council, on the other hand, explicitly pinpoints poor race relations as one of the key social problems which it has a duty to tackle (Sports Council, 1982). However, by targeting programmes specifically on ethnic minorities with the aim of integrating them into the community; that is, by tackling the symptoms of, rather than the causes of disorder in the inner cities, the Sports Council implicitly labels ethnic minorities as the cause of the problem.

With the exponential expansion of sport at the international level sports has become a focal point for the construction of a sense of national identity amongst a diverse, in some ways deeply divided, population. State aid through the Sports Council for the development of a national sports elite has been for a number of years one of the Council's top priorities and the sports elite today functions with some significant degree of success as the symbol of the nation and its fortunes. Media coverage of international events is one of the main ways in which sporting outcomes are interpreted in terms of the national interest. With the cooperation of the media the political establishment since the end of the nineteenth century has appropriated sports culture and turned the great national sporting occasions progressively into political rituals symbolizing the national virtues and national unity.

Finally, it should be understood that the articulation of the way the body is deployed in sport and the power network is neither smooth nor perfect, and that it requires constant maintenance and elaboration in order to avoid breakdown and power failures. There are many reasons. The reach of consumer culture is never even, and therefore it is limited in its capacity to accommodate subordinate groups to the social order. Unemployment, for example, virtually removes large numbers from its reach altogether. There is little evidence that state programmes, which deploy sport to compensate this section of the population for its recreational deprivation, and as a means of accommodating the alienated population of the inner cities to the social order, have been successful. The rationalization of spectator sports has had counter-productive effects in relation to audience satisfaction. Ruthless competition, violence on and off the field, the routinization of performance, financial scandals among the stars and in the boardrooms, drug-taking, and so on, tend to contradict and erode the 'wholesome fun and family entertainment' image of sport promoted by controllers and dominant groups. Politicization has proved counter-productive as well. For example, The Conservative government's attempt to have the Moscow Olympics boycotted in 1980 failed to achieve its objective; it alienated the Olympic Sporting Community in this country; and it probably destroyed for ever a key ideological tenet of sports culture, namely, that sport has no political significance.

The way football violence has been exploited by the Conservative Government in the 1980s to legitimate its move towards a more authoritarian mode is a salutary reminder, however, that what appears to negate the objectives and strategy of dominant groups may be turned to their advantage with appropriate ideological work. Conservative forces in Britain, in fact, have displayed far more practical understanding of the body-sport-power relation than the Left and the labour movement. From the time when attachment to sports crystallized as one of the main features of working-class culture, the leadership of the working-class movement has simply ignored its significance; and even today the Left still finds it difficult to accommodate the body and sport within its political programme.

Note

1 On the concept of 'articulation' see Laclau and Mouffe, 1985.

References

Atkinson, P., 1978, 'Fitness, feminism and schooling', *The Nineteenth Century Woman in the Cultural and Physical World*, London, Croom Helm.

Bailey, P., 1978, *Leisure and Class in Victorian England*, London, Hutchinson.

Bauman, Z., 1983, 'Industrialization, consumerism, and power', *Theory, Culture and Society*, Vol. 1, 2.

Bourdieu, P., 1984, *Distinction*, London, Routledge & Kegan Paul.

Brookes, C.C.P., 1974, 'Cricket as a vocation', PhD Thesis, University of Leicester.

Carrington, B. and Wood, E., 1983, 'Body talk', *Multiracial Education*, Vol. 12.

Cashmore, E., 1982, *Black Sportsmen*, London, Routledge & Kegan Paul.

Coward, R., 1985, *Female Desire*, London, Paladin.

Cunningham, H., 1980, *Leisure in the Industrial Revolution*, London, Croom Helm.

Delaney, T., 1984, *The Roots of Rugby League*, Keighley, Delaney.

Douglas, M., 1973, *Natural Symbols*, Harmondsworth, Penguin.

Dunning, E. and Sheard, K., 1979, *Barbarians, Gentlemen and Players*, London, Martin Robertson.

Elias, N., 1978, *The Civilizing Process*, Vol. 1, Oxford, Blackwell.

Featherstone, M., 1983, 'The body in consumer culture', *Theory, Culture and Society*, Vol. 1, Part 2.

Foucault, M., 1976, *Discipline and Punish*, London, Allen Lane.

Foucault, M., 1980, *Power/Knowledge*, ed. C. Gordon, Brighton, Harvester.

Gathorne-Hardy, J., 1977, *The Public School Phenomenon*, London, Hodder & Stoughton.

Gillis, J.R., 1975, 'The evolution of juvenile delinquency, 1880–1914', *Past and Present*, Vol. 67.

Gray, R.Q., 1976, *The Labour Aristocracy in Nineteenth Century Edinburgh*, Oxford, Oxford University Press.

Gray, R.Q., 1977, 'Bourgeois hegemony in Victorian Britain', J. Bloomfield (ed.), *Class, Hegemony and Parity*, London, Lawrence and Wishart.

Haley, B., 1978, *The Healthy Body and Victorian Culture*, Cambridge, Mass., Harvard University Press.

Hargreaves, J.E., 1986, *Sport, Power and Culture*, Cambridge, Polity Press.

Hebdige, D., 1978, *Subculture*, London, Methuen.

Hendry, L.B., 1978, *School, Sport and Leisure*, London, Lepus Books.

Hobsbawm, E.T., 1967, *Industry and Empire*, London, Weidenfeld and Nicolson.

Holt, R., 1981, *Sport and Society in Modern France, 1920–1938*, London, Macmillan.

Hughes, J., 1975, 'The socialization of the body within British educational institutions – a historical view', MSc(Econ) Dissertation, University of London.

James, C.L.R., 1976, *Beyond a Boundary*, London, Hutchinson.

Johnson, R., 1976, 'Barrington Moore, Perry Anderson and English Social Development', *Cultural Studies*, 9.

Joyce, P., 1980, *Work Society and Politics*, London, Harvester.

King, R., 1973, *School Organization and Pupil Involvement*, London, Routledge & Kegan Paul.

Laclau, E. and Mouffe, C., 1985, *Hegemony and Socialist Strategy*, London, Verso.

Lidtke, V., 1985, *The Alternative Culture*, New York, Oxford University Press.

Lukes, S., 1977, 'Political ritual and social integration', in Lukes, *Essays in Social Theory*, London, Macmillan.

McIntosh, P., 1968, *Physical Education in England Since 1800*, London, Bell.

Mangan, J.A., 1981, *Athleticism in the Victorian and the Edwardian Public School*, Cambridge, Cambridge University Press.

Mason, T., 1980, *Association Football and English Society, 1863–1915*, Brighton, Harvester.

Meller, H., 1976, *Leisure and the Changing City*, London, Routledge & Kegan Paul.

Metcalfe, A., 1979, 'Organized physical recreation in the mining communities of South Northumberland, 1880–1887', unpublished paper, University of Windsor, Canada.

Nowell-Smith, G., 1979, 'Television—Football—the World' in *Screen*, Vol. 19, 4.

Plumb, J.H., 1978, 'Sports and fortune', *Listener*, 19 October.

Scott, D. with Dent, C., 1984, *Borrowed Time, A Social History of Running*, Moston.

Simon, B. and Bradley, L. (eds), 1975, *The Victorian Public School*, Dublin, Gill & Macmillan.

Smith, W.D., 1974, *Stretching Their Bodies*, London, David and Charles.

Sports Council, 1982, *Sport and the Community*, London, Sports Council.

Steadman Jones, G., 1973, 'Working-class culture and working-class politics in London, 1870–1900', *Journal of Social History*, Vol. 7,4.

Veal, A.J., 1979, *Sport and Recreation in England and Wales*, Birmingham, Centre for Urban Studies.

Veal, A.J., 1982, *Using Sports Centres*, London, Sports Council.

Walvin, J., 1975, *The People's Game*, London, Allen Lane.

Wilkinson, R., 1964, *The Prefects*, Oxford, Oxford University Press.

'Boys muscle in where angels fear to tread' – girls' sub-cultures and physical activities

Sheila Scraton

Introduction

This paper considers the relationship between PE[1] in secondary schools and young women's sub-cultures. For many years PE teachers have been concerned with the apparent loss of interest and 'dropping out' of many adolescent young women from the PE lesson. This paper attempts to relate PE teaching to the sub-cultural experiences and resistances of young women and thus move beyond a biologically determined position which traditionally has explained young women's responses to PE as 'natural' and inevitable.

The paper provides 1) a brief critical introduction to youth sub-cultural analysis, 2) a more detailed examination of recent work on young women's sub-cultures and their school-based resistances and 3) a consideration of the relationship of PE to this work on young women's sub-cultures. The analysis in this third section draws on eight year's teaching experience in secondary school PE and qualitative research carried out in Liverpool secondary schools during the 1983–1984 school year. In conclusion the paper looks forward to possible initiatives which could help move towards a more positive and challenging approach to PE for adolescent young women.

Youth sub-cultures

Analyses of youth culture and subcultures can be summarized by dividing them into generational and structural explanations. The first analysis is concerned with the continuity/discontinuity of inter-generational values, and the second with the

160

relationship to social class, the mode of production and its consequent social relations. (Brake 1980)

This summary of the main analyses of youth sub-cultures which developed during the 1970's emphasised two main categories – age and class. Almost without exception 'youth' was presented as being white, working-class and male and studies of 'the lads' dominated the literature.[2] Throughout this work young women were rarely visible, appearing only in relation to 'the lads' and their experiences. Young women were defined either as extensions of 'the lads' experiences or as direct inhibitions on these experiences. Either way the judgements passed on young women focused on their sexuality and its objectification:

> Ellen was very popular among the girls – she was always
> surrounded by her mates; but she was less often seen with a
> boy. The boys had, of course, classified all the girls into the two
> familiar categories: the slags who'd go with anyone and
> everyone (they were alright for a quick screw, but you'd never
> get serious about it) and the drags who didn't but whom you
> might one day think about going steady with. (Robins and
> Cohen 1978:58)

> So the conversation went on, with Joey suggesting that the
> girlfriends should be kept in their place and not allowed to
> interfere with 'the boys' who if they were real mates would see to
> it. At this time Joey practised what he preached. He had been
> 'going with his tart' for six months and although he obviously
> liked her he would not allow his affection to change his
> relationship with the Boys . . . Basically the girls are divided
> into three categories: 'somebodies tart', 'dirty tickets' and the
> 'not having anys'. (Parker 1974:95)

In these typical examples, young women's experiences were viewed through the eyes of the lads and this vision was sharpened, as has been noted by McRobbie and Garber (1976), by the assumptions of male researchers. It was a vision which condemned young women's lives to the periphery of youth culture, leaving the centre-stage to 'the lads'. As McRobbie and Garber point out, however, the position of young working-class women is structurally different to that of young working-class men. The common sense assumptions, upon which much of the interaction between young men and young women is apparently founded, demarcate clear boundaries for 'acceptable' masculine and feminine behaviour and responses. The boundaries, however, are not derived simply from the shared assumptions of everyday life. They are structural in the sense that images of sexuality become institutionalised and legitimated within the policy responses of agencies such as schools, youth clubs and sports centres. It is here that images translate into ideologies and form part of the political management of sexuality. It is at these levels – ideological and political – that the experiences of young women and men are structured differently and provide an institutionalised process of reinforcement of commonly-held assumptions. McRobbie and Garber argue that the position of young women cannot be explained simply by a social marginality within sub-cultures but has to be located with reference to the structural location of women in a patriarchal society. Thus young women are not appendages to male sub-cultures (although to a large extent their presence within dominant male sub-cultures remains undocumented)[3] but inhabit their own specific sub-cultures. If an analysis of youth sub-cultures is to include both young women and young men then there should be generational and class considerations and, furthermore, an understanding of patriarchal power relations.[4]

An understanding of the experiences of young women requires class, race, age and gender considerations. Brake (1980) states:

> women have reality mediated not just by class location
> interpretations, but also by patriarchy, the system of
> subordination in a world which is male dominated in sexuality
> and procreative potential; a system where women's labour is
> organised economically, ideologically and politically by males.
> It is a world where sexism is the articulated, as well as the taken
> for granted unquestioned superiority of men. In this sense
> women inhabit two locations: their role in their specific social
> class and their position in patriarchy.

Furthermore race produces significant differences, for patriarchy is not experienced in the same way in all cultures. In British society black women and women of colour face different opportunities and restrictions in relation to school, family, work, leisure. They are often subjected to the patriarchy of different cultures while also experiencing the patriarchal oppression of white racist society. This duality of oppression is further intensified by class so that working-class black women have their reality mediated by the complexity of race, gender and class relations.

It is not 'just in order to tell us something about the position of women that we should make such an analysis' (Cockburn 1983). Any analysis of male youth sub-cultures must acknowledge similar complexities. Brake (1980) moves beyond the traditional concern of male cultural analysis – class and generation – by stressing that male sub-cultures are primarily an 'exploration' of masculinity. In working-class male sub-cultures the 'macho', aggressive image of masculinity, which strongly reinforces gender identity, is presented as a resistance to a collectively experienced sense of failure or rejection. However, not all men are involved in this aspect of masculinity and the 'culture of masculinity' with its aggressive, competitive, 'macho' image through choice, physique or temperament. Male sub-cultures such as the 'bikers' in Willis's ethnography (1978), demonstrate a culture of masculinity which reinforces their male identity. Those who fail to meet this expectation are excluded from the groups. Similarly, while cultures of masculinity cut across class locations there are differences *between* classes. The physically aggressive, 'macho' form of masculinity in some working-class male youth sub-cultures (Parker 1974; Willis 1978) is expressed in a similar way (although more socially legitimated) in the rugby playing 'macho' competitive culture of the male middle class (Sheard and Dunning 1973). However, 'masculinity' does not have to be physically aggressive in order to be oppressive both to women and to men outside the culture. Sexist comment and the intellectual/verbal aggression of male middle-class culture presents a powerfully oppressive 'masculine' image. An understanding of patriarchy, therefore, is not only necessary to an understanding of the position of women; it is also central to an analysis of male sub-cultures.

For young women, as McRobbie (1978a) explains:

> The culture of adolescent working class girls can be seen as a response to the material limitations imposed on them as a result of their class position, but also an index of and response to their sexual oppression as women.

Middle-class young women, while benefiting from a more privileged material position, experience sexual oppression as women. However, this oppression may take on different forms which can produce differing responses from these young women. The next section will look more closely at young women's cultures and the responses that young women make to their class location and role as young women.

Young women's sub-cultures and school-based resistances

Within the work on youth sub-cultures the invisibility of young women's lives and experiences does not reflect a simple marginalisation to the main action of 'the lads'. Rather it represents an absence informed directly by patriarchal power relations. Recent work has attempted to redress the balance by providing for sub-cultures a feminist perspective which starts from the experiences of young women (McRobbie 1978b; Griffin 1981; McRobbie and McCabe 1981; Nava and McRobbie 1984). An initial consideration in the analysis of young women's experiences is that collectivity (i.e. the 'gang' or group), which is integral to the definition of male sub-cultures,[5] cannot be taken for granted for young women (Griffin 1981). McRobbie (1978a) and Griffin (1981) in two separate projects with white working-class women, found that they tended to form small but intense friendship groups with a 'best friend' central to their experiences. However, as young women begin relationships with boys, feminine cultures based on supportive friendships begin a gradual process of breaking up (Griffin 1981). This does not occur to the same extent for 'the lads' who usually retain their male group membership. The earlier quote from Parker (1974) confirms the significance of male group membership even when girlfriends have arrived on the scene. Before heterosexual relationships begin to fragment the supportive feminine cultures, various constraints work to discourage or to restrict the possibilities for young women to form large groups or gangs. (These constraints also inhibit alternative expressions of women's sexuality.) It is in this way that young women's sexuality becomes regulated and controlled.

First women, especially young working-class women, have little access to 'space'. Social and sporting facilities are dominated by men and male groups with the pub, working-men's clubs, snooker halls, rugby/cricket clubs clearly male domains. Often the street corner where 'the lads' can be found is unsafe territory for young women as they regularly face harassment ranging from verbal abuse or put-downs to actual physical violence. This does not mean that young women are totally excluded from the street.

Research by Cowie and Lees (1981) suggests that young working-class women can be found in groups hanging around shopping centres or street corners. They acknowledge, however, that 'the extent of girls' participation or exclusion on the street would seem to be less than boys, but remains to be fully investigated'. They conclude that girls' appearance on the street is always constrained by their subordination. It would seem that for many young women the answer is, as McRobbie (1978a) suggests, to retreat to a 'home base' where best friends can meet, chat and negotiate their existence.

Working-class young women also experience material constraints which, together with a lack of access to private transport, further inhibits their movements. Middle-class young women have greater opportunity for participation in social and sporting activities. Not only do they have economic support,[6] but also parental help to transport them to the gym club, swimming pool, youth centre, etc. Despite increased access, however, the very real threat of violence on the streets exists for *all* women. Facilities remain dominated by men and within families 'free-time' is defined differently for young women and for young men. This raises the issue of domestic and childcare responsibilities which many young women unlike young men experience from an early age. Young women are expected to help with housework and the care of younger siblings.[7] The strength of the ideology of domesticity emphasises women's 'natural' domestic and childcare role. Young women also have a realistic view of their future which they see as involving domestic/childcare responsibilities. They recognise this as preparation for their future roles as wives and mothers, and although not always accepting it unquestioningly, it is regarded generally as inevitable. The extent of expectations of domestic/childcare responsibility is also related to class. Working-class young women are expected to take on these responsibilities to a greater extent (Dorn 1983) although middle-class young women often still have their share of washing up and cleaning to do!

Young women's sub-cultures, then, do not correspond to male sub-cultures in any simplistic way and an understanding of gender-, class-, race- and age constraints is important. Indeed the term 'sub-culture' takes on 'masculine' connotations. It is more useful perhaps to consider young women's 'cultures' which are structurally separate and distinct from those of male youth. McRobbie (1978a) identifies 'romance' and the 'culture of femininity' as central to the daily lives of adolescent young women. Her research highlights the importance for young women of talking and planning around fashions, make-up and boyfriends. The culture revolves around the intense task of 'getting a man' but always within the constraints of 'keeping a good reputation' (Cowie and Lees 1981) which is by no means easy or unambiguous. Young women are well aware of the inevitable future, influenced by political, economic and ideological constraints, in which a heterosexual relationship leading to marriage, home and family is the expected outcome. Within this 'culture of femininity' there are obvious class and race differences. Just as 'masculinity' cannot be viewed as a static, universal concept so 'femininity' demonstrates marked variation across class and ethnicity. As Griffin (1981) rightly asserts:

> There *are* some parallels with the position of young black and middle class women, but it is crucial to understand the ways in which young white women benefit from cultural, ideological and institutional racisms; how race and racism affect and are affected by the experiences of young black women; and how young middle class women negotiate their relatively privileged position in education and waged work.

Turning now to schooling it is important to examine its relationship to the 'culture of femininity'. There is clear evidence that young women and men experience schooling differently, and this leads to distinct outcomes (Deem 1980; Stanworth 1981). Young women and young men are prepared for their future roles in society which for young women is expected to involve becoming a wife and mother as well as being involved in the world of work. Within the curriculum this need not take the overt form of differential option choices (e.g. domestic science for girls; woodwork for boys) but as Stanworth recognises it can involve 'a myriad of subtle ways in which the educational process brings to life and sustains sexual divisions – the process of quite literally, teaching girls to be women and boys to be men'. Again this cuts across class boundaries and is experienced to some degree whether in a local comprehensive school or a privileged public school (Okeley 1978). Chris Griffin (1981) confirms this in her discussions with white middle-class girls in school:

> Whilst some of these young women clearly realised the extent of their privileges as white and middle class, as women they will always have to play second fiddle to men, denied full access to

the spheres of power in which they have apparently been
granted 'equal opportunities'.

Within school there are clearly female counter-school cultures
just as there have been shown to be male counter-school cultures
(Willis 1977). Whereas the *class* significance of male counter-
school culture has been stressed (Willis 1977), female counter-
school cultures are seen to involve negotiation around age, race,
class and *gender* relations. Resistances to schooling for young
women are not solely about gender or class but are bound up with
the complex development towards adulthood. Indeed age-based
resistances have been a part of struggles by young women and
young men within schooling since formal schooling began. It is
likely that this has been further intensified with the raising of the
school-leaving age which leaves young adults in a system geared to
childhood and based on a clear age related authority structure
(Johnson 1981).

Young women's resistances within school, however, do take on
a specifically female form and cannot simply be equated to those of
male youth. Young women who are considered 'non-academic' are
in conflict with a school system geared to examination results.
However, as research into girls' schooling has shown, schools are
concerned also with producing young women who will fit into our
society as wives and mothers. Resistance here is gender-based and
cuts across class considerations for it is challenging the school
definition of a 'nice' girl which is seen to emphasise neatness,
passivity, hard work, politeness, etc. which will result in a 'good',
'suitable' job, i.e. nursery nurse, nurse, infant teacher, etc. It is
important here to see resistance not necessarily as a 'problem' (as
viewed by the school) but perhaps a 'legitimate source of pressure'
(Johnson 1981). Young women in this situation could be seen to be
challenging the 'culture of femininity' and reasserting their right to
define their own existence. This becomes dependent on the form
of resistance taken. McRobbie (1978a) stresses the importance of
'appearance' as a form of resistance for adolescent young women.
By wearing make-up, jewellery, altering the school uniform,
young women often use overtly sexual modes of expression which
demonstrates quite clearly that they are overstepping the boundaries
of girlhood (as demanded by the school) into womanhood. As
young women constantly are judged by their sexuality, be it by the
'lads' in Willis' study or the teachers in their classrooms, it is a
powerful means of challenging 'the system'. However, McRobbie

argues that young women's own culture then becomes the most efficient agent of social control for by resisting they reaffirm and reinforce patriarchal power relations: 'they are both saved by and locked within the culture of femininity'. Clearly by asserting a more sexually orientated appearance young women run the risk of being labelled as a 'slag', 'tart', etc. However, by rejecting the image of the 'nice' acquiescent girl, a more positive assertion of femininity *is* possible such that resistances can be used to *challenge* the dominant culture of femininity. Griffin (1981) discusses this positive assertion of femininity which:

> Partly rejects the idealised notions of the 'nice' girl in a very direct manner, undermines images of the passive asexual young women waiting for her 'fella' found in teenage magazines and romantic fiction; and serves as a partial attempt to reappropriate femininity by young women, and for young women.

Young women's resistances are not restricted to those involving appearance. Griffin (1981) discusses a further strategy that young women use to negotiate their existence in schools. Most teachers would recognise her description of young women's silence and the 'sullen stare'. For many young women this is a more subtle and acceptable challenge which does not rely on the more extrovert use of appearance. This, too, cuts across class and cannot be seen as only a working-class resistance to schooling (Griffin 1981).

What becomes clear is that young women's cultures exist in specific structural forms and cannot be equated simplistically with those of young men. Within school young women's counter-school culture is complex and again cannot be viewed only in relation to issues around class location. Certainly forms of 'femininity' are used by working-class young women as class based resistances. However, as in middle-class schools, notions of 'ideal' femininity, i.e. the 'nice' girl are also challenged and can be seen not as 'locking' them within the 'culture of femininity' but indeed forming a challenge to that culture in an attempt to redefine 'femininity' for themselves. The complexities are such that counter-school resistances by young women do several things at once; they can serve to reinforce, negotiate and challenge the 'culture of femininity'. There is no clear-cut line that can differentiate between these outcomes. Cultural analysis which recognises these complexities and acknowledges the importance of gender, class, race and age considerations remains at an innovatory stage.

The final section of this paper relates the teaching of physical education in secondary schools to young women's cultures and especially their resistances. PE is a subject which receives little attention in the considerations of young women's schooling.[8] However, it is an area which experiences resistances from young women particularly around adolescence. The centrality of the 'physical' makes it an interesting confrontation, for a biologically deterministic position is attractive when dealing with physical issues.[9] This final section stresses the importance of a cultural analysis and considers the implication of this for the future teaching of PE.

Physical education – what is on offer?

PE in the majority of secondary schools is taught to single-sex groups even when part of a co-educational school system. My own research in Liverpool schools[10] demonstrates the existence of a core curriculum in the first three years of secondary schools consisting of team games, gymnastics, athletics with some schools including swimming and/or dance. Within this core component half of the total PE time is taken up by competitive team games with the other activities sharing the remaining time. A programme of 'options' including more individually based activities (e.g. badminton, trampolining) or less competitive situations (e.g. keep fit) is offered, in most instances from the fourth year upwards. The extra-curricular programme offers team games in specific age groupings, gym, swimming, and/or dance clubs for the younger girls with a badminton club a usual addition from the age of fifteen years. PE is theoretically compulsory up to the school-leaving age and is taught in mixed ability groups apart from extra-curricular representative-year team practices.

The notion of 'good practice' and 'standards' in PE has been at the forefront of PE teaching throughout its history and development. 'Good practice' centres around discipline, neatness, good behaviour, appearance, etc. It is stressed by PE teachers today as one of the most important features of their work. In 1905 the Anstey College of Physical Training Magazine[11] reported that the main aims of physical training included:

Regular attendance, good behaviour throughout the year, and general improvement in all respects.

Smart personal appearance shown by general care of the body as regards hair, teeth, skin, nails, clothing and good health.

Good posture when standing and sitting and good carriage in walking.

Attention to word of command, absence of mistakes and vigorous work in the gymnasium.

General forms and style of movement, sense of time, self-control and power of relaxation. (quoted in Crunden 1974:19)

Good behaviour and discipline whilst very much part of the general school ethos have a particular association with PE. Margaret Stansfield the first principal of Bedford PE College (founded in 1903) believed that 'the discipline of the school emanates from the gymnasium' (Fletcher 1984). The content of PE for girls has long been associated with 'discipline'. The rules and regulations of team games combined with the discipline of Swedish gymnastics[12] made girls' PE every bit as regulated as the more formal, regimented military drill associated with boys' PE. Although Swedish gymnastics tended to be associated with a freer type of movement that was less restricted than that offered to the boys, Jenny Hargreaves notes that in the Ling system:

the potential for natural, spontaneous movement was denied by the exact parameters of behaviour laid down and by the very nature of the system, which was remarkably similar to drill. (Hargreaves 1979)

Today PE continues to stress discipline. Lining up in the changing rooms in silence, entering the gym quietly and responding without question to rules and regulations of games, are an essential part of contemporary PE lessons. In many schools the 'success' of PE is still measured by the achievements on the sports field or netball court. PE often provides the 'public face' of the school when it represents them at tournaments, inter-school matches, swimming galas, gym displays, etc. Even the discipline and behaviour of the girls when outside, playing hockey, tennis, etc. is on view to the rest of the school in their classrooms and the local residents as they walk past. In many respects what occurs in PE is under far closer scrutiny than teaching in the classroom where doors and walls can provide a useful barrier to observation and comment!

Similarly appearance in relation to dress, neatness, posture, etc. can be identified as having been important in PE throughout each decade of its history. In the training of PE teachers it remains an obsession. Comments remembered by past students at Anstey include:

'How can you keep your children in order if you cannot keep your hair tidy . . .'

'if you cannot control your legs, how can you control your class.' (Crunden 1974)

The continuing emphasis on appearance for teaching practice in schools today demonstrates both its importance for teachers of PE and the values of subsequent transmission of such values to the pupils. The wearing of PE uniform is still compulsory throughout Liverpool schools. In most instances the uniform is regulated to a specific skirt/shorts/top of a defined colour. Even where this has been relaxed, which was only evident in three situations, there is an insistence on 'suitable' clothing as defined by the PE teacher.[13] A considerable amount of time is taken up in the PE lesson by the enforcement of correct PE uniform and neatness of appearance.

While 'good practice' and 'standards' inform the teaching of PE, the primary aims and objectives are dependent also on economic, social and political forces. Kane's 1974 survey of secondary school PE for the Schools Council found that women teachers ranked leisure as their fourth most important objective in PE teaching out of a table of nine major objectives. In my own research in Liverpool schools I found that in 1984 every girls' PE department placed leisure as their main or second objective for the teaching of PE especially from the third year upwards. The emphasis was on enjoyment and preparation for participation in post-school leisure time. Most teachers recognised this as a changed emphasis throughout the 1970s and early 1980s because of economic changes which they identified as producing increased leisure time, both in terms of shorter working hours, and most importantly through the reality of probable unemployment or part time work. The validity of these points will be discussed later.

The PE on offer to adolescent girls is therefore, influenced, both structurally and ideologically, by a number of interrelated factors.

In order to consider the relationship of PE to young women's sub-cultures, it is important to turn to the influences which impinge on the young women's responses to the PE experience.

Young women's responses

It is obvious that young women experience biological changes during puberty, and which therefore usually occur between the ages of nine and thirteen. These changes are often dramatic with changed body shape, related to the onset of menstruation, happening over a short period of time. How far these biological changes influence young women's responses to PE remains questionable. Menstruation was in the past regarded as an inhibition to young women's physical movement and thus a direct restriction on her participation in most physical activity. In recent times research has debunked this myth (see note 9) and it is now widely accepted that, in most situations, menstruation does not adversely affect women's ability to participate in physical activity. What would seem more important is the social construction of young women's biology, the ideology of biology, i.e. the expectations placed on young women as to how they *should* be reacting to these physical changes. It is reasonable to assume that for some young women the changes of puberty produce such distinct changes in body shape that they find it awkward to move physically in the same way as in the past, for example in gymnastics or in athletics. It is, however, the social and ideological pressures linked to sexuality and body physique that produce the inhibition rather than a biologically determined restriction on movement. As discussed in a previous section of this paper young women's experiences at adolescence centre around the culture of femininity. In terms of the 'physical' the expectation is one of inactivity, passivity, neatness (reinforced through socialisation, media, schooling, etc.). Young women are not expected to run around, get dirty or indeed sweat. The old adage that young ladies 'glow' as opposed to sweat remains firm in today's thinking.

Peer group pressure intensifies the culture of femininity. Whereas an individual may still be interested in playing netball or swimming in the team, it is often pressure from friends, which encourages her to 'drop out' or, certainly diminishes her enthusiasm. Option lists in the PE department often show names erased because a 'best friend' does not want to take part in that particular activity. Certainly many potential senior team members are lost, not necessarily through a loss of interest by the individual, but more often because of the sub-cultural influences that surround her.

So, what happens when the PE on offer encounters the young women it is intended for? The meeting place is the lesson and it is here that the relationship between secondary school PE and young women's sub-cultures becomes either a 'problem' for the teacher, or a subject for negotiation and resistance by the student.

Teacher and student: the meeting of PE and adolescent young women

Figure 1 shows the centrality of the PE *lesson* and the resultant effects for both PE teacher and student.

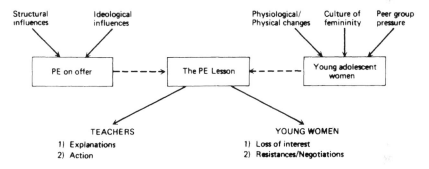

Figure 1: *The centrality of the PE lesson*

First, PE teachers attempt to explain why young women tend to lose interest in physical activity during and immediately after puberty. This 'loss of interest' of adolescent young women is confirmed by the majority of heads of PE interviewed during my research.

> 'In the second or third year they just lose interest but not just in PE. They lose interest in everything at this time.'
> 'Girls at this stage are going through . . . they're changing fairly rapidly. They get embarrassed very easily. They change shape more and feel more self-conscious than lads do. They just lose all interest in physical activity at this time – its just natural.'
> 'I've talked to my girls and they always say "we're just beginning to be interested in outside." They lose interest in PE at

school. If they go to a disco they expend more energy than they ever would in a PE lesson.'

The explanation is given as 'natural' – an inevitable problem inherent to adolescent young women. In general, PE teachers see young women at this time as less interested in physical activity, lethargic and inactive. My own research indicates that this gender expectation cuts across class, ethnic divisions and that PE teachers tend to generalise about all young women. This may indeed reflect the reality of their experience but an explanation of it must involve more than a simplistic biological determinism. However, for many PE teachers the problems faced with 3E or 4X on a Thursday afternoon are real and, in general, result in one or two coping strategies. First, many teachers, identifying the 'problem' as biologically constructed and/or individually based, tackle the solution by reiterating their belief in the value and ideals of the PE on offer. They attempt to enforce participation through disciplinary means. Obviously this has minimal 'success' for even if the young women involved continue to participate in theory, in practice they remain uninterested and unmotivated. The value of 'enjoyment' placed so highly by *all* PE teachers on their list of aims and objectives cannot be achieved by use of hierarchical disciplinarian methods. Second, teachers have attempted to alleviate their difficulties by adapting the curriculum and making it more relevant to young women's needs and requirements. During the past decade and a half this has included the introduction of a scheme of options for the upper school age group. (These options have been introduced also for economic reasons where shortage of staff, facilities, etc., affect organisation. However, the primary justification given for 'options' is that they are more 'suitable' for adolescent young women.) These 'option' activities whilst retaining the compulsory element of PE allow more choice of content. The options offered tend to be individually based since this is recognised as being more 'appropriate' for older girls. The emphasis is on indoor activities which provide 'an activity which won't mess up their hair or make them too sweaty' (interview, PE teacher). In some situations activities relating directly to appearance are encouraged with stress on the development of an 'attractive' figure and body shape. This can be through Keep Fit/Aerobic classes or the development of specialist Health and Beauty courses which cover a wide range of issues including care of the hair, nails, diet, make-up, clothes, etc. The difficulty with these last developments in PE is that they reinforce the cultural expectations of femininity and in many ways fall into the 'double-bind' described previously. Once more as McRobbie (1978a) suggests young women become 'both saved by and locked in the culture of femininity'. The message being reinforced in these situations is that young women should not be interested and involved in physical activity in order to develop strength and fitness but should be concerned in enhancing their appearance, in making themselves more 'attractive', particularly to the opposite sex.

The response from young women to the PE lesson can involve resistance to the activities and teaching of PE. These resistances take on similar forms to those described in relation to schooling in general. Resistances based on appearance take an intensified form when related to PE. As has been discussed, appearance in relation to 'standards' and 'good practice' is an integral part of the ethos of PE teaching. Young women who use their appearance to challenge their school experiences confront PE by contesting its central ideological tenet. Young women refuse to wear the required PE uniform, they wear make-up and jewellery and will not consent to the 'golden rule' of 'tying your hair back'. These challenges to authority are more obvious in the changing room than elsewhere in the school, and indeed produce a confrontation which can often be avoided by most other school staff. Whereas other teachers can choose to ignore the wearing of a ring or ear-rings which contravenes school regulations, PE teachers not only have their own standards and values around appearance to uphold, but have the added concern of safety during physical activity. Rings, ear-rings, necklaces, badges and long hair can be in fact, exceedingly dangerous in some physical situations.

The 'sullen stare' so aptly described by Chris Griffin takes on particular significance in PE. A sullen, silent 'participant' on the hockey pitch or in the gymnasium is inordinately difficult to manage. In the classroom a young woman using the 'sullen stare' often simply encourages less attention from the teacher. In a mixed group situation, where boys have been shown to dominate the lesson and receive more attention from the teacher (Spender 1982; Stanworth 1981) a silent, sullen member of the group provides little overt challenge to the successful continuation of the lesson. Indeed it provides a reinforced view of the stereotypical female pupil as more passive, quiet, less articulate, etc. In PE, however, where lively, active behaviour is demanded a silent, sullen participant produces far more conflict and can affect the

Sheila Scraton

participation of the whole group. It is a particularly successful resistance to PE for adolescent young women.

Towards a cultural explanation

A biological explanation for young women's loss of interest in PE and their resistances within the PE lesson is not sufficient. Whilst acknowledging the physiological changes of puberty I would argue that an understanding of cultural expectations is vital if young women's experiences, attitudes and behaviours are to be fully understood. It is necessary to analyse from a cultural perspective why it is that many young women 'drop out' or lose interest in PE during the period of adolescence. The PE on offer to young women conflicts with their interests and attitudes not simply because they are undergoing biological changes of puberty but because the cultural expectations of gender-specific attitudes, behaviour, role, etc. are at odds with both what is on offer in PE and the values, ideals and ethos underpinning the subject.

PE for girls in most secondary schools remains dominated by team games. Team games are synonymous with sport which in our society is problematic for female participants. The relationship of sport to masculinity is well documented (Young 1980; Hargreaves 1982). Sport celebrates a certain kind of masculinity with its sporting heroes dominating the headlines on the sports page. Young women are immersed in a culture of femininity and romance, reinforced through the magazines they read, the television they watch and their everyday experiences. PE appears incompatible with their expected lifestyle. Sport is seen primarily as a male pursuit bound up with masculine values. Young women spectate, support and admire; they do not expect to participate.

Furthermore sport in the form of team games is problematic not only in definition but also in form. Young women's cultures which emphasise the 'best friend' or small groupings do not relate easily to the collective team situation. PE stresses the collective through team sports, gym clubs, dance groups, athletic teams. Young women often reject these situations as incompatible with the expectations of adult femininity (Leaman 1984). Young, fit, virile men are expected to revel in group camaraderie and team spirit. It is less acceptable for their adolescent sisters.

'Preparation for leisure' was stated as a primary aim of PE teaching by every secondary school in my current research.

176

This confirms Kane's (1974) findings in the only major survey of secondary school PE undertaken for the Schools' Council. This, however, is problematic for adolescent young women. Recent work on women's leisure has emphasised the problem of defining leisure for women. Women's leisure is constrained by many factors including class, race, age and not least 'men, collectively and as individuals' (Deem 1984b). Both Deem and Griffin et al. (1982) question the very existence of 'leisure' for women as it has been traditionally defined. They insist that in order to explain women's leisure, or lack of it, both the public and the private spheres of women's experiences must be understood. As Griffin et al. (1982) state:

> women's position in waged and unwaged work in relation to the
> family means that the existence of 'leisure' as a pure category
> for women is questionable.

Preparation for leisure creates problems of relevance for all women especially in the realm of physical leisure activities. Deem's (1984b) research confirms this, for in her study of 168 women drawn at random from five areas of a new town, she found 'scarcely any adult women who continued with any sport or physical activity done at school once they had left, with swimming the only widespread exception to this'. Therefore 'preparation for leisure' is a dubious objective for young women's PE. Not only does leisure not exist for many women but where women have opportunities for leisure the most frequently pursued activity is swimming (Deem 1984b). My research suggests that swimming is offered to adolescent young women as an option in schools only where the school has a swimming pool on site. This is restricted further by staffing problems as most departments cannot release a member of staff to cover the numbers opting for swimming. In most schools there is no choice, as access to swimming facilities is not available.[14] The emphasis on leisure as a realistic objective for young women seems particularly illogical given that many PE teachers recognise their own personal limitations in time and opportunities at a private level. Many PE teachers described the problems they had with family and domestic responsibilities which affected their ability to spend more time on extra-curricular activities or personal leisure pursuits. This failure to recognise the problems of using leisure as a relevant and useful concept for women produces a contradictory and, in many ways, an unachievable aim for PE teaching. PE teachers need to look more critically both at the structural limitations and at the reality of everyday experiences for women in physical leisure activities in order to provide a more realistic link between school and future physical participation. The recognition of a sexual division of leisure, as well as a sexual division of labour, by all teachers, should be an important aspect of the teaching of girls in schools. Furthermore, young women themselves often recognise the constraints put on their 'leisure' time. Even where they succeed in challenging their lack of access to time, space, etc. (more easily achieved by middle-class young women) they face unequal provision of facilities and opportunities to participate. Their present reality confirms their future 'leisure' participation. When they attend youth groups, clubs, etc. they know only too well who dominates the snooker tables, gymnasium, table tennis etc (Nava and McRobbie 1984).

The resistance of young women to the discipline and control of PE, described previously as being central to the ideology of PE, is a response similar to the responses of young women to schooling in general. The actual resistance is class- and age-based although within a particularly gendered form, (McRobbie 1978a). Although these problems are faced throughout the curriculum, the importance of discipline and control which is so much a part of both the *content* and teaching of PE creates an often intensified conflict between PE teaching staff and students.

Equally resistances to school uniform by adolescent young women are resistances to the style, restriction and enforced uniformity of the dress. As Whylde (1983) states:

> Collar, tie and jacket for boys and skirt and blouse (or twin-set!) for girls imitate the conventional dress of the middle aged and middle class, a group which few pupils will identify with, and against which most will rebel.

Once more the issue of uniform is intensified during PE. PE uniform is one of the major areas of conflict between young women and PE. To many young women the wearing of a standard tee shirt, regulation navy shorts/skirt plus ankle socks is one of the greatest indignities and embarrassments placed on them. Whilst they react to school uniform for the reasons suggested by Whylde, their reactions to PE kit is enhanced as their developing sexuality, and their desire to achieve adult femininity, meet head on a PE kit which denies not only their individuality but also any hint of a developing sexual person. At a time when fashion, jewellery and make-up are central to their concern with appearance, the uniform, asexual PE kit is an anathema.

Anxiety around PE for adolescent young women is caused also by showering after a lesson and indeed changing in large, group changing rooms. This relates to the fact that girls reach puberty and mature physically at different rates. Again, whilst this is experienced throughout the school, the 'physical' nature of PE intensifies the problems. Measor (1984) found in her research a great reluctance of young women to take showers as a group:

Pat: 'I don't like showers. On the first day we were ever so shy. Everyone has got things different . . . some people have got hairs and some haven't.'

Carol: 'There is one big girl in our group . . . she is big chested, and that and she walks through the shower all covered up. It's best to be in between, we all giggle and throw our towels down. She finally went into the shower with her towel. There is one really little girl, who sits there making faces, she looks at everyone, she makes you feel embarrassed.'

The explanations for the problems faced by young women in coping with this situation are clearly grounded in physiology and the physical changes of puberty. However, it is the interaction of physical development and *cultural* expectation that is important. It is not the actual physical changes of the young women's bodies which cause the anxiety but the culturally determined responses to these changes. Those who are 'in-between' or average in their development can cope with the situation. They meet the expectations for desired body shape and development. Those who deviate from the norm face acute embarrassment and often unkind comment. When society emphasises a desired physique for adult femininity, those who become aware of their differences during adolescence are caused anxiety and often retreat or 'hide' from the situation. PE provides the platform where physical differences are unmasked. Adult women are not expected to expose their bodies and are encouraged to dislike their body shape unless it conforms to the 'ideal' feminine stereotype. During adolescence the PE changing room or shower area is an exposed situation where young women's developing bodies are put 'on view'. The problem is not the physical appearance as such, but the desire of young women to achieve the 'acceptable', sexually attractive physique of womanhood. This body shape is culturally determined and strongly informed by ideologies of woman as a sexual object to be admired, viewed and used by men.

The way forward

The 'culture of femininity' is based on the social construction of women's roles and behaviour. The ideology of biology emphasises women as passive and submissive and presents them in appearance, dress and style in terms of their sexuality. This influences not only women's work opportunities but also their use of leisure, and their domestic and family commitments. These images of women cut across class, race and age although at each of the levels (work, leisure, family, sexuality) there are differences depending on women's individual location in society. The media reinforce this imagery even when dealing with women involved in sporting activities (Graydon 1983). Women athletes are presented *positively* as conforming to the desired image: Zola Budd – 'the waif'; Donna Hartley – 'the golden girl'; Joyce Smith – 'mother of two', or alternately *negatively* as having overstepped the boundaries of femininity: Martina Navratilova – 'the machine'; Jarmila Kratchvilova – 'the man'.

School PE fails to provide 'meaningful experiences' for many young adolescent women because it appears at odds with the culture of femininity. Their resistances which are complex and not always consistent, relate to what they perceive as on offer from PE:

a) the development of muscle
b) sweat
c) communal showers/changing facilities
d) 'childish', asexual PE kit
e) low status activities.

It is acceptable for the 'tomboy' in junior or lower secondary school to participate in and enjoy these activities but not so acceptable to adult femininity.

As shown, therefore, PE remains trapped within possibilities which will 'appeal' to young women but will consequently reinforce the culture of femininity. This is intensified by the training and ideological constraints of women PE teachers. Even so-called 'progressive' moves, for example, mixed PE, provide only superficial challenges to the ideologies of femininity. Any suggestion of substantive change to give young women positive experiences in PE tends to be met with scepticism because it is assumed that young women are so steeped in the deterministic *Jackie* mentality that they will reject more positive physical values of assertiveness, strength, control, etc. There is not necessarily real substance to this argument. Adult women's experiences are not *totally* determined and the past decade and a half has seen a substantial shift through the development of new directions in the reconstruction of women's sexuality and consciousness. These include the development of self-help groups in medical care/mental health, the emergence of well-women's clinics and other all-women projects geared to giving women more control over their own health, bodies, etc. Women's groups have developed, resisting male violence with rape crisis centres, women's refuges, etc. Education has seen the introduction of 'NOW' courses, 'outreach' projects, women's writing groups, etc., where women are encouraged to gain confidence and assertiveness in intellectual situations. Women's physical control over their own bodies can be seen further in the development of self-defence/assertiveness training[15] and women's fitness programmes which are geared to developing health, strength and physical well-being rather than the traditional construction of 'womanhood' around appearance, body physique, etc. These latter developments indicate a qualitative shift in definitions of 'the physical'. Women in these programmes are reclaiming the right to physical development and appearance on *their own terms* rather than on the terms laid down in the traditions of 'feminine culture' which are learned and reinforced in youth. As Lenskyj (1982) describes from her own experience, that after years of upbringing women are:

> alienated from our bodies not knowing the extent of our
> physical strength and endurance and not daring to find out.
> Those of us who have dared have found a new avenue for self-
> realisation as women and as feminists – joyful at the discovery
> that our bodies are strong and resilient, capable of hard work
> and hard play.

It is with these developments in adult women's projects that women's PE should be concerned rather than a concentration on equal access to male-based sports, e.g. women into soccer, etc. For these are part of the same institutional relations of patriarchy (i.e. cults of masculinity) which produce young women's sub-cultures and define/constrict young women's opportunities. By contrast, women's PE needs to develop a new programme geared to assertiveness, confidence, health, fitness and the capacity to challenge patriarchal definitions of submissiveness, passivity, dependence, etc. This is by no means an easy task but nonetheless a direction in which we must, at least, begin to move.

The unifying feature of all the adult women's projects mentioned, is the emphasis on collective support.[16] PE is in the perfect situation to offer young women opportunities for collective support through co-operative and enjoyable physical activity. Whilst the relationship between teacher and student will retain an age-related power structure, young women can be encouraged to work together through such activities as dance, outdoor pursuits, self-defence, etc. Indeed Willis (1982) suggests:

> A sport could be presented as a form of activity which
> emphasizes human similarity and not dissimilarity, a form of
> activity which expresses values which are indeed immeasurable,
> a form of activity which is concerned with individual well-being
> and satisfaction rather than with comparison.

Many young men thrive on their collective 'rugby club' experiences. Young women, too, need the space for collective physical experience whilst rejecting and challenging the competitive, 'macho' values of the male sporting ethos. Adolescence is a time to develop group and collective experiences rather than the channelling of young women into individually based activities which deny the opportunities to develop group confidence and identity.

Young women also need the space to develop confidence, interests, etc. This is especially true in mixed schools for the evidence clearly indicates that in all social situations men dominate space – physically, verbally, etc. (See Spender 1982; Young 1980.) In co-educational schools the primary female-only space is in the toilets, cloakrooms and changing rooms. These are the areas where young women 'hang out', where they spend time together away from 'the lads' and the teachers (Griffin et al. 1982). It would be a positive contribution if women PE teachers could recognise the need of young women to have their own space in which to chat, plan or simply 'have a laugh'. This is clearly problematic given school organisation and the enforcement of school rules and regulations. However, it would be a positive move to open up changing rooms and facilities during breaks, lunchtime and after school and encourage young women to use the space available for their 'leisure' whether it be netball, table tennis *or* chatting with a friend. Too often young women are allowed into the PE wing only if they are taking part in organised, formal PE activities. It would be an encouraging move to give young women more control over their extra curricular PE activities and to provide the space for meeting and chatting together.

Just as adult women are beginning to reclaim the right to control and develop their own bodies for intrinsic satisfaction rather than sexual exploitation, so PE must emphasise these values for young adolescent women. They must be encouraged to enjoy physical movement; to develop strength and muscular potential; to work together to discover body awareness and confidence. It will be only when young women collectively become confident and assertive with control both physically and mentally over their own bodies that they will move towards redefining their position. PE has an important contribution to make towards the denial of ideologies of 'femininity'. For this to occur it requires a critical self-appraisal and a more sensitive understanding of young women's position in our schooling system and in wider society.

Acknowledgments

Many thanks to Pat Craddock, Rosemary Deem and Phil Scraton for their help, support and critical comments. Also personal thanks to Sally Channon.

Notes

1 For the purposes of this paper PE will denote young women's physical education.
2 This point is noted across a wide range of literature. For example 'juvenile delinquency' invariably has focused on boys' criminal or deviant activities – see Campbell, A. (1980) *Girl Delinquents*, Blackwell, Oxford.
3 See Shacklady-Smith (1978) for a further discussion of this point.
4 In this paper 'patriarchy' represents male domination of women. See Beechey (1979) for a detailed consideration of the complexity of this concept.
5 For example, see Brake (1974); Hebdige (1976); Willis (1978).

6 However, many working-class teenage women do have paid jobs outside school hours, e.g. Low Pay unit report on children and work.

7 My research in Liverpool schools indicates that young women have considerable domestic and childcare responsibilities which restricts their opportunities to take up extra-curricular PE opportunities. See also Dorn (1983).

8 ILEA (1984) and Leaman (1984) provide specific work. See also Browne et al. in Whylde, J. (ed.) (1983).

9 Physical *sex* differences have been taken for granted until recently. See Ferris (1978) 'Sportswomen and Medicine', *Report of the Ist International Conference on Women and Sport*; Mees (1979), 'Women in sport: a review of physiological factors', *Physical Education Review*, Vol. 2, No. 1, pp. 44–9; Dyer, K. (1982), *Catching up the Men*, Junction Books, for evidence that challenges many of the 'myths' surrounding physical sex differences.

10 This research examines how images of 'femininity' and the construction of gender-appropriate behaviour are reinforced or challenged by the structure, content and teaching of girls PE in Secondary schools. The qualitative methodology has involved extensive interviews with Heads of Girls' PE Departments in Liverpool Secondary Schools (state), periods of close observation in selected schools and structured interviews with PE advisers, lecturers in the specialist teacher-training college and education committee members involved in reorganisation.

11 One of the original PE teacher-training colleges founded in 1897.

12 Swedish gymnastics originated from the work of Per Henrik Ling. The gymnastics was based on scientific principles of anatomy and physiology and was introduced into the English school system primarily by the work of Madame Bergman-Osterberg.

13 The definition of 'suitable' PE clothing consists of plain tee shirt, shorts or games skirt. It varies from a formal uniform only in so far as colours are not specified.

14 The issue here rests on political and economic factors rather than the individual decisions of PE teachers.

15 For a discussion of the redefining of women's strength and power and the development of self-defence techniques see Quinn, K. (1983).

16 See Dixey and Talbot (1982), *Women, Leisure and Bingo*, Trinity and All Saints College, pp.78–9 for a discussion on the importance of contact and support for women during their leisure.

References

Ardener, S. (ed.) (1978), *Defining Females*, Croom Helm, London.

Beechey, V. (1979), 'On patriarchy', *Feminist Review*, 3, pp. 66–82.

Brake, M. (1974), 'The skinheads – an English working class subculture', *Youth and Society*, Vol. 6, No. 2, December.

Brake, M. (1980), *The Sociology of Youth Culture and Youth Subcultures*, Routledge & Kegan Paul, London.

Cockburn, C. (1983), *Brothers*, Pluto Press, London.

Corrigan, P. (1979), *The Smash Street Kids*, Paladin, London.

Cowie, C. and Lees, S. (1981), 'Slags or drags', *Feminist Review*, 9, Autumn.

Crunden, C. (1974), *A History of Anstey College of Physical Education: 1897–1972*, Anstey CPE.

Deem, R. (ed.) (1980), *Schooling for Women's Work*, Routledge & Kegan Paul, London.

Deem, R. (1984a), 'The politics of women's leisure', paper presented to Leisure Studies Association International Conference, 4–8 July.

Deem, R. (1984b), 'Paid work, leisure and non-employment: shifting boundaries and gender differences', unpublished paper presented to BSA conference 'Work, Employment, Unemployment', April.

Dorn, N. (1983), *Class, Youth and Drink: Historical Analysis of Policy and Contemporary Ethnology of Youth*, Croom Helm, London.

Dorn, N. and South, N. (1983/4), 'Youth, the family and the regulation of the 'informal', *Resources for Feminist Research* XII, 4 Dec./Jan., OISE, Toronto.

Fletcher, S. (1984), *Women First – The Female Tradition in English Physical Education 1880–1980*, Athlone Press, London.

Graydon, J. (1983), But it's more than a game. It's an institution: 'Feminist Perspectives on Sport', *Feminist Review*, 13, Spring.

Griffin, C. (1981), *Cultures of Femininity: Romance Revisited*, Centre for Contemporary Cultural Studies.

Griffin, C. et al. (1982), 'Women and leisure' in Hargreaves, J. (ed.), *Sport, Culture and Ideology*, Routledge & Kegan Paul, London.

Hall, S. and Jefferson, T. (1976), *Resistance through Rituals*, Hutchinson, London.

Hargreaves, J. (1979), 'Playing like gentlemen while behaving like ladies', MA Thesis submitted to University of London Institute of Education.

Hargreaves, J. (ed.) (1982), *Sport, Culture and Ideology*, Routledge & Kegan Paul, London.

Hebdige, D. (1976), 'The meaning of Mod' in Hall, S. and Jefferson, T., 1976.

ILEA (1984), *Providing Equal Opportunities for Girls and Boys in Physical Education*.

Johnson, R. (1981), *Education and Popular Politics*, E353 Block 1 Unit 1, The Open University Press, Milton Keynes.

Kane, J.E. (1974), *Physical Education in Secondary Schools*, Macmillan, London.

Leaman, O. (1984), *Sit on the Sidelines and Watch the Boys Play: Sex Differentiation in PE*, Longman (for Schools Council), London.

Lenskyj, H. (1982), 'I am Strong' in *The Women's News Magazine*, University of Toronto, March/April.

McRobbie, A. (1978a), 'Working class girls and the culture of femininity' in *Women Take Issue*, Hutchinson, London.

McRobbie, A. (1978b), *Jackie: An Ideology of Adolescent Femininity*, Stencilled paper. Centre for Contemporary Cultural Studies.

McRobbie, A. and Garber, J. (1976), 'Girls and Subcultures' in Hall, S. and Jefferson, T., 1976.

McRobbie, A. and McCabe, T. (eds) (1981), *Feminism for Girls*, Routledge & Kegan Paul, London.

Measor, L. (1984), 'Sex education and adolescent sexuality', Unpublished manuscript.

Nava, M. and McRobbie, A. (eds) (1984), *Gender and Generation*, Macmillan, London.

Okeley, J. (1978), 'Privileged, schooled and finished: boarding education for girls' in Ardener, S. (ed.), 1978.

Parker, H. (1974), *View from the boys*, David and Charles, Newton Abbott.

Quinn, K. (1983), *Stand Your Ground*, Orbis, London.

Robins, D. and Cohen, P. (1978), *Knuckle Sandwich*, Penguin, Harmondsworth.

Shacklady-Smith, L. (1978), 'Sexist assumptions and female delinquency – an empirical investigation', in Smart, C. and Smart, B. (eds), *Women, Sexuality and Social Control*, Routledge & Kegan Paul, London.

Sheard, K. and Dunning, E. (1973), 'The Rugby Football Club', *International Review of Sport and Sociology*, Vol. 3–4, pp. 117–24.

Spender, D. (1982), *Invisible Women: The Schooling Scandal*, Writers and Readers Co-operative, London.

Spender, D. and Sarah, E. (1980), *Learning to Lose*, The Women's Press, London.

Stanworth, M. (1981), *Gender and Schooling*, Women's Research and Resources Centre, London.

Weiner, G. (1985), *Just a Bunch of Girls*, Open University Press, London.

Whylde, J. (ed.) (1983), *Sexism in the Secondary Curriculum*, Harper and Row, New York.

Willis, P. (1977), *Learning to Labour*, Saxon House, London.

Willis, P. (1978), *Profane Culture*, Routledge & Kegan Paul, London.

Willis, P. (1982), 'Women in Sport in Ideology', in Hargreaves, J. (ed.) 1982.

Young, I.M. (1980), 'Throwing like a girl: a phenomenology of feminine body comportment, mobility and spatiality', *Human Studies*, Vol. 3, 1980.

The exploitation of disadvantage: the occupational sub-culture of the boxer

John Sugden

Introduction

While there are more objective and accurate research techniques which can be employed to discover who lives in the poverty trap, there is little doubt that a survey of amateur and professional boxing is one of the quickest ways of discovering which groups are the poorest of the poor in the modern industrial world. As Michener (1976) has observed, reviewing the boxing results in the sports pages of the American press provides a reasonable parody of the succession of working-class, racial and ethnic minorities who have been involved in a century-long struggle to gain access to that country's melting pot: the fighting Irish giving way to the fighting German; the German to the Jew; the Jew to the Italian and the whole ladder to the fighting Afro-American (Weinberg and Arond, 1952). More recently, particularly at the lighter weights, the fighting black's dominance of the international arena has been seriously challenged by the rise of the fighting Hispanic. Woven within this shifting pecking order, for the most part just outside the boxing's contemporary hall of fame, is a healthy representation of white, lower working-class Americans and Europeans.

While the specifics of the nexus of economic, class, ethnic and racial links within amateur and professional boxing are exceedingly complex, it has been suggested that there is a tendency for them to overlap around the experiences of young males within structures of urban poverty (Hare, 1971). However, observing that there are long-standing relationships between urban poverty, youth culture and boxing does not, of itself, enable us to understand the nature of these relationships. From the back pages of the newspapers or from the television screen in the lounge, we are able to understand little in terms of the experiences, feelings and motivations of young men who live in the inner city, living through both poverty and boxing. We are not certain why and how male youth and urban poverty appear to have an unbroken bond with the prize ring. By and large, we have left interpretative explanations to the cliché-mongers of Hollywood: the 'hungry fighter', the ragged youth who walks off the city streets and into a boxing club with anger in his eyes, fire in his heart and dynamite in both fists and proceeds to bludgeon his way to a world title and its attendant riches.

As with most myths, there is a grain of truth which underpins this characterisation, but the full reality of why people get involved, and stay involved, in boxing is far more complex. Unlike the farm systems of many other professional sports, which tend to be embedded in the school system and a range of other visible and accountable institutions, the world of professional boxing is subterranean, located in pockets of urban poverty and largely unexposed to the public gaze. This paper is based on a study conducted in 1980–1981 which sought to penetrate the hidden world of the boxer, to reveal the sub-cultural context and patterns of interaction through which inner-city youngsters become professional fighters.

A note on method

The following is a summary of a larger study based upon a two-year-long investigation into the workings of an inner-city boxing club in the north east of the United States. Throughout history, alongside, but less visibly than recognised institutional avenues, sports have provided an ongoing and varied context for the construction of distinctive social networks and the inspiration for a rich cultural tradition. Because of the variegated nature of the sport-order (Loy et al., 1978) and the emphasis within sport on long term social interaction of one kind or another, the patterns of behaviour associated with sports are often characterised as 'sub-cultural' (Polsky, 1971; Hoyle, 1971; Yiannakis et al., 1977). Whilst it has been both theoretically and methodologically useful for the analysis of the social forms of sport, the concept of sub-culture, by being invoked and operationalised in different ways by diverse traditions in sociology, has also become a problematic one.

As a point of departure, I adopt and adapt a framework

emerging from work done by the Centre for Contemporary Cultural Studies at the University of Birmingham in the 1970s. This movement, characterised by Brake (1980) as a New Wave of sub-cultural research, takes the snap-shot ethnographic traditions of the Chicago School developed in the 1920s and 1930s (Wirth, 1928; Cressey, 1932; Sunderland, 1937), divests them of the functionalist emphasis added in the post-war period (Gordon, 1947), and relocates the concept of sub-culture in the context of critical theories of social structure and social relations (Hall and Jefferson, 1976). These theoretical developments provide a useful working model of the sub-cultural process.

A sub-culture is the social product of people who find themselves at a common point, and confronting common problems and opportunities, within a complex webbing of social structures and ideological representations. This commonality determines the boundaries within which a distinctive style of life is worked out. Once established, a sub-culture develops its own institutional practices and processes which become part of a framework for its longevity; sub-cultures have histories. In this way, while a sub-culture begins as a lived relation among various elements in social structure, it develops, over time, a distinctive vitality and a relative autonomy, which set it apart from more routine social formations and imbue it with a certain power to act back upon the overarching social order.

Methodologically, the appropriate approach for the study of sub-cultures is necessarily interpretative, and takes, as a point of departure and return, ordinary people as social actors doing their best to make life as meaningful as they can within the limitations and opportunities of the complex world which surrounds them. Set in a transcending social context, the principal research strategy of this study was participant observation, augmented by recorded interviews. The research process culminated in the reconstruction of the boxing sub-culture as an ideal type. The following is thus a relatively open-ended construct, subject to alteration or abandonment as the nature of the structure which it purports to represent changes, or new and more valid interpretations emerge.

Finally, in this study, for the most part, I have used the term sub-culture to refer to localised and bounded contexts of ongoing, face-to-face interaction and not to more general, less bounded, cultural sub-divisions, such as class cultures, youth cultures, or ethnic cultures.

John Sugden

The setting

Hidden in the shadows of the sky-scraping office blocks which dominate Insurance City's profile, there is a loosely connected ring of low-income housing estates, an area of ghetto-overspill, into which the poorest of the city's poor families have been drawn. Amongst them is the Burnt Oak housing project, a decaying, barrack-like settlement which typifies modern American urban poverty. Burnt Oak is a pocket of human subsistence, populated by blacks and hispanics and kept from the view of respectable middle America. Unemployment is high, with up to two-thirds of the adult population not involved in regular work. There are many single-parent families and the local economy tends to boom and slump with the cycle of welfare payments and food stamps. People with better jobs or better prospects simply do not come to, and certainly do not linger long in, the likes of Burnt Oak.

In the heart of the area stands an oblong block-house, somewhat larger than any of the warren of dwellings which surround it. This is the Burnt Oak Community Centre and, like its neighbouring buildings, it is heavily daubed with multi-coloured graffiti and in a poor state of repair. Most of the windows are either bricked or boarded up and the rest are screened with heavy, wire-mesh grills. Large sections of cement and plaster on the outer walls have crumbled away, leaving the building with a mottled and camouflaged appearance. This is not the place for community singing, amateur dramatics, bridge or other forms of family recreation and the city's housing development executive has given up trying to impose a formal timetable of rational community use.

In the daytime, when the heavy steel door which guards the entrance to the hall remains barred, local youngsters use the exterior of the building for a variety of improvised sporting activities. The broad and flat rear of the centre looks on to an open square, making an ideal backdrop for a variety of ball games. The meshed window grills, together with the drain pipes, make the north face of the building a tricky climb and the concrete canopy which overhangs the main door is an excellent highboard from which to execute acrobatic leaps into the tangle of shrubs and bushes below. If this becomes too exhausting, there are always the folk murals to add to and, as the daylight begins to fade, the sheltered doorway becomes a favourite gathering area for talking, horse play, listening to music and shouting comments to anyone who happens by.

In the early evening, a troubled caretaker pushes and curses his way through the crowded porch and unlocks the steel door. The inside of the community centre is little better than its exterior. With broken doors and window frames, flaking paintwork and crumbling plaster, the whole place is badly in need of renovation. A large hall, complete with stage and gallery, dominates the centre. Originally intended for public meetings and other forms of community entertainment, the seating has been removed to make way for the spontaneous local drama acted out in the chaotic game of basketball, which is the main event of each evening. There is no obvious structure to the game: no referees; no official teams; no formal scoring system; no out of bounds; no stoppages for fouls; and no time keeping. It appears to be every man for himself as players join and leave the game as they please and attack baskets at either end of the hall. A pass is rare and most of the time the ball is carried end to end through dazzling displays of dribbling, to arrive in or near the basket after an acrobatic lay-up or shot from an improbable angle and distance.

The atmosphere is thick and scented with a mix of cigarette smoke, reefer, alcohol and the more pungent odour of the poorly maintained washrooms. Around the edges of the game, on the stage and in the hallways, young men and women hang out, half watching the play, teasing and joking with each other and calling out to the players as they go hurtling by.

The conversations are necessarily loud, shouted above the pandemonium of the basketball game and competing with a confusion of rhythm, blasting out from the large portable tape recorders spread throughout the company. In a parallel social world, gangs of younger boys and girls dash in and out of the rubble-strewn rooms which open into the main hall, demonstrating their own spontaneous athleticism as they weave in and out of the basketball game, shrieking at one another and adding their own shrill commentary to the general discord.

The boxing club

Beneath the unrestrained youth culture surrounding the basketball game there is a more formally organised drama taking place. Each evening, in a basement room directly below the main hall, the members of the MBC (Memorial Boxing Club) gather to share in a different sort of ritual. Anybody wishing to enter the club has first, as we have seen, to thread a path through the throngs gathered in the entrance to the community centre, and turn across the crowded lobby before descending a short flight of stairs into the darkness below. At the foot of the stairs there is a reinforced wooden and steel door which is barred from within and it takes a sustained drumming to coincide with a lull in the activity taking place inside, before the bolts are drawn and the visitor is invited into a different world.

The club consists of a single, rectangular room, no larger than 30 feet by 35 feet. Immediately in front of the door, like a muted belfry, hang three large, worn, sail-cloth punch bags: heavy, heavier and heaviest. Flush to the near-side wall and sited ominously next to a set of scales, stands a small, electrically powered turkish bath. It is hard to imagine the need for such a device since the ceiling of the gymnasium is slung with the central heating pipes for the rooms above. Owing to a defective thermostat, they carry a volume of boiling water twenty-four hours a day, throughout the seasons, ensuring that the whole room heats up like one big sweat box. When it rains, a steady flow of sluggish grey water drains in from the streets above and gradually evaporates in the unnatural heat of the basement, exaggerating the sweated body heat of the boxers and making the atmosphere in the gym fetid and steamy.

One half of the club is dominated by an undersized boxing ring with loosely hanging ropes and a worn canvas, long since rendered threadbare by ten years of dancing feet and falling bodies. Surrounding the ring are a series of rough wooden benches; on these and on the hooks above are draped a mixture of sports gear, street clothes and the general bric-à-brac of the boxer's trade: gleaming red and black boxing gloves; high-waisted shorts; flashy robes; protective headgear and defensive equipment for the waistline and groin; a selection of mouth-guards; multicoloured boxing vests; jump ropes; hand wraps and several pairs of boxing boots. Every inch of wall space is covered with a colourful array of photographs, posters, magazine features and yellowing newsprint, blending to herald the past and present achievements of the club's own heroes and the feats of boxing's legendary champions.

The most important figure in the club, its manager and patron, J 'Mack' Murphy, leans on a broom in the centre of the gymnasium, taking a break from a vigorous spell of sweeping which has left the bottoms of his $350 business suit speckled with mud and dust. In opposite corners of the ring, two dark-skinned youths wearing gloves and protective headgear move slowly from tiptoe to tiptoe, loosening and flexing their muscles and gulping in precious draughts of the warm and clammy air. One or two others lean across the ropes to give advice, tie a loose glove, offer a drink and generally act as seconds. Throughout the rest of the room, skinny boys, athletically-developed teenagers and powerfully-built young men sit on the benches or rest against the walls, likewise breathing heavily in competition for the scarce oxygen.

Apart from the fidgeting of the youths in the ring, the scene is relaxed and sedentary until the red second hand of the large clock on the wall sweeps around to twelve and, in the baritone voice and brisk manner of a Boston bar tender, Mack bellows, 'Time!'. The gymnasium errupts into life. The boxers in the ring gingerly leave their respective corners to begin an ever-diminishing circular dance around the faded canvas. As they draw close, there is a sudden change of tempo and direction as one or other of them darts inside and both fighters momentarily become engulfed in a blur of jabs, hooks, crosses and upper-cuts, before breaking away to recommence orbiting soft-shoe. The sporadic slaps and thuds of leather against flesh and muscle blend into the steadier beat of more measured energy and aggression being unleashed outside of the ring: muffled combinations as they are hammered into the heavy bags; the metronome rhythm of jump-ropes slapping off the concrete floor and the jarring rat-tat-tat-tat of the speed bag. Meanwhile, several young fighters manage to exhaust themselves without equipment, boxing shadows or stabbing and snorting at their own image reflected in a full length mirror which dominates one wall. In the remaining space, other club members balance on mildewed matting and execute an exhausting series of callisthenics: sit-ups; push-ups; sit-ups; squat-thrusts; sit-ups; toe-touching and inevitably back to the stomach hardening sit-ups.

Even the manager takes some aggressive sweeps with his broom, guiding a dark trickle of dust mixed with the evening rain water towards a small drain in the middle of the floor. At the same time he provides his audience, real or imaginary, with a loud and abrasive running commentary, shouting advice and insults to the fighters in the ring and encouragement and abuse to the characters working throughout the gymnasium. The whole performance builds to a frenzied physical climax and deafening crescendo as the second hand sweeps towards twelve for the third time and, without looking up, Mack interrupts his own diatribe once more to call, 'Time', bringing the scene to a gasping halt.

The athletes in the ring, the young men boxing their own shadows, the powerful men hammering the heavy bags, the manager in the $350 business suit and the physical structure of the basement gymnasium are at the core of an occupational sub-culture: a social process which connects the impoverished streets of Burnt Oak and the leisure practices of its inhabitants at the MBC to the multi million dollar atmosphere of the sports entertainment industry and Madison Square Garden. The roots of this process and the bedrock of the sub-culture are to be found in the everyday practices of boys and young men growing up in and around the streets of Burnt Oak.

Street life

Play time

The story of the MBC begins in the maze of houses, apartments and streets which hem in the Burnt Oak Community Centre. It is here that the overwhelming majority of boxers who use the club live or originate and it is through their early experiences in this modern ghetto that most of the current members developed an appetite for boxing and were drawn into its sub-culture. Most of the club members first became actively involved with boxing during or before early adolescence, between the ages of ten and fourteen. Asked why they became involved, they provide no single, simple reason. There is a complex range of motivations, some complementary, others less so, which encouraged and continues to encourage their association with the sport.

From more searching enquiries, it became clear that the boxing sub-culture was grounded in the social relations which emerge as child's play becomes embroiled within the aggressive, male-dominated and brutally athletic youth culture of the housing project and the surrounding neighbourhood. To a greater or lesser extent, all sports can be thought of as relatively formal extensions of activities made up and encountered within play. Playing is something which children do naturally, as a facet of growing into an unknown physical and social environment. Through play, the child learns concepts of time, space, things, people and develops the social and physical skills to move among them. Amongst other things, children learn to run and jump, to catch and throw and to rough and tumble. They also begin to learn the appropriate social skills to accompany a nascent athleticism.

However, while the impulse to play might be a universal one, the style and product of the process of play vary according to the cultural surroundings within which the child grows up. Play begins within touching distance of the youngster, but gradually develops out of reach and, in many respects, out of control, to include the objects, people and sentiments which comprise an expanding social and physical environment. In this way, the child's urge to play is progressively harnessed to a pattern of social practice already established in the home and in the streets and school yards of the local community. Whereas in upper- and middle-class communities children are kept within the adult-patrolled sanctuary between home and school, often until they are teenagers, in a community such as Burnt Oak, at a relatively early age, children do their playing and socialising in and around the local streets. In terms of physical capacities, attitudes and motivations, it is at this point that the foundations of the boxing sub-culture are laid.

Messing around

Ask the young boys of Burnt Oak what they do when they are not at home or at school and they will tell you that they 'hang out' or 'mess around', doing nothing in particular. Watching them, eavesdropping on their conversations and consulting with adults who live in the neighbourhood confirms Corrigan's (1979) observations: that when unsupervised, working-class kids get together in and around the city streets to 'do nothing', they actually become involved in a wide range of energetic activities. Messing around in Burnt Oak includes a range of standard and improvised sports and games, commando-style assaults up the walls and across the roof-tops of local buildings, break-neck gang chases and skirmishes around the project, individual and gang-fighting, disruptive forays into the city's main shopping area, and a variety of petty illegal and anti-social activities which often result in real games of cops and robbers with the local police.

The kids of Burnt Oak do not need to attend gym classes or go to summer sports camps to develop the athletic ability and temperament suited to boxing. Many of the delinquent activities of inner-city juveniles are aggressively athletic and contain an element of risk. As has been argued elsewhere (Sugden and

Yiannakis, 1982), while anti-social, within the context of urban deprivation, such activities can also be thought of as local improvisations, inspired by a more generally displayed youthful need for mastery, competence, challenge and adventure. This is the core of messing about for the youngsters of the project and through a prolonged involvement in the local street scene, they grow to be physically assertive, to be quick on their feet and they learn to have fast hands: attributes of some importance in an environment within which youngsters learn at a tender age that the weakest go to the wall.

Fighting

Amongst the retinue of activities involved in messing around is an established pattern of street fighting. Much of this begins as semiplayful, rough and tumble, but as kids get older it develops into more serious and exacting trials of strength and courage. There is nothing exceptional about this. It has been observed that at a certain stage in their social development, boys everywhere seem to settle disputes and build reputations around competitive demonstrations of physical prowess (Tiger, 1971). Veblen (1953) referred to this feature of boyhood as 'the predacious interval', a passing phase of growing up which occurs between the protective custody of the home and the regulative institutions of adulthood, wherein less abrasive and more socially acceptable strategies for settling disputes and earning status are made available. While a potential for fighting has been observed to be a common amongst all boys, as Lefkowitz et al. (1977) argue, whether or not they do fight and how long the predacious interval lasts, is culturally, rather than biologically, determined.

In the ghetto, where boys spend a considerable amount of time hanging around the streets, social conditions ensure that the 'predacious interval' begins early and lasts long, until the early teens, when patterns of individual fighting begin to merge with a more sinister, and potentially more deadly, network of gang affiliations. This atmosphere of 'might is right' guides certain individuals to the boxing club, but not all for the same reasons. As would be expected, some youngsters get involved because they are good at fighting and have a proven record of 'good hands'. For them the boxing club is viewed as a place where they can extend skills and reputations already established in the streets and spotlight otherwise deviant skills for more formal approval.

For others who lack weight, strength or natural fighting ability, the MBC is viewed as a place where they can learn to take care of themselves. Burnt Oak affords rough justice to those who cannot or will not fight. The pecking order of the streets is generally indifferent to relative factors of size, weight, skill or experience and the toughest kid on the block is generally the biggest kid on the block. The boxing club turns out to be a good bet for adolescents who have learned the importance of being physically assertive, but invariably lose out in a meritocracy where brute strength counts for everything. In the first place, regular work-outs at the gym improve their overall chances of survival, if not victory, should they be caught up in a brawl at school or in the streets. Secondly, and of greater significance in the long term, these youths find that within the boxing sub-culture they are given the chance to earn respect, using the aggressive currency of the streets, but within a neutral structure which, as much as possible, equalises inherited physical differences and takes account of different levels of skill and experience.

Even some of the hardest cases in the neighbourhood are attracted by the MBC's neutrality. Burnt Oak is notorious for its youth gangs and their violent conflicts. Boys who live in the estate are expected to show allegiance to one or other of these local street gangs by taking a colour of affiliation and participating in confrontations with rival organisations. As they grow older, the stakes are raised and their chances of getting seriously hurt increase as fist-fights give way to skirmishes with knives and, occasionally, guns. Those wishing to opt out of this potentially deadly factionalism face a major problem insomuch as the activities of the gangs are focal to the process through which young men are supposed to display their masculinity and earn respect in the local, male-dominated youth scene. The MBC offers a solution to this dilemma by concentrating on aggressive skills which are broadly similar to the cut and thrust of adolescent street life, but practising them in a controlled and relatively safe environment. Moreover, because boxing is a sport having a traditional following in the inner city, particularly amongst blacks and Hispanics, the prestige which youths can earn within the boxing sub-culture tends to travel with them outside of the club. Carried outside on the backs of jackets and on the sides of kit bags, the symbols of the boxing club act as a neutral colour and give the carrier a kind of informal immunity, while at the same time enabling him to hold

John Sugden

his head high. Learning how to fight in the streets, and developing strategies of avoiding fighting in the streets, emerge as powerful complementary motivations for embracing the boxing sub-culture.

Being tough

While learning how to cope physically with a cycle of confrontation and challenge, the young men of Burnt Oak pick up a streetwise repertoire of attitudes and sentiments: a stoic, male code of honour and courage: a simmering 'machismo', requiring cool-headedness and resilience in the face of danger. These values, activated by a streak of machiavellian opportunism, invest social encounters with an atmosphere of ruthless self preservation and a sense of timing whereby 'to get in first' becomes the rule of thumb. As one fighter remarked, in order to get through the day in the ghetto, a youth has to be 'tough-tough', that is to be cool and calculating and able to stand up for himself. When translated into the ring, toughness and coolness blend to provide the foundations of 'a fighting heart', a quality much valued in a business built around the spectacle of giving and taking punishment.

The sports creed

The push of inner-city youth culture in the development of a boxing sub-culture is augmented by the sport's traditional affinity with the urban poor. As Edwards (1981) argues, sport in general takes on an enlarged significance in the ghetto. An overarching ideology, or sports creed, penetrates areas like Burnt Oak, stressing the all-American virtues of sport and its capacity to serve as an escalator to wealth and status for those who are effectively barred from other avenues of social mobility. Because only a tiny minority of the multitudes who try can ever make a decent living from professional sport, Edwards views this promise as false and damaging to the general development of black communities in America. This view is endorsed by Brown (1978) who views the massive commitment to sport by minorities as an indication of oppression and a buttress to racism, rather than a sign of integration or equality.

From the perspective of a young man growing up in a pocket of urban poverty such as Burnt Oak, the image of the black or

198

Hispanic professional sport super-star is undoubtedly a powerful one. Other careers and educational opportunities tend not to be available. Even if they were, in a largely unsupervised adolescent world, given a choice between training to be a professional athlete or preparing for a career in the law or teaching, the vast majority of teenagers would opt for sport. Also, because the farm system of professional boxing is not tied up with survival in the education system, unlike American football, basketball and, to a certain extent, baseball, it is held in special regard by the children of the inner cities who traditionally underachieve at school.

The stable

It would be mistaken to conclude from the evidence presented so far that all inner-city areas like Burnt Oak spontaneously produce professional boxers. Not all pockets of urban poverty produce and sustain boxing sub-cultures. They provide the raw materials, measured in terms of muscle and blood but, by themselves, the urban poor do not have the resources to organise and finance the farm system for the production of professional fighters. This is generally done from the outside, by people who, at least in part, view the deprivations of the people of the ghetto and their special relationship to sport as an opportunity for developing and marketing athletic talent. The MBC is no exception and, as a material and ideological presence, it is not an initiative of the residents of Burnt Oak.

The manager

The club was established by Mack, who continues to be its leading patron and general manager. He is a successful criminal lawyer, with expensive offices in the heart of Insurance City. While he likes to refer to his humble, Irish-emigré heritage, Mack is third generation and from solidly upper middle-class stock. His motives for being involved in boxing revolve around two sets of values, which seem to be ethically incompatible, but which have been operationally welded together to form the guiding philosophy of the club: missionary amateurism and commercial professionalism.

In the first instance, his exposure in the home and at school to middle-class values on sport, in concert with his own experiences as a boxer as a young man, have instilled in Mack a firm belief in the character-building qualities of the ring. This has been reinforced through an ongoing involvement with law enforcement, wherein he is professionally associated with some of the more serious social problems arising out of urban decay. Sport is traditionally valued by a variety of public agencies as a deterrent to juvenile crime and as a vehicle for the rehabilitation of young offenders. Mack supports this view and is an active member of the PAL (Police Athletic League), an organisation dedicated to the provision of sport for kids in the inner city. Several of Mack's best young fighters have been in trouble with the law and a few were actually recruited by him as they passed through the City's criminal justice system.

While the PAL provided some of the equipment which helped Mack set up the MBC, most of the moral and financial support for the club has been his own. Mack suggests that he selected Burnt Oak as the site for his club because of its poverty and high rates of juvenile crime. He claims that the MBC tempts at-risk youngsters away from the trouble-filled streets, keeps them on the straight and narrow and, for a gifted few, offers them opportunity for fame and fortune.

Despite the caring rhetoric, it is this last aspect, the production of professional fighters, which in practice, emerges as the most powerful driving force behind the MBC. Mack might well have had a certain amount of concern for the youth of Insurance City's urban poor when he went prospecting for a home for his boxing club. But when he settled on Burnt Oak, there can be little doubt that he was mostly influenced by its potential in terms of yielding street-hardened recruits for training for the prize ring. The MBC is an amateur club, but at the same time and in the same space it is a professional stable. The vast majority of the forty or more youngsters who come regularly to the gym understand it not as a temple of Muscular Christianity, but as a meeting place, where they can get a good work-out, exchange information about the local street scene, box a little, improve their standing in the neighbourhood and rub shoulders with the professional fighters in whose footsteps they may tread. While this might be a slowly dawning aspiration for most of the new members, as they take their first steps through the doors of the basement, whether they realise it or not, Mack views each and every one of them as a potential professional.

Occupational training

Indeed, while all of the newcomers to the club are aware of its professional dimension, initially at least, most of them are more concerned with non-occupational issues such as having a good time, staying in shape, winning junior and amateur titles and travelling to tournaments. One of the more significant features of the boxing sub-culture is the way in which the young fighters' original, avocational definitions of the situation are gradually and subtly remodelled around commercial objectives which are clearly professional. This is achieved through the structure of the club in tandem with the instrumental interventions of the manager who guides the boxers through three levels of participation: junior; amateur; and professional.

The juniors

The most numerous attenders are the juniors, the bottom tier and foundation of the pyramid-like boxing sub-culture. The youngest age at which a person can be officially registered as a boxer is twelve years. In practice, however, nobody checks birth certificates and, so long as a boy looks big enough and tough enough to handle himself in the ring, he is allowed into the gym to train. Thus, the age range of the juniors who frequent the MBC is somewhere between ten and sixteen, the point at which a boxer must either become an amateur or give up the sport. To begin with, for most of the juniors, their commitment to boxing is open-ended and a matter of individual choice, coming and going as they please and putting in as much or as little effort as they see fit. This intermittent pattern of participation is a trial period during which time the youngsters test their own ideas, aspirations and capacities against the established procedures of the club.

Once inside the gym, they become involved in a straightforward pattern of training, which all of the fighters share. It begins with a period of warm-ups involving stretching exercises, callisthenics and light work-outs with jump ropes and the heavy-bags. The warm-up period is followed by sessions of gloved sparring in the ring. Once the sparring is over, the boxers commence a second, but more intense circuit of training outside of the ring. The whole sequence of warm-ups, sparring and circuit training is paced at three-minute intervals, with a minute rest in between, emulating the rhythm of rounds and breaks of a professional boxing match.

While each cohort of fighters experience the same pattern of training, more or less, at the same time and in the same space, the quality of the experience is different. For the juniors, the routine is not very vigorous. They do not have to spend much time getting fit for the ring, but tend to rely on the natural fitness of youth to carry them through. A junior boxing match is fast and furious, but it is also very short and while there are many punches thrown, most tend not to have the weight to do much damage or sap much strength. The juniors spend most of their time in the club acquiring the boxer's style: learning how to look, feel, think and sound like a boxer. They receive little formal tuition from the manager and, for the most part, the youngsters learn to be boxers by playing at being boxers. They hang around the gym, taking in the performances of the older fighters and doing their best to copy them. Any coaching they do receive tends to come informally from their more established peers or from older fighters. Sometimes, one or other of the club's professionals may take time out of his own schedule to correct a stance or offer a word of advice to a newcomer.

This is an important and unique feature of the boxing sub-culture. All professional sports have some kind of farm system, formal or otherwise, through which athletes of professional potential are recruited, trained, tested and from which an elite is selected for the sports entertainment industry. In most cases, such a farm system is structured in such a way that the stages of occupational socialisation are contained within relatively independent organisations. For instance, the stages of the farm systems of American football and basketball are contained within the structure of interscholastic and intercollegiate sports as well as training programmes built beneath the professional leagues.

In the MBC, junior boxers learn their trade alongside and under the same roof as their amateur and professional mentors. Boys of twelve and younger come to the gym and find themselves involved, shoulder to thigh, in an unbroken pattern of training with boxers of local, national and international repute. They undress alongside one another on the same rough wooden benches, share the same clothes hooks, use the same equipment, drink out of the same water bottles and dance to the tune of the same manager. There can be little doubt, that learning the role of the boxer while actually performing and training under the gaze of experienced amateurs and professionals, is a most powerful mechanism of anticipatory socialisation.

Mack simply fine tunes this process. He provides the facilities and the incentives, recruits the performers and, from a distance, stage manages the interactions among them. He observes the youngsters as they spar and monitors their progress in local tournaments, such as the Junior Olympics and the Silver Mittens, events which themselves appear as microcosms of the big time. The diffusion of attitudes and motivations which occurs through the role playing which accompanies this pattern of competition, in concert with the status given to winners within the sub-culture and in the immediate community, ensures that when the most gifted juniors reach the age of sixteen, the vast majority of them accept the invitation of Mack, the gatekeeper, and register as amateurs.

The amateurs

From the short-term perspectives of the fighters, amateur boxing is taken seriously and can be considered as a sport in its own right. But, as a critical feature of the sub-culture, in the long run, this level of performance provides the dynamic link between the fun-filled, itinerant and piecemeal pattern of junior boxing and the no-nonsense occupational world of the professional fighter. Unlike the juniors who become involved in a reasonably homogeneous pattern of participation, the social organisation of amateur boxing is itself informally broken down around three integrated categories of ability and expectation negotiated between the boxers and their manager.

First, in keeping with the ethic of moral and social development, which is the official rationale of the club, there is a small group of boxers who, in terms of their own motivations and ambitions and in terms of the managers view of them, are pure amateurs. They maintain an involvement in the sport for a range of mostly recreational reasons, including health and fitness, friendship and 'having something to do' with their spare time. Through their amateurish approach to training and performance and general lack of ability, they exclude themselves from consideration as pro-fessionals and are happy to stay on the periphery of the main activities of the club.

Second, the rest of the amateurs, the overwhelming majority, start out as potential professionals by subscribing to a structure of training and competition which, if they are good enough, will, in time, edge them towards a career in the ring. A few will begin as amateurs with clear aspirations to become professionals, but most carry forward an ill-defined interest, picked up as juniors and balanced against the increasing demands and challenges of adolescence as it is experienced in and around the streets of Burnt Oak. Not all of this second category of apprentices make the grade. Whether they do or not is a feature of their physical abilities, personal motivations and ambitions as they are worked out within the more demanding routines of the sub-culture. A minority opt out of their own accord, some are forced out by changes in their personal circumstances, many others are 'cut' by the manager or informally 'cooled out' by their peers and a small number are encouraged steadily to increase their commitment to become professional understudies.

From the manager's perspective, the main purpose of supporting amateur boxing is the development of this third, elite cohort of professional understudies. These are the fighters who have a proven physical capacity to become professionals and who, through their participation within the sub-culture, have adopted this role as a central feature of their identities. Mack expects more of this group. He pushes them harder in training than the other amateurs and pays more attention to points of style and technique. In the mean time, he ensures that his professional understudies maintain a serious challenge in the national network of amateur boxing championships, such as the Golden Gloves. These operate as clearing houses for talent in much the same way as the junior tournaments, but on a grander scale. Fighters can build up an impressive record through these competitions which stands them in good stead when they turn professional. If a fighter gets to a national final, win or lose, such an encounter provides him with valuable experience of the nature of the competition to come, while at the same time giving Mack the opportunity to assess an understudy's performance under professional-like conditions.

Also, the manager consistently involves the understudies in the pre-fight training itinerary of the club's existing professionals: uses them as sparring partners in the basement gym; takes them to his country farm as part of the team for the final preparations; takes them on the road to the big professional 'shows'; puts them up in hotels; and uses them at ring-side as seconds when the fights are in progress. Occasionally, he will pack one or other of them off to a different stable in another city, on loan to do some sparring with other professionals. Generally, Mack keeps this small amateur elite as close to the professional experience as possible. In this way, they are able clearly to anticipate the role of professional and get a carefully edited preview of some of its rewards. By engineering it so that the professional and amateur circuits merge around certain individuals, Mack helps to create an environment within which the transition between amateur and professional boxing seems as natural and as reasonable as the movement from the juniors to the amateurs.

The professionals

The world of professional boxing is the most critical dimension of the boxing sub-culture, being both its product and its progenitor. Within the MBC there are two relatively simple criteria which qualify a person for entry into the professionals. To begin with, a boxer must have demonstrated through his record as an amateur that he has the dedication and the blend of skills and attitudes to enable him to survive and perhaps thrive in the prize ring. Unless there is a chance of selection for the Olympic team, the most visible showcase of preprofessional achievement, amateur boxers with exceptional talent are generally encouraged to turn professional at eighteen as soon as they are old enough. For the remaining pool of apprentices, however, having established their pedigree, they must wait for a space to become available on the local professional circuit before they are offered a contract.

It is not in the long-term interests of a boxing manager to graduate too many professionals if there is not enough work around in the local boxing scene. If they are not getting enough fights they may lose their edge, lose interest or be forced to seek other ways of making money, ending up weakening the calibre of local boxing and depressing demand even further. Mack, and stable managers like him, are the gatekeepers in this network of recruitment. Amongst the eager amateurs who operate out of his gym, Mack decides who turns professional and when. It is also through his agency that boxers are assigned to one of a number of informal status groups shortly after embarking on their professional careers.

In the MBC, all of the fighters who turn professional believe they have a chance of 'going all the way' and making the big time. However, as their careers progress and their potential, or lack of it, is realised, they find themselves allocated to one of four categories. First, there are the local boys: fighters who rapidly reach a ceiling in their progress, but show sufficient ability and 'heart', measured in terms of staying power and aggression, to please the crowds in a network of small-time promotions, or on the under-card of a more prestigious event. Most of these fighters retire after a few years in the lower reaches of the sport, but a few box on until they lose what edge they had and finish up being knocked to the bottom of the professional boxing heap to join the flotsam and jetsam of the boxing sub-culture in the 'meat market': has-beens, stumble-bums and never has-beens who have been plucked straight off the street or hurried through inglorious amateur careers, all for a handful of cash, to make up the time and numbers at the wrong end of a fight card in some small-time promotion. To end up in the meat market is the professional boxer's dread. While Mack does not encourage his fighters to continue their careers after they have experienced a string of defeats, he constantly invokes the image of the meat trade as a means of inspiring extra effort from those more successful boxers who are showing signs of slacking.

Thirdly, there is a small group of likely-lads, fighters who have had their 'shot', or who are in the process of having it, and, to a greater or lesser degree, are maintaining a level of performance in the mainstream of professional boxing: the structure of events which leads directly into the national and international rankings and ultimately, for those who continue to be successful, to the role of contender. Most of these fighters graduate directly from the elite group of amateur understudies and continue to receive special attention from the manager who carefully monitors their progress in training and matches and moves them gingerly through an introductory series of professional contests. The aim is to accumulate a respectable tally of wins against losses in the local scene. This gives Mack the currency to bid for the matches he wants outside of the State and enables him to gradually move his best professionals towards the threshold of an international ranking. If he achieves this, and produces a contender, purses counted in hundreds of dollars are rapidly displaced by those measured in tens and hundreds of thousands of dollars.

While the research for this study was in progress, there was one fighter who broke away from the pack of professionals to become a world-ranked contender in the welter-weight division. The short term pay-offs of becoming a contender are made obvious to a fighter by the size of his next purse, however, it is the long-term and indirect pay-offs which are even more significant. To begin with, he gets automatic national and international exposure through the media. If he wins, his reputation is boosted globally, enabling him to be moved closer to a shot at the world title and its attendant glories and riches. The better his record against fellow contenders, the higher he is ranked and the more power his manager has in terms of arranging his next contests: whom they are against; where and when they are fought; and the size and relative share of the prize money. In this manner, the further he goes, the further he is likely to go and, even if he does not 'go all the way', if he is carefully matched, he can linger long enough in the top rankings to make for a relatively comfortable retirement.

The production of a contender is also a major milestone for the home club. There is a band-wagon effect which travels in the wake of a contender's success and changes the status and practices of the club within which he learned his trade. The spotlight shining on a contender illuminates the other up-and-coming professionals, increasing the demand for their services and indirectly improving their chances of making a go of it themselves in the mainstream. Secondly, his success will increase the number and range of opportunities for all the local professionals by attracting bigger promotions to the region. This gives Mack the space to allow more of his pool of professional apprentices to pass through the gate into the local professional circuit. Also, having a contender in and around the gym electrifies the atmosphere and inspires the younger members of the club. At the same time, it improves the club's standing in the neighbourhood and swells the crowds of youngsters begging admittance at the doorway. All of which, alongside his share of the profits, serves to improve the good will of Mack's business.

In this way, the long-term stability and development of the boxing sub-culture is both conditioned by its roots in the ghetto and guided by the achievements of its elite professionals. Through the husbandry of the manager, the club is set up to produce world-class fighters. The various stages of the sub-culture are essential experiences in the passage of a contender and once he makes the big time, it is that sub-culture which, more than anything else, keeps his consciousness anchored in the streets of Burnt Oak, sharpens his edge and fuels an appetite for the ring. In return, as his career progresses, so too does the fame and fortune of the stable within which he learns and refines his trade.

Thus, the determining is likewise determined as the formative layers of experience which produce professional boxing are themselves contained within, and changed by, structures generated by the specific needs of the professional circuit. The essentially exploitative nature of this process is disguised by the rhetoric of amateurism and the gradual manner through which fighters are encouraged to grow into the occupational role of the boxer. The has-been professional fighter is the ultimate expression of this deception: a person who has developed a self-concept and an accompanying repertoire of skills, attitudes and desires which are unsuitable for any other trade apart from the one which he can no longer safely play.

Conclusion

The centre stage of the basement gym is a boxing ring. The ring is in fact square and this is symbolic of the paradox around which the boxing sub-culture is constructed. The main, but largely unspoken, objectives of the club revolve around the production and training of professional fighters. For the most part, this is achieved through a framework of junior and amateur boxing. The exploitation of disadvantage which takes place is made to appear laudable by locating the boxing club within a pocket of urban poverty: a declared ideology of moral and social development legitimates the club's targeting on the male youth of the urban poor, offering itself as a deterrent against juvenile delinquency and a series of related social ills. However, the states of mind and physical skills displayed by male youth in Burnt Oak, which the boxing club purports to deter, are precisely those attributes required by the professional boxing stable as its raw material. In this way, Mack, the manager, is in the same position as the preacher who is dependent upon the devil for the size of his congregation.

Once involved in the club, recruits share a process through which their streetwise qualities are honed and controlled in the service of professional boxing. Their volatile aggression and physical assertiveness, their courage and pride, their 'tough-toughness' are given new rhythms and disciplined around the timing of the professional ring. Their identities gradually become centred on the role of boxer and, as they mature through adolescence and become aware of a world beyond Burnt Oak, it is the light of the professional ring which is construed to offer them hope in the shadow of urban poverty.

Thus, through the intervention of Mack into the social life of

Burnt Oak, the circle is squared. Through his agency, self improvement and character development are tied to an individual's progress through the various hurdles of a boxer's career. Going all the way to the top is appraised as a sign of moral transubstantiation, as well as commercial and occupational success. For a few, at least for a while, the squaring of the circle offers a genuine chance for self-fulfilment. But, to make one contender it takes the exploitation of many others who will not succeed. The boxing sub-culture takes them as boys off the streets and shows them a glimpse of the big time: a vision which can only reinforce a sense of failure when they find themselves without their gloves, without an education and without jobs, back amidst the poverty of Burnt Oak.

References

Brake, M. (1980), *The Sociology of Youth and Youth Subcultures*, London, Routledge & Kegan Paul.

Brown, R. (1978), '"The Jock Trap": How the black athlete gets caught', in Straub, W. (ed.), *Sport Psychology*, Ithaca Movement, pp. 171–84.

Corrigan, P. (1979), *Schooling the Smash Street Kids*, London, Macmillan.

Cressey, P. (1932), *The Taxi Dance Hall*, New York, Greenwood.

Edwards, H. (1981), *The Sociology of Sport*, Homewood, Illinois, Dorsey Press.

Gordon, M. (1947), 'The concept of subculture and its application', *Social Forces*, 6, 26 (Oct): 40–2.

Hall, S. and Jefferson, T. (eds) (1976), *Resistance Through Rituals*, London, Hutchinson.

Hare, N. (1971), 'A study of the black fighter', *The Black Scholar*, November: 2–9.

Hoyle, E. (1971), 'Organisation theory and the sociology of sport', in R. Albonico and K. Pfister-Binz (eds), *Sociology of Sport*, Switzerland, Bickhauser Verlag Basel: 82–93.

Lefkowitz, M., Eron, L., Walder, L. and Huesmann, L. (1977), *Growing Up to be Violent*, New York, Pergamon.

Loy, J., McPherson, B. and Kenyon, G. (1978), *Sport and Social Systems*, London, Addison-Wesley.

Michener, J. (1976), *On Sport*, London, Secker and Warburg.

Polsky, N. (1971), *Hustlers, Beats and Others*, Harmondsworth, Penguin.

Sugden, J. and Yiannakis, A. (1982), 'Sport and juvenile delinquency: a theoretical base', *Journal of Sport and Social Issues*, 6, 1:22–7.

Sunderland, E. (1937), *The Professional Thief*, Chicago, University of Chicago Press.

Tiger, L. (1971), *Men in Groups*, London, Longman.

Veblen, T. (1953), *The Theory of the Leisure Class*, New York, Mentor.

Weinberg, S. and Arond, H. (1952), 'The occupational culture of the boxer', *American Journal of Sociology*, March, 57: 460–9.

Wirth, L. (1928), *The Ghetto*, Chicago, University of Chicago Press.

Yiannakis, A. (1977), 'Sports groups as subcultures: a conceptual analysis', unpublished paper, University of Connecticut.

The politics of women's leisure*

Rosemary Deem

Leisure is an aspect of women's lives which has been greatly neglected, not only by male leisure studies researchers, but also and more surprisingly, by feminists too. The latter neglect has only been partly because leisure is considered by many feminists to be a male concept, developed in relation to analyses of the working class and their non-work time, and with a history closely tied to the hours worked by men in paid employment (Chambers, 1985). Additionally feminist writers have been centrally preoccupied with analysing the structures and ideological forces shaping women's oppression rather than with considering some of the less overt consequences of that oppression. As anyone who has ever tried to research women's leisure will confirm, what is most obvious is the apparent absence of leisure as a significant force in the lives of many women. Hence the political significance of examining both what leisure women have and why they have so little has escaped attention. It is the intention of this article to go some way towards remedying this omission by considering the political importance of women's leisure (including its absence) and by exploring the social, political and economic factors which underlie the politics of that leisure.

In tracing the history of feminist theory in the contemporary period, Eisenstein (1984) points to the political nature of that theory and its roots in not only liberal theory of the seventeenth and eighteenth centuries, but also in the traditions of socialist and utopian theory of the nineteenth century and in the nineteenth- and early twentieth-century exploration of the social context of sexuality. Feminism and feminist theory are not just abstract analyses of the subordination of women by men, but contain a political commitment to changing women's position in the world

* Originally presented at the Leisure Studies Association International Conference, 'Politics, planning and people' University of Sussex, 4–8 July 1984.

(Gordon, 1979). There are, of course, several different varieties of feminist theory, ranging from the liberal 'improve women's rights' through socialist feminism, which sees the source of women's oppression lying in both capitalism and male patriarchal relationships of power and control over women, to radical feminism, which sees male power as the major cause of women's inferior position in society. But all feminist theory concerns itself with change, with what Eisenstein calls

> an element of visionary, futurist thought. This encompasses a concept of social transformation that, as part of the eventual liberation of women, will change all human relationships for the better. Although centrally about women . . . feminism is . . . also fundamentally about men and about social change. (Eisenstein, 1984, p.xiv)

The study of women's leisure makes a contribution not only to feminist theory and our knowledge about the situation of women, but also towards a programme of social change. Accordingly, the final section of the paper deals with suggestions for the reform of social life, so that leisure becomes something available to women as well as men.

The exploration of women's leisure brings into play almost all the issues, debates and concerns raised by contemporary feminist analysis, because like housework, for example, leisure, although analytically separable, is part of women's lives as a whole. The forms which it takes in women's lives and the reasons for its lack of prominence in many of those lives can be related to women's responsibility for domestic work and childcare; their relationship to men at an individual and collective level; their paid employment; the extent to which men control women's sexuality; the low physical power possessed by women; the state's policies (centrally and locally) on women and a whole range of welfare and other services; and the provision that capitalist societies (especially in the form of commercial producers and providers of services) make for consumption of leisure and enjoyment. The consideration of women's leisure emphasises the importance of the women's movement slogan 'the personal is the political' (Coote and Campbell, 1982) by showing that there are individual as well as structural and ideological influences on what, where and how women experience leisure. Furthermore, the myth that women belong mainly in the private sphere of the home rather than in the public sphere, which is exploded by Siltanen and Stanworth (1984), is further debunked by the revelations both about the centrality of the 'community' to women's leisure and by the realisation that the public and private domains of women's leisure are closely linked. What follows is some attempt to document both the constraints on and the nature of women's leisure, an area which is beginning to attract increasing attention from all quarters (Sport and Leisure, 1985).

Men and the politics of women's leisure

As Tomlinson (1983) has pointed out, leisure is not just facilities or institutions but is an integral part of social relations, and women's leisure is no exception. Virtually all the national surveys of leisure done in Britain suggest that women's leisure experiences are less varied and less numerous in their extent than men's, but do not tell us why (Talbot, 1979). We must remember that women are not, in any case, a homogeneous category; although gender divisions ensure points of commonality, there are women whose leisure patterns are similar to male ones. There are also, as Green, Hebron and Woodward (1985a) found in their study of over seven hundred women in Sheffield, a few who have too much leisure. Age, employment and partner's job, social class, marital status, life-cycle stage, ethnicity, disability are all factors which can crucially affect women's leisure (Deem, 1986).

Nevertheless, despite the differences between women, the dominance of men over women in British society, at every level from individual households to government and the media, means that there are also common factors and constraints affecting the leisure of all women. These include the real as well as perceived risks of rape, violence and sexual harassment in both public places and in the home; the virtual exclusion of women from some public places (private clubs are exempt from the requirements of the 1975 Sex Discrimination Act) and the profound intolerance of them in others, whether pubs or city streets at night; the continued assumptions made by men about whose responsibility it is to carry out domestic work and child-care (it is usually only done by men in dire emergencies or it is seen as *help* to be given out of the goodness of a man's heart, not out of duty). Of course well-off women can evade some of these constraints – for example, it is easier to go out at night, or in the daytime, to distant places for leisure if you have a car, than it is if you have to use and pay for public transport, which may involve a long walk to and wait at a lonely bus stop or railway station (Deem 1982a and 1982b, 1986). But few women feel really relaxed about going out alone in urban areas, especially at night and sometimes not in the day time either.

The Sheffield study (Green, Hebron and Woodward, 1985b) found that sports and health clubs were the only public leisure venues where unaccompanied women of all social classes felt safe from sexual harassment by men, and a study of Armley in Leeds by Dixey and Talbot (1982) noted that bingo was popular because it offered a friendly women-dominated atmosphere and was also an acceptable place for husbands to allow their wives to visit. Thus men both make public places 'unsafe' for women by 'policing' them and exercise control over which places it is 'appropriate' for women to be allowed to go to. Green, Hebron and Woodward (1986) found that places involving the consumption of alcohol or those where 'other' men might be met, were considered particularly problematic by the husbands and partners of the women in their study.

Although few married women have financial independence, middle-class women with an independent income may have husbands who 'help' them, or be able to pay others to do their housework or look after their children. Single women too, may be more socially accepted into 'male' social spaces, and need only do their own housework if they live alone (as Delphy, 1984, notes, it is really only housework if it is done for others). But only a few employed women (married or not) have genuinely equal pay with men and so most are financially dependent on men. Hence those who become divorced may find life as a female single parent hard, although as Wimbush (1985) has shown, it has the advantage of giving a woman control over her own social life again. But in any case, marriage and male social control over women by men affect all women, regardless of whether or not they as individuals live with a man or not. So, for example, our taxation and social security systems assume that women are the dependents of men, unless they are single and live alone; a married woman may, if she is unusually well paid elect to be taxed separately from her husband so far as job earnings are concerned – but her investment income remains regarded as the property of her husband. Only a male-dominated society allows such injustices to continue, and they are a symbol of the constraints that men have placed on the autonomy of women's lives and leisure.

But there is also another and crucial sense in which men affect women's leisure, and this is in regard to their own enjoyment of leisure. As Burns (1973) has pointed out, the male working class in Britain has fought since the onset of the Industrial Revolution to preserve time free from paid employment for the purposes of leisure and recreation. But it has been quite happy for women to continue to work in the home to make that leisure possible. Men believe they have an entitlement to leisure; neither I nor other researchers have found more than a handful of women who believe that they have a similar entitlement. As Clarke and Critcher (1985) argue, 'the family embraces a sexual division of labour if anything more exaggerated than that which prevails outside it' (p. 165) and it is this division of labour which contains within it the belief that leisure is a male privilege. Even unemployed men do not necessarily turn to domestic labour and childcare when forced to stay at home, and despite the constraints which unemployment itself places on leisure, unemployed men engage in more leisure and less unpaid work than do unemployed women (Deem, 1984; Campbell, 1984; McKee and Bell, 1984).

Of course not all leisure, male or female, takes place in gender-segregated ways. Mixed leisure is a familiar part of the social scene in Britain, often involving couples. But the fact that it is mixed does not make it an equal experience for both sexes. As Griffin (1981) has shown in her studies of adolescent girls, not only does the leisure of this age group revolve around preparing for, meeting and going out with men, but it does so in a context where all the dice are loaded on the male side; it is men whose wages are high enough not to make marriage an economic necessity, men who make the major decisions about which women they will go out with, live with and marry; men who apply the double standard of having sex with women they then regard as 'slags' or other terms of sexual abuse (Willis, 1977). Mixed leisure often involves elements of sexual relations and is conducted on a basis of male superiority as well as an assumption of heterosexuality. Many of the places where mixed leisure take place are precisely those locations where women alone feel vulnerable and where men are reluctant to allow 'their' women to go (Green, Hebron and Woodward, 1986), yet unaccompanied males or groups of men find those places no problem.

Men have much to lose if women are to gain their leisure entitlement; the household equivalent of demands for a thirty-five hour working week would find a lot of pubs empty, football pitches devoid of players and political meetings even less well-attended than usual. It is not men alone who are responsible for constraining women's leisure; capitalist societies, employers and governments have a large part to play too. But, of course, men operate at all these levels too, for example, in policy-making and in refusing to cook or clean their houses. Until men recognise that the quality of their lives is made possible by the reduced quality of life most women experience, then this aspect of the politics of leisure will change little.

Children: pleasure and work

For most women dependent children are both pleasures and ties. As one woman in my Milton Keynes research said 'Children stay dependent on women a long time; even when they're adults they still expect mum to do things for them'.

Children are a major source of enjoyment in many women's lives but women recognise that there are economic as well as other costs in living with children. Ironically, the older a child, the greater may be the constraints on the mother; a tiny baby can often be taken along to a social club, meeting, or other activity, although the time-consuming nature of care for very young babies does not allow much leeway for outings or household peace. But whilst an older child may attend school, and be less prone to waking up every two hours at night, that same child will also be developing their own leisure interests and requiring an escort or transport to the BMX track, leisure centre or dance classes.

One aspect of my research was to look at the usage of leisure centres by women. Busy times of the day revealed considerable numbers of women entering the centres. Only a few were actually wanting to use the centre facilities themselves; the remainder were accompanying children who were about to use sports facilities or attend classes. Yet few men, even at weekends, were observed to attend *only* on their children's behalf. Men have both the money and the legitimacy to use such visits for themselves too. But children are a constraint not only because it is often women who are assigned to look after their offspring's leisure activities.

If women with children want to take part in leisure activities, they have to make arrangements for their children (few men will take this on board). Whilst public leisure provision is beginning to offer crêches, commercial provision is only rarely accompanied by childcare facilities. And children are not conducive to wanting to sit down with a book, or take a nap, or ten minutes of quiet thought, all important to women's 'at-home' leisure. Theoretically, of course, there is no reason why men cannot also take responsibility for children; a few actually do so. For the remainder of fathers, looking after children is considered women's work, because it either interferes with men's paid work or their leisure, or more usually both of these. Hence children are both a source of everyday enjoyment for women (and therefore part of their leisure) *and* a source of constraints on leisure and leisure time.

Women in the community

Whilst participating in commercial and public sector leisure plays a relatively minor role for women as a group, many middle-class women over 40 belong to a variety of clubs and organisations, most of which are women-only groups (Deem, 1983, 1986). These include political groups, the Women's Institute, Inner Wheel, Ladies' Circle and flower-arranging clubs. Whilst some are purely leisure-oriented, others are directed at a variety of community activities, from charity fund-raising to organising competitions in public speaking for schoolgirls. There are, of course, male equivalents of some of these organisations, for instance, the Rotary Club, although these figure less strongly in male leisure than do their equivalents in female leisure. But for women, community organisations have a dual political significance. First, they are important because there are relatively few places where women (especially those without paid jobs) can discuss any issues of common concern outside of the isolation of their own homes and without men or children being present. Second, community-oriented organisations are significant because there is a strong cultural assumption that community tasks are mainly appropriate for women, an extension of their caring role and their domestic labour (Finch and Groves, 1983). Thus community organisations are not only welcomed by some women as a way of both relaxing and talking or acting about community issues with other women, but are also seen by men, and increasingly the government, as an appropriate place for women to be. For example, the Women's National Commission, first set up in 1969 to advise government on women's affairs, has under the Thatcher government achieved a new prominence. Its membership is drawn from community organisations like the W.I. and it is seen by the current government as representing the interests of all women, and has produced reports on a variety of topics including sexism in girls' education and women's health.

Whereas Siltanen and Stanworth (1984) note that researchers have often seen women as politically passive, the W.N.C. demonstrates that some women are political and often far from self-centred in their leisure pursuits. By contrast, men's leisure pursuits are often far from community-oriented – and frequently no more political either. Women's organisations and their history indicates that the autonomous formation of women-only groups is not something confined to contemporary feminist groups but an important part of female culture in Britain, for both working- and middle-class women (Campbell, 1984). Yet leisure researchers and policy makers have virtually ignored both the existence of such organisations and their importance in understanding the nature of women's leisure (although see Tomlinson, 1979).

Education: liberation or control

The unfair treatment of women in schools has been extensively documented over the past few years by educational researchers and feminists. But here, too, the significance of the connections between what happens to women in schooling, and their experience and use of leisure has largely been missed by leisure researchers. There are three important aspects of women's education which are particularly relevant to their leisure. The first is that in emphasising women's future destination as marriage and child-rearing, especially in relation to the curriculum offered to girls, schools help to shape women's leisure interests in particular directions. So, for example, many adult women have sewing, knitting, cooking and other crafts associated with women as major non-work activities when they are relaxing at home; out-of-home activities often relate to domestic or caring roles, as noted in the previous section. Schools teach particular craft skills to girls which emphasise domestic and caring roles. Woodwork, metalwork, or car mechanics, which like most craft skills, can relate to employment, unpaid work *or* leisure in adult life, are not usually offered to them. Nor do schools emphasise sufficiently that adult life is about leisure and work for *both* sexes.

The second aspect of schooling relevant to women's future

leisure is the teaching of sport and physical activities. As Sheila Scraton (1985, and in this volume) points out, PE is one of the most gender-segregated areas of the curriculum in secondary schools (even in primary schools there is often gender differentiation at the upper end of the age-range) yet relatively little attention has been paid to it by either researchers or feminists. Girls are much more rarely than boys introduced to outdoor adventure pursuits like climbing or canoeing, and where both genders do get involved in the same sport, women's achievements are expected to be less (e.g., shorter cross country runs; see Stantonbury Sexism in Education Group, 1984). Most girls are quickly turned off sport and physical activity, because they find the activities boring and competitive or find it difficult to associate femininity with sport and the 'healthy living and showers' atmosphere of most school PE departments. In a study of 168 women drawn at random from five areas in a new town, I found scarcely any adult women who continued with *any* sport or physical activity done at school once they had left, with swimming the only widespread exception to this (Deem, 1984). The Sheffield study found only one quarter of their sample of adult women played sport (Green, et al., 1985a, 1985b). Sports and physical activities which adult women do enjoy, from walking and cycling to yoga and keep-fit, are rarely taught in schools, although they may form part of adult educational provision.

This brings us to the third point about education. As the most female dominated sector of education, adult education is a major source of leisure, retraining and providing new learning opportunities for women whose school education may have been far from adequate. Yet Jane Thompson (1983), in a radical attack on the structure and organisation of women's adult education, argues that female prominence is confined to student numbers. All other decisions about courses, content, location and teaching methods are taken by men, resulting in an adult education which men think women should want (whilst many middle-class women appear to want what is provided, working-class women in particular reject it as too much like school).

My own research suggests that middle-class and single women make far more use of existing adult education classes and courses than working-class women, and not just on financial grounds (Deem, 1982a, 1982b). One attraction of adult education, apart from its intrinsic enjoyment and sociable atmosphere, is that men 'allow' women to attend, just as community and women-only activities are approved of by husbands as suitable for their wives, where pubs and discos are 'unsuitable'. This, of course, does not mean that adult education should *not* be a valuable part of women's leisure, but it does suggest that women ought to have much more control over what, where and when they learn.

Employment and time-compartmentalisation

Women's employment is at the present time an extremely political issue for a number of reasons; there are debates about the rights of women and mothers to be employed at all, about the relative job-loss of women and men, and about the widening of pay differentials between males and females.

Women's average earnings are still only just above seventy per cent of men's average earnings, despite the Equal Pay Act. Employment is also, however, very much connected to leisure for women, in a way closer to the male experience than generally considered. My own research suggested initially that employed women have more leisure interests and activities than non-employed women. This was partly because the employed had money of their own, and if married or co-habiting, were slightly more likely to get assistance with housework than their non-employed sisters. This left them a little more time for themselves (Deem, 1982a and 1982b). Subsequent research and data analysis suggest that there is another reason why the employed are more likely to have leisure time and a range of leisure interests. Coyle's (1984) study of women made redundant from the clothing industry found that those women unable to obtain new jobs not only suffered financial and identity loss after being made redundant but also found their daily routine, previously well adapted to coping with both a job and housework/childcare, was drastically upset by the absence of paid work.

In a recent paper I compared employed and unemployed women (Deem, 1984) and found that the former were more able to compartmentalise their lives. Employed women not only think of themselves as having timeslots which are for leisure but they are also able to plan their leisure, whatever that involves, to a greater extent than women who do only unpaid work, have no fixed hours and a very fragmented day as a result (and also usually live in a situation of financial, emotional and other dependence on men). Some writers have argued that the daily lives of women,

219

'unconstrained' by paid work, are enviable in their flexibility and potential for the development of leisure (Gregory, 1982). However, my own research and that of Coyle (1984) suggests that women value the development of a routine for their own. This allows them the possibility of allocating time specifically to leisure.

Women's employment, then, is not just an important political issue because women have economic needs and because for many, their job is a central part of their identity and social activity. Jobs also provide women with both economic independence (even if this is only partial) and a degree of time-independence which allows them far more control over their leisure and lives as a whole, than if they have no job.

Public leisure provision for women

There are a number of important issues here, but fundamental to the politics of women's leisure are '*who* decides to provide' and *what* is actually provided. There is some documentation now of women's involvement in political life (through formal and informal channels) which suggests that women are more politically active and aware than they are often given credit for, but which also indicates that women have very far from their fair share of political power and involvement (Siltanen and Stanworth, 1984; Rogers, 1983).

There are many more women who are active in local politics as compared to national politics, and so there is a slightly increased possibility that they can influence local provision. But many such women conform only too readily to stereotypes of femininity themselves, and are hence fairly traditional in what they perceive women as requiring (swimming pools and sewing classes but not student-negotiated discussion groups or electronics). There is often a strong class bias (and an ethnic one too) amongst both politicians and local authority officers; working-class life is rarely understood or appreciated. Working-class women are often deterred from adult education because of the need to pay for classes and courses a term in advance, whereas activities paid for on an 'as you attend' basis might widen access. But when this issue was raised with one local authority, the Treasurer, asked to investigate more flexible methods of payment, responded with the suggestion that a system of credit-card payment be implemented. Similarly, although many leisure centres now offer some limited form of crêche provision, this is not always free, it often does not cater for babies or school age children, is sometimes tied to particular forms of provision (ladies' mornings, for example) and fails to recognise that some women may be reluctant to leave their children with strangers.

Leisure policy itself is rarely flexible enough. The organisation of responsibilities between different tiers of local authorities means there is often no recognition of the fact that leisure, like many other local services, requires some degree of co-ordination across different kinds of provision. Public transport is vital to women's leisure outside the home, since many have none of their own, yet the relationship between transport and leisure, or between safe roads and paths and leisure, and between housing developments and local rather than city or town wide leisure facilities, to take but a few examples, is rarely realised or acted upon. Because women are less apt than adolescents or ethnic minorities to riot or crowd the streets, and are less publicly 'visible' when unemployed, the issue of leisure for women is rarely seen in overt terms of social control or as what Clarke and Critcher (1985) term 'leisure as compensation'. There is however often an implicit assumption by both national and local government leisure planners that families and household tasks come before women's own needs, and also that leisure is an individualised 'problem' with individualised solutions which can safely be privatised or left to localised or voluntary initiatives. Only a few local authorities have shown that it is possible to take radical and group action on issues and provision for women as a social category, (for example the GLC) and some of these are threatened with abolition because of what is seen as 'luxury' expenditure. Some national bodies like the Sports Council have recognised the need to take positive steps to involve more women in leisure activities, but appeals to women on the basis that 'sport benefits your health' do not necessarily strike a ready chord with women, and may fail to take account of the many and varied reasons why women are not very involved in sport.

The lesson which still needs to be learnt about women and leisure in public provision, is that it is not sufficient to recognise women as a target group or to provide *what men think women need*, under male control. Women actually need to be part of the policy-making and planning processes, not as tokens and not just in the form of pressure groups. Only then can women at least start to provide what women need under their *own* and not patriarchal and paternalistic control.

Commercial provision of leisure

There are of course many areas of women's leisure which fall under neither public nor commercial leisure provision, and some of these are dealt with earlier in the section on 'Women in the community'. But there are obviously important areas of commercial leisure provision for women, from the marketing of leisure and 'jogging' clothing to computers and bingo halls, as well as pubs and dance halls or private sports facilities. Many of the same criticisms can be levelled at commercial planning and provision as at public provision; a failure to grasp women's actual needs and interests as opposed to the stereotyped needs and images portrayed in the media and elsewhere. The relative absence of women in positions of power in commercial organisations means that more often than not men organise and decide, whilst women consume. So, pubs in Britain generally do not have children's or family rooms, most computer software is directed at male interests, women's magazines focus on family and domestic issues (Earnshaw, 1983) rather than on leisure activities or non-home based interests, and a leading cycle manufacturer advertises and sells women's bikes on the basis of colour schemes rather than the quality of components and without explaining that so called 'women's' frames make cycling harder work than necessary. There are some areas of commercial provision where women are the most important consumers, for instance romantic novels and bingo, but here the appeal is to the stereotypes of women and their needs rather than trying something new (although Virago, Pandora Books and Women's Press have made courageous attempts in the field of publishing).

Dixey and Talbot (1982) in their study of bingo found that many women went because it was cheap, unthreatening, a way of meeting other women and getting out of the house rather than because they found bingo itself intrinsically interesting. There is obviously potential here for new forms of commercial leisure provision for those women with any disposable income at all. Commercial leisure in a capitalist society cannot realistically be expected to take on board the difficulties of unwaged women, although public provision has not always taken this issue seriously either. But commercial provision could be a lot more adventurous than it presently is, and perhaps take the lead of the National Association of Licensed Bingo and Social Clubs which funded the Dixey and Talbot (1982) study of women players in at least trying to find out why women are not customers and what particular problems or advantages there are for women in a given activity, service or consumer good.

The politics of women's leisure – policies and changes

I noted at the beginning of the article that a feminist analysis is not just one which points out what is and is not wrong with the present position of women. It must also set out to achieve change and to develop what Eisenstein (1984) describes as placing 'women's needs and women's goals at the centre of a progressive political programme'. There is, as we have seen, a lot wrong with women's leisure at the present time and there are pressing needs for some far-reaching changes, some of which are fundamental ones and others of which can be super-imposed on the present largely male dominated society. Women's leisure cannot change unless men and their leisure change too, however, and change in ways which recognise the legitimate right of women to 'time-off'. There are two different sets of changes which are needed; one is in leisure, its provision and conceptualisation, and the range and location of that leisure. The second set is to do with the conditions under which leisure takes place – the structures, institutions and ideas which shape what is possible in our society. We ought not (despite many efforts to the contrary, particularly in relation to the unemployed) to legislate or lay down what women should do with their leisure, *but* it is possible to create social conditions under which women have a wider range of options and choices than they do presently. Leisure is partly a personal and private phenomenon, unique to each individual, but it is essential to recognise the wider implications and politics too. Leisure which is more responsive to the needs of women should fulfil at least some of the following:

– it should be unconnected to gender stereotyping, just as the 'catching up' of male performances by women in sport has shown that centuries of keeping women out of certain sports was totally unjustified (Dyer, 1982). This would mean, for example, encouraging women in pursuits where women have not been welcome or where (as in photography) women have been the objects of leisure rather than the participants.
– it should take place in locations where women feel safe, including venues easily reachable by public transport, and women's homes.

- it should utilise locations where women already go – health centres, shopping precincts, for example – as well as purpose-built or institutional bases.
- leisure should be available locally as well as in town and city centres – which may mean moving away from the notion of huge multi-purpose leisure centres for example.
- there should be childcare provision available, at weekends and evenings as well as during the day time, in places where leisure takes place; this could also be a valuable addition to children's leisure.
- leisure should be available as of right to those with low or no incomes.
- all kinds of women should have their leisure needs catered for, not just middle-class, middle-aged mothers of teenagers, but older women, disabled women, women from ethnic minority groups.
- leisure provision should be more imaginative, assuming until proved otherwise that potentially women may be interested in all kinds of diverse activities; women should also be consulted about what they would like, rather than it being assumed on their behalf.
- leisure provision should be by a mix of public, commercial and voluntary organisations, which would recognise the importance of the last-named to women's leisure.
- leisure should be available in single sex groups and locations as well as mixed settings, both because autonomous women's activities are very important but also because women should not feel excluded from mixed activities if they are not accompanied by a man.

But these kinds of changes in leisure provision need at the same time to be accompanied by other kinds of changes, both in the organisation of the sexual division of labour and in women's rights and in the way leisure policies, services and goods are conceived of. The following are priorities:

1 A recognition by men of the control they exercise over women collectively and individually, and an attempt to reduce that power by recognising that women are capable of organising their own lives, without the patriarchal interference and domination of men, but with the active co-operation of men at all levels, from households to work places.

2 Childcare should be shared between women and men wherever possible. There should be a coherent national policy on the care and education of the under-fives, and better provision for care of older children when not at school, so that women's and children's needs are not irrevocably tied together, to the detriment of women's free time and leisure requirements.

3 Men should be encouraged to be as active in caring roles in the community as women; neither should be expected to perform tasks for free which should properly be paid for and organised by the state, such as care of patients discharged early from hospital because of NHS charges, or sole and unaided care of disabled children or infirm old people. Many women would probably still choose to spend leisure time on community-oriented activities, but no longer in a framework where these are an expected and largely unsupported extension of their household roles (Finch and Groves, 1983).

4 A determined shift towards a non-sexist education at all levels, from nursery schools to adult education should occur so that women's education is no longer controlled and determined by men. The education of adults should endeavour to draw fully on the experiences of its students and reduce the power differentials between teachers and taught, so that women in their quest for self-education are not overwhelmed by masculine knowledge and male authority hierarchies.

5 The teaching of sport and physical activity in schools should cease to be so strongly gender-differentiated and cover a wider range of non-competitive activities for all students.

6 Not only should women's rights to a job and independent income (the latter means changes in taxation as well as equal pay) be recognised, but also, the importance to every adult of a day which includes time slots for leisure as well as work. This would imply changes in household divisions of labour as well as changes in the organisation of paid working hours and conditions. Housework would have to be done by both sexes.

7 There should be determined efforts by men as well as women to get more women involved in formal as well as pressure group politics, so that decisions are not taken about women's concerns and facilities (including leisure provision) without the full involvement of women in that decision-making process.

8 Leisure planning should recognise that many aspects of public and social policy need to be integrated for successful leisure facilities and services to be provided for women. These would

include transport, education, social services and more general forms of planning including housing and local developments.

9 Leisure researchers should try to persuade commercial leisure providers, whose clients and consumers are women, to fund research to investigate the quality of what is provided and the extent to which women are satisfied or dissatisfied with what already exists, so that new and more adventurous provision can be attempted.

10 The right of women to leisure should be fully recognised, understood and acted upon, but not in ways that prevent women from being actively involved in the planning and organisation of leisure.

Of course, it would be unrealistic at the present juncture to think that any of these priorities could easily be implemented, or even straightforwardly put on the political agenda. Not only do we have a government whose policy on women has many internal contradictions, from the theoretical belief in equal opportunities to practical steps to dissuade mothers and married women from being employed or seeking jobs. We are also in the midst of an economic recession and most improvements in the position and treatment of women have occurred in conditions of economic prosperity (Deem, 1981). Nevertheless, leisure itself, if not women's leisure, is very much on the political agenda, albeit for bad reasons (to do with pacifying the young, poor and unemployed, see Clarke and Critcher, 1985) but there is no reason why this concern cannot be turned to good advantage. As Dunleavy and Husbands (1985) have pointed out in their study of the political implications of the 1983 British General Election, women voters are a sector of the electorate to whom it is becoming increasingly necessary for the winning political party to appeal. So some changes, for example, in the integration of leisure with other policies or greater involvement of women in national politics, could come through this route. Others require a recognition on behalf of individual men, including researchers into leisure, that political change can begin at the individual level, for example by doing housework which will enable a woman to be released from her domestic duties so that leisure is possible. Still other changes may need to await a more fundamental social and economic upheaval. But it is now also opportune, with the availability of research on the poverty of women's leisure, for feminists to recognise and incorporate into their vision of the future and their political programme the right of all women to participate in leisure. Leisure, like charity, often begins at home!

References

Burns, T. (1973), 'Leisure in industrial society' in M. Smith, S. Parker and C. Smith (eds), *Leisure and Society in Britain*, Allen Lane, the Penguin Press, London.

Campbell, B. (1984), *Wigan Pier Revisited*, Virago, London.

Chambers, D. (1985), 'Conceptualising the work-leisure complex', presentation to 'Women, leisure and well-being' workshop, Dunfermline College of P.E., April.

Clarke, J. and Critcher, C. (1985), *The Devil Makes Work: Leisure in Capitalist Society*, Macmillan, London.

Coote, A. and Campbell, B. (1982), *Sweet Freedom: The Struggle for Women's Liberation*, Pan Books, London.

Coyle, A. (1984), *Redundant Women*, Women's Press, London.

Deem, R. (1981), 'State policy and ideology in the education of women 1944–1980', *British Journal of Sociology of Education*, Vol. 2, No. 2, pp. 131–43.

Deem, R. (1982a), 'Women, leisure and inequality', *Leisure Studies*, Vol. 1, No. 1, pp. 29–46.

Deem, R. (1982b), 'Women's leisure: does it exist?', unpublished paper presented to British Sociological Association Conference 'Gender and Society', April.

Deem, R. (1983), 'Gender, patriarchy and class in the popular education of women', in Walker, S. and Barton, L. (eds), *Gender, Class and Education*, Falmer Press, Barcombe, Lewes, Sussex.

Deem, R. (1984), 'Paid work, leisure and non-employment: shifting boundaries and gender differences', unpublished paper presented to British Sociological Association Conference 'Work, Employment, Unemployment', April.

Deem, R. (1986), *All Work and No Play*, Open University Press, Milton Keynes.

Delphy, C. (1984), *Close to Home*, Hutchinson/Explorations in Feminism Collective, London.

Dixey, R. and Talbot, M. (1982), *Women, Leisure and Bingo*, Trinity and All Saints College, Horsforth, Leeds, England.

Dunleavy, P. and Husbands, C. (1985), *British Democracy at the Crossroads*, G. Allen and Unwin, London.

Dyer, K. (1982), *Catching up the men*, Junction Books, London.

Earnshaw, S. (1983), 'Women's magazines and culture, ideology and the oppression of women', unpublished PhD thesis, University of Liverpool.

Eisenstein, H. (1984), *Contemporary Feminist Thought*, Allen and Unwin, London.

Finch, J. and Groves, D. (eds) (1983), *A Labour of Love*, Routledge & Kegan Paul, London.

Green, E., Hebron, S. and Woodward, D. (1985a), 'Leisure and gender: women's opportunities, perceptions and constraints', unpublished report to ESRC/Sports Council Steering Group, Women and Leisure project.

Green, E., Hebron, S. and Woodward, D. (1985b), 'A woman's work is never done', *Sport and Leisure*, July–August, pp. 36–8.

Green, E., Hebron, S., and Woodward, D. (1986), 'Women, violence, gender and social control', in J. Hanmer and M. Maynard (eds), *Gender, Violence and Social Control*, Macmillan, London.

Gregory, S. (1982), 'Women amongst others', *Leisure Studies*, Vol. 1, No. 1, pp. 47–52.

Gordon, L. (1979), 'The struggle for reproductive freedom: three stages of feminism', in Z. Eisenstein (ed.), *Capitalist Patriarchy and the Case for Socialist Feminism*, Monthly Review Press, New York.

Griffin, C. (1981), 'Young women and leisure', in A. Tomlinson (ed.), *Leisure and Social Control*, Brighton Polytechnic, Sussex, England.

McKee, L. and Bell, C. (1984), 'His unemployment: her problem: the domestic and marital consequences of male unemployment', paper presented to the British Sociological Association's Conference 'Work, employment, unemployment', April.

Rogers, B. (1983), *52%: Getting Women's Power into Politics*, Women's Press, London.

Scraton, S. (1985), 'Boys muscle in where angels fear to tread: the relationship between physical education and young women's subcultures', paper given to Leisure Studies Association conference 'Leisure and Youth', Ilkley.

Siltanen, J. and Stanworth, M. (1984), *Women and the Public Sphere*, Hutchinson, London.

Sport and Leisure (1985), Special section on 'Women and sport', Sports Council Publication.

Stanley, L. (1980), 'The problem of women and leisure: an ideological construct and a radical alternative', Capital Radio/Centre for Leisure Studies, University of Salford 'Leisure in the Eighties' Forum, September.

Stantonbury Campus (Bridgewater Hall), Sexism in Education Group (1984), 'The realities of mixed schooling', in Deem, R. (ed.), *Co-education Reconsidered*, Open University Press, Milton Keynes.

Talbot, M. (1979), 'Women and leisure: a state of the art review', Social Science Research Council/Sports Council, London.

Thompson, J. (1983), *Learning Liberation: Women's Response to Men's Education*, Croom Helm, London.

Tomlinson, A. (1979), 'Leisure and the role of clubs and voluntary groups', Social Science Research Council/Sports Council, London.

Tomlinson, A. (1983), 'The new hope for leisure: some comments on Labour's manifesto', in *The Politics of Leisure*, Leisure Studies Association Newsletter Supplement, ed. G. Jarvie.

Willis, P. (1977), *Learning to Labour*, Saxon House, London.

Wimbush, E. (1985), presentation to 'Women, well-being and leisure' workshop, Dunfermline College of P.E., April.

Leisure, the state and collective consumption

Dave Whitson

Introduction

This essay will argue that an analysis of leisure policy which elucidates the political context of state interventions in respect to leisure, and which thereby politicises a number of issues which have typically been framed in apolitical terms, is an important priority for the sociology of leisure. The discussion will briefly review the growth of a government presence in recreational provision and regulation. It will go on to situate contemporary debates about the merits of public and private provision in the context of long-standing divisions around what is the legitimate role of the state, and to relate specific policy alternatives to economic and political pressures which have led states, in all the capitalist democracies of the West, to assume increasing responsibility for the provision of social infrastructure.[1] Finally, an analysis of the current fragility of popular support for the public services will lead to a reconsideration of the 'relations of consumption' which have characterized the provision of recreational and other services within a bureaucratic framework.

Common sense has seen leisure as an aspect of 'private life', a sphere of individual choices, which is not properly the object of public policy. However, recent work in social history and cultural studies (c.f. Cunningham, 1980; Waites et al., 1982) has drawn to our attention a long history of state intervention designed to contain and regulate a variety of the entertainments traditional to popular culture. Less direct but no less significant in their effects have been regulations on land use. The enclosure and privatisation of formerly common land gradually reduced the space in which poor people could entertain themselves without admission charges of some form; and restrictions on what could be done in public spaces (whether the harassment of street games, or the prosecution of swimming in canals and urban waterways) had the effect of legally aligning the 'public interest' with the wishes of commerce and/or of genteel sensibilities. Indeed it was out of just this kind of regulation of the uses of public space that demand for state-sponsored provision first grew. In cities where people could not play because there was no room, or because the only facilities were in clubs which ordinary people could not join, demands arose for parks and playing fields and swimming baths. Outside the cities, where enclosure of common lands and the use of the law to prosecute trespassers and poachers meant that countryside recreation was available only to the land-owning classes, organized civil disobedience led eventually to state sponsorship of access agreements and, in the end, national parks (c.f. Lowerson, 1980).

Thus although the history of actual state provision of recreational opportunities is briefer, we are becoming more aware of the political contexts in which local and national governments have progressively assumed responsibility for services as various as libraries and swimming baths, parks and broadcasting. Today it is possible to identify at least five different ways in which state policies affect the nature and distribution of leisure opportunities in the mixed economies of Western Europe and North America.

1 Direct provision and grant support. This includes, at the most direct level, municipal operation of libraries, community centres, and various kinds of sports facility. Such provision has been for the most part consensual, though political divisions and national contrasts exist in the extent to which local authorities are supported by grants from national government as opposed to the extent to which they must fund such provisions themselves, out of property taxes or user fees. Contrasts can also be drawn in how far-reaching municipal provision attempts to be; an interesting instance would contrast the impact of the Swedish policy of supporting municipal indoor tennis facilities with that of the British and Canadian traditions of leaving tennis to private clubs. Clearly, opportunities to develop tennis skills are more widely available in Sweden. In addition the growth of organizations like the Sports Council and the Arts Council (and their Canadian counterparts, Sport Canada and the Canada Council), and the presence of publicly supported broadcast networks in the UK and Canada, point to a dimension of national government provision that is both more far-reaching

and more politically contentious. Macintosh et al. (1986) point out that although the formal relationship of such organizations to government is an 'arm's length' one, designed to protect institutions with their own logic and traditions from direct political 'interference', the effect of sports governing bodies' dependence on government for unprecedented levels of funding has been to transform the administration of amateur sport, and to integrate the practices of sports governing bodies more closely with the broader policy objectives of government. The debates surrounding government support of the arts raise issues which are beyond the scope of this paper; but the tensions of the arm's length relationship are, if anything, magnified.

2 Regulation and taxation of popular enjoyments. Examples include restrictions and taxes on drinking and gambling (including gambling on sport), as well as on sport, hunting and fishing. It is also important to remember here the role which social control objectives, especially in respect to youth, have played historically in the expansion of recreational provision (c.f. Carrington and Leaman, 1983; Olson, 1985).

3 Subsidies and incentives to the leisure industry. This can include small grants and business advice designed to assist local residents, for example in tourist destinations, to set up independent businesses which would keep tourism-related income and employment in the community. It can also include large subsidies to consortia developing resorts or erecting stadiums for commercial sport. The government of Ontario, for example, is committed to contributing thirty million dollars towards the construction of a domed stadium in Toronto which will be owned and operated by a consortium of large Canadian and multinational corporations. In addition, it is necessary to recognize as a form of subsidy the provision of infrastructure (e.g., roads and municipal services) which effectively socializes the development costs of ventures like ski resorts and marinas.

4 Business environment. At the same time that government policy subsidizes selected kinds of private sector activity, it also establishes the regulatory climate in which the leisure industries, like all other industries, must operate. Sometimes this is a matter of a strict or lax attitude towards the enforcement of safety or employment regulations, or the presence or absence of consumer protection legislation (a contemporary case in point here relates to fitness clubs). More importantly, however, it revolves around land-use regulation, specifically the protection

(or not) of parkland and greenbelt against pressures for various forms of more intensive and revenue-producing uses (recreational as well as non-recreational).[2] Finally, of fundamental importance is a government's policy in respect to privatisation, which can either offer a series of opportunities to private entrepreneurs or can reaffirm the public operation of facilities which private operators often regard as subsidized competition.

5 Professionalization of recreation and leisure. It is worth noting that the scope of state interest and involvement in all of the above areas has played a considerable part in the emergence of recreation and leisure as a profession. As the state began to formulate policy in areas which recognizably related to leisure, it began to institutionalize the participation of 'experts', both in the policy formation process and in the 'effective' delivery of leisure services. Arguably the institutions of leisure provision described in (1) above have been a major source of legitimation for recreation professionals; certainly they have been a major source of employment, without which the emergence of courses leading to professional qualifications would have been problematic.

Despite all these developments, however, there have been only isolated attempts to relate conceptual and empirical work on leisure to new developments in social theory, to theorise the significance of state policies for leisure in the reproduction of social inequalities, or to consider how a more theoretically informed 'politics of leisure' might contribute to the transformation of these unequal relations.[3] This paper will argue that once we have recognized leisure policy as a not insignificant dimension of social policy, we can see more clearly the importance of recognizing the wider implications of free market and public welfare approaches to leisure policy. It will contend that the de-commodification of recreational opportunities, and likewise the regulation of private economic initiatives which threaten to narrow the availability of leisure options, each constitute important dimensions of efforts to assert the needs of people against the logic of capital accumulation.

The politicization of leisure, it will be argued, is one site in a broad politics of 'collective consumption', Castells's term for popular struggles which developed around the inadequacy of public housing and transport in the working-class suburbs of French cities (Castells, 1977). The significant fact about these mobilisations, in Castells's view, was that common interest had been registered not so much as arising from the status of workers or through workers' organizations, but as arising from the interest of the consumers of services which have become essential to the reproduction of everyday life in a modern capitalist society. Castells's discussion of collective consumption has been subject to much debate (c.f. Saunders, 1981 and Forrest et al., 1982). However, Dunleavy has refined and operationalized the concept to refer to any services which are publicly managed and subsidized from public funds, so that access is not solely dictated by market criteria (Dunleavy, 1980, pp. 52–3). He suggests that collective consumption, thus defined, is a major factor in the availability of education and health care, old age security and cultural and recreational facilities as well as housing and transport in Britain and Western Europe today. He also suggests that although land use regulation is not itself a service, it must be considered an integral dimension of any politics of collective consumption. This is because it is only through regulation of land use, real limitation of property rights and intervention in the property market, in the name of communal rights and of non-market criteria, that land is reserved for public use, whether as parkland or as any kind of built facility.

Collective provision and consumption of the necessities of everyday life are integral to the structure of advanced capitalism, in Castells's analysis, because they are indispensable to the reproduction of labour power both on a daily and a generational basis. At the same time, they are indispensable to the viability of life for substantial and indeed increasing sectors of the population. Castells argues that the significance of this is twofold. First, there is the potential for forming broader alliances, incorporating a variety of groups who have not traditionally identified their own interests with working-class political objectives but who nonetheless become ready to oppose what they experience as inroads on the support structures and the environment of their daily lives. Even more important to Castells's overall analysis, however, is the fact that as the state has become more visibly enmeshed in the provision of social infrastructure, the *political* nature of decisions to improve or to cut back on services becomes increasingly exposed.

Dave Whitson

Debates about the state

It is indisputably true that the role and scope of government is now a major issue in most Western nations. The consensus which supported or at least accepted the growth of the welfare state and of Keynesian-style management of the economy has come under increasing attack from both left and right. The Western state has developed out of classical liberal understandings of freedom and individual rights, and much of the contemporary criticism of both the effects of political intervention on economy and civil society revisits the central themes of the early liberal debates. Two currents of thought within liberalism are worth identifying here. The first of these has tended to identify human rights with property rights; it has generally viewed the regulation of business activity and taxation itself, as interference with the natural and inalienable right of the individual to the enjoyment of property and to its use in the pursuit of livelihood. This kind of thinking was central to the possessive individualism of Locke, and to the market model of man employed by Hobbes, Smith and Bentham. Its advocates saw the protection of economic activity from political interference (i.e., the 'free market') as one of the necessary conditions of a free society.

Another tradition of liberal thought, however, harking back to Mill and Paine and the Declaration of Independence, embodies a broader, sometimes religious, vision of human potential, and places more stress on civil and political freedoms associated with the pursuit of individual and collective development. It sees the most important freedoms, to be underwritten by political institutions, as being connected with speech, worship and association, and ultimately with the right to develop one's God-given individuality and talents. In its later versions, at least, what Macpherson (1973) has called 'developmental individualism' also embodied the recognition that the constraints of poverty and economic dependence limit freedom at least as severely as do politico-legal restraints; and it articulated a role for government in the provision of facilities and programmes which would open up life choices and new possibilities for whole groups or classes of people whose lives had been historically constrained by economic necessity. Libraries and municipal recreation facilities, as well as opportunities to pursue excellence in sport or in the arts, each in their own way, manifest this new appreciation of the material dimensions of freedom and constraint. They also manifest a new and broader conception of the role of government in seeking to open up more opportunities for more people. A similar division of perspectives is embodied in the difference between Hayek's (1960) 'negative' definition of freedom, as the absence or at least minimum of politico-legal constraints on individual action, and Berlin's 'positive freedom' (1969) which sees a legitimate and even necessary role for government in providing the material conditions in which the fuller development of human potential becomes possible.

Macpherson (1985) proposes that we can see, in the subsequent evolution of the liberal-democratic state, an ongoing tension between property rights and developmental rights which, despite the growth of the welfare state, remains unresolved today. Early liberals like Mill, in Macpherson's view, did not perceive any real contradiction between developmental and possessive individualism. In an era when liberalism was the philosophy of the new bourgeoisie who palpably expanded their own life chances by breaking free of the constraints and obligations of the feudal order, property rights and developmental rights were conceived as synonymous. However, Macpherson argues that the effect of nineteenth century legislation and common law was to give systematic priority to property rights and ultimately, to the logic of property maximization. This laissez faire liberalism effectively traded off other kinds of human rights for economic growth, justifying this where necessary with a Benthamite logic which foreshadowed the contemporary vocabulary of 'wealth creation' and 'trickle-down' economics.

It has become apparent, however, from the actual development of capitalism, that in a society with freedom of private economic activity, only political/legal constraints can offset the tendency of market forces systematically to advantage the strong at the expense of the weak. With the extension of democracy, moreover, increasing pressure for social arrangements which afford developmental opportunities to the non-propertied sectors of the population has served to highlight fundamental oppositions between the two kinds of rights and freedoms outlined above. Indeed Macpherson contends that today we have no excuse for failing to acknowledge that if the state abstains from intervention in the marketplace, the political system is effectively being used to reinforce economic power (1985, pp. 46–54). In a similar vein, Bosanquet points out that 'the natural state of society is not one in which, in the absence of government, freedom flourishes even in the negative sense.' It is rather one in which economic and physical power routinely create

Dave Whitson

opportunities for private coercion, one in which in principle, the case for government arises precisely from the need to protect the more vulnerable members of society from this. He goes on to point out the historical irony of our current concern to protect the individual from coercion by the state, given that much current state intervention has its origins in legislation designed to protect individuals, either from private coercions or from the effects of the market (1983, pp. 192–5).

Certainly the last hundred years have seen a steady, if always contested, growth in the scope of the welfare state, and in the scope of regulations containing the activities of private capital, interventions which have been ameliorative in intention, if not in effect. It is fair to say that for a period of time the case for some measure of 'distributive justice' (Rawls, 1971) became the consensus of serious contenders for government. Debates centred not so much on the principle itself, as on matters of degree and of institutional form. However, both financial and regulatory dimensions of redistributive programmes have led to increasing infringements of property rights (i.e., to greater taxation and to controls on business activity); and these have led in turn to a renaissance of interest in the ideas of neo-liberal economists and political theorists (Hayek, 1960; Friedman, 1962; Nozick, 1974) who have advocated a return to the minimal state, and called for the recommodification of many of the public services whose growth I have outlined.

Contradictions of the Welfare State

Before examining the implications of these debates and developments for the leisure services, however, and before exploring the outlines of a politics of leisure appropriate to a time in which 'restraint' has become the new commonsense, it will be useful to consider what Offe (1984) and others have described as the 'contradictions of the welfare state'. Conservative as well as marxist scholars have pointed to the problems generated by increasing demands upon the state, problems which have become increasingly acute as liberal-democratic states in capitalist economies encounter political limits to their capacity to raise the revenues they need in order to satisfy these demands.

For conservatives, the problems of 'overloaded government' are a product of the democratic political process, of 'rising expectations'

236

fuelled by the promises of party politicians in a pluralist electoral system. They are problems that can be contained, however, at the level of politics, by politicians who are firm enough to tell groups, grown accustomed to government support, that they must support themselves, and who are committed to withdrawing the state from responsibility for a wide range of services which can then be left to the private sector. In this 'privatization' scenario, public spending is substantially reduced at the same time that public expectations of government become much more circumscribed. According to this diagnosis, the trend to the politicization of economic issues and issues of 'personal' life has deeply corrosive effects: on the economy, on the political capacity of the state to fulfil those functions which *are* proper to it, and upon acceptance of individual responsibility.[4] In respect to the last, Ingham (1985) makes a powerful case that the current discourses surrounding fitness and 'lifestyle', which frame health as a matter of individual responsibility, have the effect of deflecting attention away from a series of what should be recognized as public, and therefore political, issues: (among them workplace environment, child care and access to recreational opportunities).

For marxists, the problems of the welfare state reside in the structural contradictions of a specifically capitalist democracy. These can be traced to the fact that in order to respond to democratic pressure for more services, the state becomes ever more reliant on economic growth and hence more dependent upon capital. Yet when the state responds to pressures from capital to reduce expenditure and to redirect resources from the support of labour power into programs which contribute directly to capital accumulation, the same problems reappear, and often in a sharper and more politically charged form. This has led both to legitimation crises (Habermas, 1975) and to fiscal crises (O'Connor, 1973) which are not resolvable by changes in attitudes, even if these could be accomplished.

In the first instance, the legitimacy of any purportedly democratic state depends upon its sustaining an appearance of responsiveness to the needs and interests of all sectors of the population. The material reality behind this appearance has been the growth of all those services Castells has theorized as collective consumption. Quite simply, Saunders maintains,

> The state cannot perform its structurally determined function of maintaining system cohesion, without responding to the

political pressures exerted upon it from the dominated, as well as the dominant classes. (1981, p. 191)

In addition, however, O'Connor (1973) has pointed out that labour's acceptance of the 'social wage', institutionalized in the welfare state and in various forms of collective consumption, has made possible reduced levels of conflict over real wages (compare Offe, 1984, p. 288; Macpherson, 1985, pp. 65–6). From this perspective, the welfare state also offers real benefits to capital, through its subsidization of the costs of the reproduction of labour power. It is for these kinds of reasons that Offe contends that the welfare state has served as the major peace formula in the advanced capitalist democracies since World War II.

At the same time, though, any state which is not a direct producer of wealth (i.e., any non-socialist state) is dependent for the budget out of which these services are provided upon taxation of wealth generated by the private sector. In other words:

> the welfare state, rather than being a separate and autonomous source of well-being which provides incomes and services as a citizen right, is itself highly dependent upon the prosperity and continued profitability of the economy. (Offe, 1984, p. 150)

This means that in order to finance its programmes of legitimation, the state is required to maintain conditions favourable to business activity and to 'privilege' the needs of capital. The problem is, as Lindberg et al. (1975) suggest, that while 'one cannot be sure that the claimed "needs" of business are strictly needs; governments challenge the claim that these are needs at their peril'. The uneasy compromise which has been embodied in the 'peace formula' has been that business has acquiesced in taxation levels adequate to the support of the welfare state, but has in turn extracted a variety of subsidies and incentives to industry, of the types discussed above, as well as benign policies towards the regulation of the 'business environment'. However, each of these has their own costs, and all of these costs add to the fiscal burdens of the state.

What are theorised as structural contradictions can thus be summarized as follows. As the state has assumed increasing responsibility for social and material infrastructure, and for buffering the effects of the market economy on capital and labour alike, the costs of these supports has led to fiscal crises for a state whose scope for raising revenues is limited by its dependence on the private sector. At the same time, because strategies for crises resolution (e.g. tax policies, or choices between public spending versus incentives to industry) have so clearly become political (and because they so profoundly affect the fates of individuals, communities, and particular capitals), the state encounters legitimation problems of a sort it could avoid when its role in the economy and in daily life was both smaller and less visible.

Offe and Macpherson suggest that it is difficult to predict how these crises will develop, particularly whether resolutions will involve encroachments on the fundamentals of capitalism or of democracy (see Offe, 1984, chs 6,7; Macpherson, 1985, ch. 5). One possible scenario lies in sustaining the common belief that individuals' chances in life (and opportunities for development) are dependent on the 'health of the economy', and thus in sustaining public support (however precarious) for cuts in services and other measures favourable to capital. Another depends upon making connections in popular understanding between different fights against cutbacks, against neighbourhood destruction, etc., and translating disenchantment with the limitations of the capitalist state into disenchantment with capitalism. Macpherson and Offe are in agreement, though, that the particular way in which these contradictions are resolved will not be determined by objective forces alone, but will depend very importantly on the outcome of hegemonic and counter-hegemonic political work which frames public understandings of what is at stake, and of what is possible.

Two issues require further development here. The first is that the state is acting on behalf of capital when it institutes cutbacks in the public services. Thus the ultimate opponent in specific struggles against cutbacks in the schools, in the staffing and maintenance of parks or transit services, is not the public employees who must then offer a deteriorating service, or even that popular target 'the government'. It is capital. Similarly many disputes which appear to pit local groups seeking to preserve the environment of their homes against municipal officials who have re-zoned their neighbourhood, or projected a motorway through it, or failed to enforce pollution control bylaws, are on a deeper level struggles between the dynamics of capital accumulation and those who must live in close proximity with its consequences. These connections must become the subject of public discussion, for there to be even a possibility of the second scenario described above.

The second issue concerns the relationship of politics to

economics. We have seen that the independence of market forces from political controls which was at the heart of the classical liberal model of society is also central to the neo-liberal prescription for our contemporary difficulties. We can now observe that at the centre of the current counter-offensive against the maximal state is the effort to mobilize a new 'common sense' (incorporating many former supporters of the welfare state and Keynesian supports to business) around the 'realization' that economics has a logic which is independent of political or ethical issues, and which is tampered with only at great cost. It is central to the thesis of overloaded government, moreover, that fiscal and legitimation crises alike derive from the tendency of democratic processes to lead to the politicization of more and more aspects of life. The corollary of this is that democracies can survive and prosper economically only if economic decisions and policies, including questions of spending priorities, are effectively insulated from democratic pressures (Brittan, 1975, and Bell, 1976), so that economic decisions are made by economists and business people, according to economic criteria alone.

Against this hegemonic belief in the independence and primacy of economics, we can remind ourselves that in most pre-capitalist societies it was routine to put the 'requirements' of communal or religious traditions before economic considerations, or at least to seek a livable balance between them. It is only capitalism that has institutionalized and naturalized the logic of material accumulation and made society serve the economy rather than the economy, society (c.f. Polanyi, 1968; Baum and Cameron, 1984). Indeed Macpherson suggests that the recent politicization of the economy can be seen either as a return to a pre-capitalist pattern, or alternatively as a transitional step to a post-capitalist order. For the latter to be a political possibility, however, requires *positive* experiences of alternatives to market provision which could provide the basis for a popular conviction that it is both possible *and* desirable to fight for institutions which put human purposes above economic ones. On this analysis, the running down of the public services has an important political side effect, in undermining the credibility and attractiveness of non-market provision. Conversely flourishing public services, incorporating positive 'relations of consumption', could prefigure the viability of a different order, and a different relationship between economic and social purposes. It is precisely for these reasons that Castells insists that the politicization of issues of collective consumption is of the utmost importance. It is crucial because it constitutes a confrontation with capital which is on absolutely fundamental issues: over the proportion of wealth produced by a society which is to be channelled into social provision, and over the extent to which the democratic process can subordinate private economic interest, in the name of priorities other than economic.

Towards a 'politics of recreation'

It is now time to try to indicate some of the questions that a politics of recreation might focus on. Following the categories developed in the introductory section of this paper, we will identify five related strategies.

1 The first of these involves the protection and even extension of public recreation programmes. This means first of all vigorous opposition to any privatization of recreational facilities, even when state withdrawal from responsibility is coded as a 'revitalization of the voluntary sector' (see Gruneau, 1984). Secondly, it means opposition to any extension of the 'user pays' principle. Because privatization programmes form an important dimension of policy towards the 'business environment', we will briefly postpone a fuller discussion of it (see 4, below). We must observe at this point, though, that either reductions in subsidy which require users to pay the economic costs of provision, or the sale or contracting out of facilities to private entrepreneurs who must *necessarily* operate them on this basis inevitably creates barriers for those who have the smallest disposable incomes. To the extent that opportunities for sporting and artistic practice, as well as the non-formal educational programmes which often fall within the remit of 'leisure services', all constitute opportunities for people to develop aspects of themselves which are rarely developed in the course of specialized and often deskilled labour, it becomes necessary to insist that any policy whose effect is to tie leisure opportunities more closely to financial resources constitutes a further limitation on the developmental freedoms available to those who are already the least privileged.

Beyond this, however, a consideration of patterns of usage of existing public facilities suggests that new thinking is necessary if this provision is to meet the needs of populations who have been

241

Dave Whitson

excluded from (or have excluded themselves from) conventionally managed facilities. This may require the provision of ancillary services such as child care for young mothers, or some form of transport (or even support for home-based recreation) for elderly or disabled persons. It may also involve hiring 'community sports leaders' drawn from the ranks of ethnic communities or disaffected youth, and management policies which are sensitive to ethnic or to class-specific cultures (c.f. Carrington and Leaman, 1983; Wimbush and Duffield, 1985). All of these embody the recognition that many constraints on leisure participation are constituted outside the sphere of leisure, and that facilities are part of the answer but not the whole answer. To make developmental rights more than rhetoric will require a variety of innovatory steps to equalize access across divisions of gender, age and ethnicity, as well as class.

2 In respect to the regulation of popular cultural forms, the major issue we would wish to raise relates to the history (referred to above) of the use of youth recreation programmes as media for the inculcation of discipline and 'good work habits'. Carrington and Leaman (1983) suggest that social engineering themes which have never been far below the surface of policy papers for British recreation are even less veiled today, in programmes which are conceived as low-cost palliatives to unemployment. To point this out is not to say that sports facilities cannot constitute real gains; but rather to insist that they not be substitutes for more direct attacks on unemployment. It is also to raise the 'system-serving' ideology which has characterized much leisure practice, in the state and voluntary sectors alike, as a problem which needs to be confronted by leisure professionals, if they are not to be perceived as on 'the other side' in what is still a struggle over what are 'legitimate' uses of free time and of public spaces.

3 The issue of subsidies to leisure industries is a vexatious one. We have indicated that the largest and most problematic ones, in North America at least, involve subsidies to resort development and to commercial sports stadiums. Yet these stadiums in particular, are often the focus of intense popular interest and support amongst the many males for whom watching sport is an important leisure pastime. To cite Bruce Kidd's suggestion that domed stadiums ought properly to be called 'men's cultural centres' is perhaps the best way of making the point that such expenditure allots disproportionate resources to the interests of

242

one sector of the population, while doing nothing to meet the real needs of others. Thus there is certainly a case for opposing large expenditures on mega-projects, at a time when less visible but more accessible recreational services are being cut back.

Yet, politically, there is also a case that the left loses from being seen as spoilsports, and indeed ought not to be caught in opposition to major focal points of popular culture.[5] Thus, given the pressures on the state to give some support to processes of capital accumulation, this may be one area where subsidies to capital may afford some dividends to the community as well. For this to be the case, however, would require much more careful negotiation than has typically been the case. Such negotiations would address the specific terms of financing, infrastructural support (e.g., transit and parking), tenancy agreements, and operational responsibilities and policies. The state's objective in the negotiations would be to ensure that in return for public subsidy of private enterprise, the community is getting a facility that is financially accessible, is suitable for a variety of community uses and is publically accountable. This would constitute an intermediate step, at least, in the direction of Taylor's proposal (1985) that the left needs to 'municipalize' sport. In the meantime, it is worth reminding ourselves of Gruneau's observation (1984) that the interests of capital have articulated with shifts in the character of state support for sport and recreation. He is referring to a shift towards *national* government support for *elite* sport programs and facilities on the one hand, which create high profile opportunities for nationwide interests in the private sector, and a shift away from forms of grant support which enable *local* governments to fund lower-profile community *recreation* projects on the other. Such shifts are clearly connected to the contradictions of the welfare state discussed earlier.

4 As indicated in (1) above, the major issue in relation to the business environment is privatization. It is contentious because state withdrawal from potentially profitable services opens up opportunities for the private sector, at the same time as it changes the conditions of access we have described. Private operators have pressed to take over a range of public services, and opposition to this is at the heart of any defence of collective consumption. Our discussion will focus on parks, partly because there have been significant moves towards the privatization of parks in several parts of North America, and partly because

camping constitutes a significant form of working-class leisure in North America, as well as one that has had little attention in the sociology of leisure (but see Cerullo and Ewen, 1984). With parkland, the issue is not so much the provision of expensive facilities, but simply maintaining the fact of public or common lands, ranging on a continuum from urban playgrounds and gardens through to conservation areas and wilderness parks of various sorts. Parkland seldom requires major capital expenditure, although operating expenditure (e.g., on staffing) is usually necessary to protect and maintain the character of the park; and the tax revenue that might be derived from alternative forms of land use is foregone. Both operating budgets and tax revenue are at issue in the current climate however.

Clearly governments can rid themselves of ongoing operating costs by privatizing parks services. The privatization policy of the former Conservative government of Ontario, according to which twenty-one provincial parks were leased to private operators over a period of eight years,[6] was publicly justified in precisely these terms. Yet the real savings, since the government has continued both to bear the costs of renewing the facilities between leases and to fund those reduced habitat maintenance programmes which still survive, were negligible as a percentage of the department's budget. This supports the suspicion that the real reasons behind the policy were ideological: to create opportunities for the private sector, and to curtail government competition with existing private campground operators. A more permanent kind of privatization is instanced in the British Columbia government's 1984 sale of Manning Park Lodge and the Gibson Pass ski facilities, near Vancouver. The Minister of Lands, Parks and Housing, Tony Brummet, said, 'Selling these facilities gets government out of a business that can best be run by the private sector'. The effect, however, has been to move the hotel 'up-market', to introduce charges for cross-country skiing, and generally to change the conditions of access to one of the major recreational playgrounds within half a day's drive of Vancouver (see *Mountain News*, Vol. 2, No. 4, 1984). Governments can also 'co-operate with the private sector' in park development, through the granting of concessions for the operation of food, accommodation, and other recreation or amusement oriented businesses along corridor roads or at 'focal points' within parks. Although such services undoubtedly find a market, to permit them *within park boundaries* is progressively to close off the option of access to nature in an undeveloped and uncommodified form (see note 2).

Of course a more final threat to parkland comes from pressures to allow the exploitation of it in other ways, which either destroy or seriously impinge upon its recreational character. This is especially acute in urban areas, where greenbelts are always a prime target for developers seeking new spaces to commoditise, and where the apartment blocks or plazas they construct promise lucrative sources of property tax (as well as the immediate capital gain from the land sale) to municipal authorities experiencing financial pressures. The *Sunday Times*, in one week in early 1984, noted the sale of parks and sports fields in Camberley, Aylesbury, and Shrewsbury. In the case of rural parks offering mountain, forest or water-based recreation, the conflict is typically with resource extraction industries promising tax revenues and, especially, jobs. The Queensland government's encouragement of oil exploration on the Barrier Reef is an especially flagrant example; pressures to expand logging within parks are endemic also in Canada.

Each of these ways of turning parkland to more 'profitable' uses illustrates Lefebvre's (1976) argument that a central dimension of capitalism has been the progressive commoditisation of space, until the survival of undeveloped or 'natural' space is something which can be preserved only by state intervention which prohibits some spaces (i.e. parks) from being developed in profit-yielding ways. In these pressures to make space 'pay its way' Lefebvre proposes that we can see in a very basic form the conflicts between the logic of capital accumulation and the needs of people. A politics of collective consumption would see access to uncommoditised recreational land, in urban and natural environments alike, as an important dimension of the quality of everyday life and as an important developmental option. It would therefore oppose moves to privatize parks; and it would seek to mobilize support for the protection of existing parkland and greenbelt, and for the extension of public provision wherever opportunities arise.

5 Finally we come to the impact of professionalization on recreation and leisure. The history of aspirant professions is one of efforts to establish and mark out a 'turf', efforts which are characterized by strategies which seek to associate expertise with credentials, and to privilege their 'own' forms of knowledge by distinguishing them wherever possible from the discourse of

ordinary people. Yet Aronowitz and Giroux (1985) suggest that there is an abundance of evidence in the literature on professionalization which 'shows that the professional is constituted as much by his or her ideological preparation as by technical education' (p. 188; c.f. also Johnson, 1972). Indeed in a field like recreation and leisure, it is arguable that technical expertise in sport or the arts, for example, is becoming less and less necessary either to admission to the profession or to effective job performance. What is becoming increasingly a central feature of professional training, and a necessary condition for certification, is that a student learns to function within an occupational culture whose domain assumptions are those of 'management'. In the public services, we can identify two kinds of consequences of this development.

In the first of these, management preoccupations combine with the tendencies of professionals in most fields to assume that they know best what are the needs of client individuals and communities to produce an impatience with client questioning of their professional judgment, and with pressure for client involvement in planning processes. This professional self-confidence rarely acknowledges peoples' well known dislike of being told by experts what is good for them. Neither, in the leisure field, does it take account of evidence that the 'providers' have been seriously out of touch with the issues that really matter to users (Haworth and Veal, 1976, especially articles by Haworth and by Pearson). It is perhaps worth suggesting that the public service bureaucracies could learn much from the respectful and accommodating stance which most private sector personnel adopt towards their customers, however self-serving this stance may be. Indeed Hall (1984) argues that one of the attractions of the consumer society for many working class people has been that its relations of consumption offer a welcome contrast to those demanded by the representatives of the paternalist state. You only get respect if you've got the money, 'but at least you aren't required to look "deserving" as you approach the till'.[7]

Secondly, Butterfield (1984) is surely correct in observing that 'value-for-money, cost-effectiveness, and the virtues of the marketing approach' have become common currency in the discourse which now characterizes recreation management. Now few would deny that it is incumbent upon all those working in the public services to seek cost-effective means of service delivery, or that careful planning and operational management are not important if this responsibility is to be fulfilled. At the same time it is necessary to insist that the public services embody goals and purposes which are different from those of corporations, purposes which have to do with the development of individuals and communities, and which can never be automatically subordinated to economic calculations if the public services are to retain any of their original meanings. Thus it is widely acknowledged that leisure centres whose policy it has been to keep their facilities easily and profitably full with club bookings, etc., have seldom played the developmental and redistributive roles in their communities which were part of their explicit purpose. Generally, management in the public services must seek economic practices which best serve social purposes, rather than the reverse; and leisure managers must guard carefully against discourses and practices which reverse these priorities in favour of a 'bottom-line' approach. The weighing-up of economic costs against benefits of a less tangible sort is a political and social issue, as well as an economic one. It has to do with the kind of society we want to live in; and, moreover, it is something which everyone, and not just experts, has a legitimate say in.

Indeed on a deeper level, Offe (1984) suggests that the professionalization of a range of service functions has contributed to the effective depoliticization of a series of questions which have real political implications. To the extent that social planning in general and recreation planning in particular can be defined as complexes of technical problems, requiring specialist and certified forms of expertise, the claims of non-experts (even those who will be directly affected) to a real say in the decision-making process can be effectively limited. In such a 'scientization of politics' (Offe, 1984; Habermas, 1975), the consensus of professionals and technocrats can be presented to the public as the limits of the possible, and non-political forms of decision-making have effectively reduced the influence of democratic process. Of course, this reversal of the expansion of citizenship rights is precisely the project of those who would limit the impact of democratic pressure on the making of economic and social policy (see note 4, above).

Conversely, the politicization of collective consumption advocated by Castells would go beyond the provision of more and better services by knowledgeable and dedicated professionals;

it would seek to change the 'relations of consumption' within which these services are planned and managed. The objectives of such a change would be not simply the provision of more appropriate and responsive services, important as this is; they would include the development of political skills within client communities and individuals. However Pine (1984), commenting on a recent Council of Europe study of community cultural development initiatives in European towns (Goodey, 1983), indicates that it was exceptional even in this context for administrators and planners to have among their objectives the creation of more meaningful consultative mechanisms, let alone structures of citizen control. Pine and Goodey each cite Arnstein's 'ladder of citizen participation' to illustrate how structures of professional-citizen interaction can range along a continuum from manipulation and information-giving, through token and genuine forms of consultation, to effective and ongoing structures of citizen control which are politically 'skilling', in the process.

It has to be acknowledged that community development models of service delivery have their own problems and limitations. These can include manipulation and co-option, limitations on the autonomy of state employees, and different perspectives on the boundaries between politics and leisure which working people can experience as yet another form of cultural imperialism (for sensitive discussions of the last issue, in particular, see Tomlinson, 1983; and Wimbush and Duffield, 1985). Encouraging community activism almost certainly complicates the work of government for, as Habermas and others have pointed out, public discussion always throws up questions which challenge the assumptions of experts' plans and impede the smooth functioning of bureaucracies. However if the scientization of politics is not to produce an irreversible political de-skilling, the appropriation by professionals of opportunities for problem-solving and decision-making in respect to community life must be halted and reversed. Indeed to the extent that one of the necessary conditions of *social* development (as well as one of the most important developmental freedoms open to individuals in a purportedly democratic society) involves the fuller development and wider distribution of those skills and self-expectations necessary to successful operation in the public sphere, it behooves all those who care about the future of democracy to work to institutionalize structures of public participation in which these habits of mind and these forms of cultural capital are actively developed rather than systematically denied.

Conclusion: rebuilding support for the public services

Gruneau (1984) has suggested that we need to understand debates about state policies towards leisure as an instance, and not a trivial one, in a struggle over what shall be the rationale for all forms of public expenditure. From one side, he has argued, there are endemic and structural pressures on the state in a capitalist society to provide material and other forms of support to private entrepreneurship. From the other side, political demands from the non-propertied sectors have articulated with broader visions of human rights to produce pressures for services and for developmental opportunities which, as commodities, had been accessible only to the better off. Thus the growth of publicly subsidized and operated services, when combined with incentives to capital accumulation and a legal framework in which limitations on the freedoms of capital were exceptions rather than the rule, constituted a system which satisfied enough interests to sustain an uneasy peace. Now, however, Gruneau suggests that the state is coming under renewed pressure from capital which is aimed not just as containing, but cutting back, welfare-oriented expenditures and also at achieving a situation in which government expenditure at all levels has assistance to capital accumulation as its primary objective. It is in just this context that we have to understand current attacks on public expenditure.

Yet this is also a political campaign as well as an economic one, which features attacks on the public services, and efforts to win hegemony for a discourse in which the private sector is popularly perceived as being able to provide *better services* than can government. That such a discourse could become a 'commonsense' is, of course, filled with historical irony; yet it finds a hearing, we have argued, because professionals who are providing services within the framework of a state bureaucracy find themselves in the difficult position of mediating, in all their relationships with clients, both the authority and the fiscal limitations of the state. Oppositions between officials and clients are at their sharpest, of course, when the authority of the state is in question. However, even in the routine provision of service the credibility of service personnel has been eroded by cutbacks which have left them unable to provide services which the public experience as adequate. The net result is that it is all too often the teachers (or the bus drivers or the parks staff) who find themselves the targets of public dissatisfaction and resentment, while the underfunding and understaffing which structures and limits the service they can provide remains a more difficult and less satisfying focus for criticism. It is indeed difficult today to disagree with Elliott and McCrone's (1982) contention that the squeeze on public expenditure has been assisted by an attack on those who work in the public services, which are themselves part of the strategy

> in which the new middle class . . . and the bureaucrats of the service class are to be put in their place no less firmly than manual workers. (p. 150)

In addition, however, we have argued that the 'relations of consumption' which have followed from the professionalization of service work, and which have become characteristic of the public services, have themselves been important contributors to antipathy to the public sector. Certainly, service professionals and bureaucrats have been slow to acknowledge the common interests they share with clients and with other public sector workers. Indeed the ideologies of professionalism discussed in the previous section have instead claimed a special status which has contributed to divisions of interest and barriers to cooperation. It will require a considerable change of perspective, on the part of those leisure professionals who are still concerned with establishing their legitimacy as experts or managers, to see the role of the leisure professional as a community development one. Yet to the extent that the fate of all the public services will depend on the success of hegemonic and counter-hegemonic efforts to frame public under-standings of 'the problem' and of possible solutions, we contend that the discourse of leisure management can only leave the leisure services vulnerable to whatever strategies of retrenchment or privatization are perceived to suit the interests of capital. These are issues which leisure professionals who care about the nature of the service they are likely to be able to work in, as well as those who are involved in their professional preparation, need to consider very carefully.

Notes

1 On theories of the capitalist state, see Lindberg et al. (1975), O'Connor (1973), Habermas (1975), and Offe (1984). On 'the urban question' (i.e. efforts to theorize relationships between the state and capital in the structuring of everyday life) see Castells (1977). Dunleavy (1980), Lefebvre (1976), Saunders (1981), Forrest et al. (1982), and Elliott and McCrone (1982).
2 Proposals for downhill ski development, for example, are often opposed by coalitions of environmentalists and devotees of less capital-intensive recreational pursuits. See for example, the debates concerning the development of the mountain parks in the southern Alberta Rockies, sharpened of course by the tourism potential of the imminent Winter Olympic Games in nearby Calgary. See also the debates which led to the refusal of permission to develop Lurcher's Gully in the Scottish Cairngorms for downhill skiing, and to the granting of permission for hotel and ski-tow development in Kosciusko National Park in Australia.
3 The work of Gruneau (1983,4) and Aronowitz (1982) stand as important exceptions to this point, as does much of the work of Stuart Hall. Also important in stimulating debate about these relationships are the projects of the journal *Theory, Culture and Society* and of the 'Channel Five' section of *Marxism Today*. This of course constitutes a further attempt to move these debates forward.
4 See Bell (1976), Brittan (1975), and Crozier et al. (1975). For commentary on conservative analyses of the crises of democracy, see Offe (1984, ch. 2) and Bosanquet (1983).
5 Hall (1984), for example, argues that the left in English-speaking countries has historically distanced itself from the people by adopting disapproving postures towards important aspects of popular culture. Contrasting this to the involvement in popular life which has characterized the CPI, he argues that there is no popular occasion or event where the left can afford *not* to be present. Some of the cultural and sport-related initiatives sponsored by the Greater London Council prefigure what such a presence might involve.
6 As of 1985 this policy was placed on hold by an incoming minority Liberal government, but information supplied by the Ontario Public Services Employees Union indicates that another seventeen parks were slated for privatization.
7 See also Connell et al. (1982) on the 'relations of consumption' characteristic of private and state schooling in Australia (especially pp. 128–39).

References

Aronowitz, S. (1982), 'On the theorization of leisure', in R. Forrest et al., *Urban Political Economy and Social Theory*, Aldershot, Gower.

Aronowitz, S. and Giroux, H. (1985), *Education Under Seige*, Boston, Bergin & Garvey.

Baum, G. and Cameron, D. (1984), *Ethics and Economics*, Toronto, Lorimer.

Bell, D. (1976), *The Cultural Contradictions of Capitalism*, New York, Basic Books.

Berlin, I. (1969), *Four Essays on Liberty*, London, Oxford University Press.

Dave Whitson

Bosanquet, N. (1983), *After the New Right*, London, Heinemann.

Brittan, S. (1975), 'The economic contradictions of democracy', *British Journal of Political Science*, 5,2. pp. 129–59.

Butterfield, J. (1984), 'Leisure and the New Right', in *Contributions to the Politics of Leisure*, LSA Newsletter Supplement.

Carrington, B. and Leaman, O. (1983), 'Sports as community politics', in *Sport and the Community. The Next Ten Years: Problems and Issues*, LSA Newsletter Supplement.

Castells, M. (1977), *The Urban Question*, London, Edward Arnold.

Cerullo, M. and Ewen, P. (1984), 'The American family goes camping: gender, family and the politics of space', *Antipode*, 16, 3.

Connell, R.W. et al. (1982), *Making the Difference*, Sydney, George Allen & Unwin.

Crozier, M. et al. (1975), *The Crisis of Democracy*, New York, New York University Press.

Cunningham, H. (1980), *Leisure in the Industrial Revolution*, London, Croom Helm.

Dunleavy, P. (1980), *Urban Political Analysis*, London, Macmillan.

Elliott, B. and McCrone, D. (1982), *The City: Patterns of Domination and Conflict*, London, Macmillan.

Forrest, R. et al. (1982), *Urban Political Economy and Social Theory*, Aldershot, Gower.

Friedman, M. (1962), *Capitalism and Freedom*, Chicago, University of Chicago Press.

Goodey, B. (1983), *Urban Cultural Life in the 1980s*, Strasbourg, Council of Europe.

Gruneau, R. (1983), *Class, Sports and Social Development*, Amherst, University of Massachusetts Press.

Gruneau, R. (1984), 'Leisure, freedom, and the state', Plenary address to Leisure Studies Association International Congress, 'Politics, Planning and People', University of Sussex, 4–8 July.

Habermas, J. (1975), *Legitimation Crisis*, London, Heinemann.

Hall, Stuart (1984), 'The culture gap', *Marxism Today*, January.

Haworth, J. and Veal, A. (1976), *Leisure and the Community*, University of Birmingham, Centre for Urban and Regional Studies.

Hayek, F. (1960), *The Constitution of Liberty*, London, Routledge & Kegan Paul.

Ingham, A. (1985), 'From public issue to personal trouble: well-being and the fiscal crisis of the state', *Sociology of Sport*, 2,1.

Johnson, T. (1972), *Professions and Power*, London, Macmillan.

Lefebvre, H. (1976), *The Survival of Capitalism*, London, Allison & Busby.

Lindberg, L. et al. (1975), *Stress and Contradiction in Modern Capitalism*, Lexington, D.C. Heath.

Lowerson, J. (1980), 'Battles for the countryside', in F. Gloversmith (ed.), *Class, Culture, and Social Change*, Brighton, Harvester.

Macintosh, D. et al. (1986), *Sport and Government*, Montreal, Queen's-McGill Press.

Macpherson, C.B. (1973), *Democratic Theory: Essays in Retrieval*, London, Oxford University Press.

Macpherson, C.B. (1985), *The Rise and Fall of Economic Justice*, London, Oxford University Press.

Nozick, R. (1974), *Anarchy, State and Utopia*, Oxford, Blackwell.

O'Connor, J. (1973), *The Fiscal Crisis of the State*, New York, St Martin's.

Offe, C. (1984), *Contradictions of the Welfare State*, London, Hutchinson.

Olson, H.E. (1985), 'The development of youth leisure policies in Sweden', *Leisure Studies*, 4,1, pp. 57–68.

Pine, R. (1984), 'Leisure planning and public policy: the social responsibility of the administrator', Leisure Studies Association International Congress, 'Politics, Planning and People', University of Sussex, 4–8 July.

Polanyi, K. (1968), *Primitive Archaic and Modern Economics: Essays of Karl Polanyi*, New York, Anchor.

Rawls, J. (1971), *A Theory of Justice*, Boston, Harvard University Press.

Saunders, P. (1981), *Social Theory and the Urban Question*, London, Hutchinson.

Taylor, I. (1985), 'Putting the boot into a working class sport: British soccer after Bradford and Brussels', North American Society for the Sociology of Sport Congress, Boston.

Tomlinson, A. (1983), 'The illusion of community: cultural values and the meaning of leisure in a gentrifying neighbourhood', in Tomlinson, A. (ed.), *Leisure and Popular Cultural Forms*, Brighton, Chelsea School of Human Movement.

Waites, B. et al. (1982), *Popular Culture: Past and Present*, London, Croom Helm.

Wimbush, E. and Duffield, B. (1985), 'Integrating education and leisure: conflict and the community school', *Leisure Studies*, 4,1.